THE ENLIGHTENED SOCIAL WORKER
An Introduction to Rights-Focused Practice

Donald Forrester

First published in Great Britain in 2024 by

Policy Press, an imprint of
Bristol University Press
University of Bristol
1–9 Old Park Hill
Bristol
BS2 8BB
UK
t: +44 (0)117 374 6645
e: bup-info@bristol.ac.uk

Details of international sales and distribution partners are available at
policy.bristoluniversitypress.co.uk

© Bristol University Press 2024

British Library Cataloguing in Publication Data
A catalogue record for this book is available from the British Library

ISBN 978-1-4473-6765-9 hardcover
ISBN 978-1-4473-6766-6 paperback
ISBN 978-1-4473-6767-3 ePub
ISBN 978-1-4473-6768-0 ePdf

The right of Donald Forrester to be identified as author of this work has been asserted by him in accordance with the Copyright, Designs and Patents Act 1988.

All rights reserved: no part of this publication may be reproduced, stored in a retrieval system, or transmitted in any form or by any means, electronic, mechanical, photocopying, recording, or otherwise without the prior permission of Bristol University Press.

Every reasonable effort has been made to obtain permission to reproduce copyrighted material. If, however, anyone knows of an oversight, please contact the publisher.

The statements and opinions contained within this publication are solely those of the author and not of the University of Bristol or Bristol University Press. The University of Bristol and Bristol University Press disclaim responsibility for any injury to persons or property resulting from any material published in this publication.

Bristol University Press and Policy Press work to counter discrimination on grounds of gender, race, disability, age and sexuality.

Cover design: Nicky Borowiec
Front cover image: AdobeStock/natrot

For Tonya

with love

Contents

List of figures, tables and boxes … vi
Acknowledgements … vii

PART I Rights and social work
1 Social work: tensions, conflicts and rights … 3
2 The Enlightenment, social work and progress … 13
3 On rights and social work … 27
4 Liberty, helping and protection … 35
5 Social work, positive freedom and need … 53
6 Human connection, community and love … 63

PART II Theories for rights-focused practice
7 Humanist social work … 79
8 The social model … 89

PART III Rights-focused practice
9 Assessment as theory development … 103
10 Assessment, formulations and rights … 114
11 Working with individuals and families … 131
12 Rights beyond the individual and the family … 152
13 Social work, rights and society … 159

References … 172
Index … 187

List of figures, tables and boxes

Figure
4.1   The ladder of consequences   39

Table
4.1   Worker responses to parents   45

Boxes
10.1   Janet and her family   122
11.1   Simulated interview scenario   134

Acknowledgements

A huge number of people helped me to develop the ideas in this book, whether they were aware they were doing so or not. As will become obvious in reading the book, probably the key influence have been the children and families I worked with as a social worker, and the many who have generously agreed to be part of research studies. I have also benefited from working with kind, wise and thoughtful practitioners and academics throughout my career. We became foster carers in 2021, and seeing a variety of social workers from a different perspective has also influenced my thinking. Some have been wonderful, and I hope I have captured some elements of the best of social work.

Thank you to my colleagues in the CASCADE Centre at Cardiff University who provide a supportive, stimulating and caring place to work. I feel enormously grateful to work with such wonderful people.

Particular mention should go to the people who have read chapters or the whole book. Your input, corrections, suggestions and disagreements have enormously improved and enriched this book, though I know many of you would disagree with some of the arguments that I make. Thank you Andy Pithouse, Charlotte Waits, Clive Diaz, David Wilkins, Kieran Lord, Lucy Sheehan, Richard Devine, Sally Holland and Tom Batterby for providing such helpful feedback. Particular thanks to Lucy Johnstone for giving permission for me to use the case study that she and Rudi Dallos used in their book on *Formulation in psychology and psychotherapy*, as well as her insightful comments on my chapter on that topic.

Finally, I wanted to thank my family. Six of you have actively made writing this book more difficult by filling my life with fun, play, stress, love and everything else that goes with family life. Nonetheless, I cannot imagine having written it without you, so thank you Hannah, Ruth, James, Rowan, Toby and Charly. One has made it possible through her endless love, patience and kindness. So I dedicate this book to Tonya, with thanks and love.

PART I

Rights and social work

1

Social work: tensions, conflicts and rights

As a social worker I have always felt there was a gap between the theory and ideals of social work and the messy realities of practice. The social work described in lectures and books, and in official definitions of the profession, seemed far removed from what I did. It also seems different to the practice I observed in research studies once I became an academic. Of course, there is always a gap between the ideals of a profession and the realities it actually delivers, but this disjunction seems more fundamental than that. It felt, and still feels, as if the theory and the practice are often talking about different things. The theory emphasises helping people and promoting social justice, yet frequently social workers do not seem to be doing either, or if they are they are doing so in ways that seem far removed from the ideals of the textbooks. This book is an attempt to understand what social workers might actually be doing, why they are doing it and to begin to outline a rather different idea of what social work is, and what it might be. In doing so it aims to bridge the gap between practice and theory by providing a description of social work that is, I hope, coherent, inspiring and can help us understand and improve actual social work practices.

In fact, the word gap perhaps underplays the difference between theory and practice in the profession. It often feels to me as if they are talking about different worlds. Such a gap is dangerous for a profession. If practitioners do not feel theory relates to what they do, then they will ignore it. This can contribute to the development of practices that are misguided, unhelpful or even oppressive, because without theories and evidence to undergird our work it can become defined solely by organisational needs. Such practice is unfortunately often found in research that directly observes what social workers do in child and family settings (for example, Ferguson, 2017; Forrester et al, 2019; Ruch et al, 2020). Setting out a vision or theory for social work that is at odds with what social workers actually do also runs a second risk – it makes it likely that the vision is incorrect, that it is not an accurate understanding of what social work actually is. An extreme outcome of such a position can be a conclusion that we should abandon social work altogether, because its practices are so far removed from the lofty ideals we believe it should represent – indeed this has recently been argued in the *British Journal of Social Work* (Maylea, 2021), and similar arguments can be found in the American movement to abolish child protection services (Roberts, 2022).

This book is in part a response to such fundamental challenges about doing social work and being a social worker. It seeks to articulate a vision of social work that can understand current practices while helping us strive to be better, both as individual workers and as a profession. It does this by focusing on rights and interpersonal tensions and conflict. As a result it has a different focus to most social work books: it sees tensions and conflicts as a central element of social work. Indeed, the draft title was 'Social Work as Conflict'. Understanding the nature of these tensions and disagreements, seeing them as an essential part of a humane society, and considering what we can do to make them positive and constructive is at the heart of the book. My argument is that this vision of social work can be applied across settings: it is a vision for social work in general. However, both my practice and my research experience are embedded in child and family social work. That area is therefore the focus of this book. I hope those working in other settings will find sufficient resonance from the arguments and examples that they can apply them to work with other groups or situations.

Social work and conflict

Myriad approaches to social work have been outlined over the decades. These include relationship-based (for example, Howe, 1998; Ruch, 2005; Howe et al, 2018) and radical traditions (for example, Bailey and Brake, 1975; Ferguson and Woodward, 2009), pragmatic helping associated with casework or community work (such as Christensen et al, 2020 or Twelvetrees, 2008), attempts to synthesise or provide frameworks that allow for an eclectic choice of methods (see Coady and Lehmann, 2016) or a focus on a particular orientation, such as feminist or anti-racist social work (Dominelli, 2002, 2017). All of these have much we should learn from, and as the book progresses it will become apparent that there is a place for all of these contributions to social work. Yet, at the heart of all these approaches there is an assumption that social work is there to help people. Some perspectives focus on helping individuals, others focus more on changing their social circumstances, and some try to integrate these two positions: yet they all share the assumption that the basic idea, the thing we seek to do, our purpose as a profession, is to help people. Of course they recognise that social work is not the same as counselling. The issues we work with are often the individual manifestation of social problems – and social work therefore needs to take not only a critical view of the nature of such 'problems' (problems for whom and why?) but also recognise the social causes and emphasise social change to combat them. Yet, nonetheless, the underlying aim is usually some form of helping. This is true even in texts that take a more critical stance. For instance, *The Essential Social Worker* by Martin Davies is a book that influenced this one so much that the title is in part an homage to it (Davies, 2007). In his book Davies argued that the aim of social work is not usually transformation of individuals or society, but is more likely to be simply maintaining people with problems in the community. This does not seem as aspirational as some accounts of social work, yet it is a more accurate description of the type of crucial work social workers and others do to keep children in families that are struggling or to help people with dementia to stay at home. Davies' argument is that this is essential work in two senses: it is essential for those who need help, and it is essential for a good society. Yet even here, there is a focus on helping – as the social worker is helping the individual stay in their community and helping society by doing so. While agreeing with key elements of Davies' argument – and in particular the idea that social work is essential for individuals and for society – this book focuses more on conflict in social work, seeking to understand why it is so common and how we can best work with it.

Many social work texts recognise that not everyone might want to be helped. They may have sections or chapters on working with involuntary clients – often providing helpful practical tips on how to deal with this issue (see Foren and Bailey, 2014). The crucial work of Ferguson, Barber and others on working with involuntary clients provides useful insights and suggestions (Barber, 1991; Ferguson, 2011). There are a few texts focused specifically on working with involuntary clients, like Trotter's interesting combination of task-centred and behavioural work (Trotter, 2015. Yet even here, the challenge of helping involuntary clients is treated as a specific issue – how to help people who do not want to be helped but for whom society has decided 'help' is necessary. The involuntary nature of our involvement with many of the people we work with, and the frequent conflict associated with it, does not lead to a fundamental questioning of whether social work is actually primarily about helping people, whether directly or by changing the world. At the very least there seems a mismatch between the literature of social work, which has comparatively little to say about working with people who do not want social work involvement, and the reality of much practice in the United Kingdom, which is so often with people who do not, at least initially, want a social worker involved.

This focus on 'social work as helping' also dominates definitions of social work. This can be seen in the older International Federation of Social Work (IFSW) definition of the profession: 'The social work profession promotes social change, problem solving in human relationships and the empowerment and liberation of people to enhance well-being. Utilising theories of human behaviour and social systems, social work intervenes at the points where people interact with their environments' (IFSW, 2001). The current 2014 definition is even more aspirational, with a focus on empowerment and liberation. Thus, social work:

> Promotes social change and development, social cohesion, and the empowerment and liberation of people. Principles of social justice, human rights, collective responsibility and respect for diversities are central to social work. Underpinned by theories of social work, social sciences, humanities and indigenous knowledge, social work engages people and structures to address life challenges and enhance wellbeing. (IFSW, 2014)

A focus on helping, broadly understood, is also central to most or all of the current frameworks we use – whether systemic or restorative, outcomes focused or strengths based, they all emphasise helping people. Indeed, most interventions are adapted from therapeutic approaches, for instance Signs of Safety is the application of solution-focused practice for child protection (Turnell and Edwards, 1999), Family Safeguarding uses Motivational Interviewing (MI) (Miller and Rollnick, 2012; Forrester et al, 2017) and several incorporate systemic therapeutic approaches (Bostock et al, 2017).

I have also had a tendency to focus on social work as helping. My last book, written with David Wilkins and Charlotte Whittaker, was about Motivational Interviewing and social work. It began by saying: 'This book is concerned with one apparently simple but actually very complicated question: how can we talk to people in helpful ways? And, in particular, how can we have helpful conversations in the context of child and family social work, when there might be serious concerns about children's safety (Forrester et al, 2021 11). I co-wrote that book because, with colleagues, I have been researching the use of MI in child and family social work for 20 years. My interest in MI emerged from my first study, which focused on parental substance misuse and identified that often social workers felt stuck and unsure how to work with parental alcohol or drug issues (Forrester and Harwin, 2011). The challenge of how workers might work in better ways with parents and families became an enduring focus for my research, with a specific interest in how MI could be used in child and family social work.

What became apparent is that social work seemed very different to the way I had thought about it, both as an academic and practitioner. Indeed, this book can be thought of as a prolonged answer to questions that arose from these attempts to help social workers to help parents more effectively. Many of these studies involved recording meetings between social workers and parents. It was these interviews that seemed to be very different to the social work described in textbooks, or indeed my own assumptions about the profession. Most obviously they were characterised by constant tensions, disagreements and sometimes conflicts. This was sometimes because of an obvious disagreement, for instance because the worker has serious concerns about a child. However, it was more often low-grade tension, where it could be quite hard to put your finger on what was happening but there was some apparent lack of alignment between what the worker was saying and the parent's responses. The worker might be trying to persuade the parent that something was true or that a course of action was necessary, but the parent did not seem convinced. Or the worker and the parent seemed to have different priorities for the conversation, and were muddling through the complexities involved in negotiating these differences. Sometimes these tensions were explicit, but often they were below the surface – manifesting as a mismatch between what the worker seemed to be interested in and what the parent or young person wanted to talk about.

Qualitative studies of social work have described beautifully some of these tensions. Chris Hall and colleagues used conversation analysis to unpick the complicated dance between social worker and mother in defining terms such as being a 'good mother', with the mother portraying herself as already a good mother and the worker emphasising what needed to be done in order to become a good mother (Hall et al, 2006. Similarly, ethnographers such as Harry Ferguson and my own students, Lucy Sheehan and Lucy Treby, have described what one might call the 'micro-tensions' involved in practice (Ferguson, 2011, 2016, 2017; Ferguson et al, 2020; Sheehan, 2022; Treby, 2022). Sheehan unpicks the ways in which parents and professionals dispute whether a pregnancy was 'concealed' or simply an unexpected surprise. Social workers, and other professionals, do not simply say 'I don't believe you' or 'I think you are lying'. Rather there is a complex interaction around the reasons for believing it was concealed, which includes consideration of medical evidence, previous history and level of concern for the child. In later chapters this book explores why saying such things is so difficult, how social workers and others approach the challenge of doing so, and some of the key elements of good practice. For this chapter a rather different point is important. This type of conversation is not, at least in any very obvious way, about 'helping'. It seems to me at odds with much of the theoretical literature about social work, and differs in substantial and important ways from the assumptions about social work that have undergirded much of my study and practice. Social work, or at least statutory social work, is characterised by almost constant tensions and sometimes conflicts. One reaction to this is to throw up one's hands and declare that this is so far from what social work should be that we should abandon the enterprise altogether. Some have been brave enough to write this in public (Maylea, 2021), but I know many more who express similar reservations in private. There are certainly grounds for serious concerns. Our research recordings tended to find a practice that was often lacking in clarity about its purpose and authoritarian and prescriptive with parents. Yet I think it is a misunderstanding to think that social workers are not striving to do something worthwhile. The argument of this book is that social workers are performing an essential role – both for the children and families they work with and for a liberal and humane society. The problem is that too often they are not being supported to carry out that role well enough. In part that is because there seems to be a misunderstanding about the core purpose of social workers. To some degree this starts from the mistaken belief that the foundation of the role is that social workers are there to help people, and addressing this misunderstanding is at the heart of this book. At the least such a focus makes it difficult for us to help social workers understand and work with the tensions that are so pervasive in practice.

Of course, if everyone has always thought that helping people is fundamental to social work then it must be: and it is. Much of this book is devoted to how social workers *can* help people and the central importance of social justice in what we do. Yet I argue that seeing social work as *primarily* about helping is a mistake, that it is a mistake that fails to provide an adequate account of what social work actually is, or what it can aspire to be, and that this has profound consequences for … well, for everything social work related. I want to articulate a different view of social work – one that sees tension and conflict as a core element of the work, something that is central to our practice, and something which is so ubiquitous that understanding why that is the case helps us understand what social work is and what it should be in contemporary society. At heart these tensions arise because social work is focused on rights, and in particular it is often involved when there are conflicts about rights.

As a result, social work is at least as likely to be characterised by conflict as it is by helping, though even more common is a combination, albeit sometimes a rather uneasy combination, of the two. When I was a social worker most of the families I worked with involved actual or potential conflict of some type; difficult meetings were the norm. I had to tell parents that I thought they were not being truthful, or that we (social services) could not pay for something, or that we were starting care proceedings. And it was not just parents. I had to explain to children that even though they wanted to live with their mother they could not, and tell teenagers that we would not pay for the new trainers they wanted. These sorts of difficult conversations, involving actual or potential conflict, were not occasional features of the job. They were a feature of probably most meetings and certainly a daily occurrence. Social work – at least in the statutory setting of local authority children's services – was fundamentally conflictual; people who were cooperative tended to get a support service or have their case closed. Of course, over time relationships were built and more positive work would start to happen but, rather like Nanny McPhee in the eponymous films, I tended to feel 'When you need me, but do not want me, then I must stay. When you want me, but no longer need me, then I have to go.'

There is more to social work than statutory services. Yet given the high proportion of social workers in the United Kingdom who work in such settings, our description of social work has to be able to incorporate these types of conflicts. Furthermore, the tensions and conflicts were not just with parents or children, they were often with the organisation. I argued for payments for a family, lobbied housing to try to get a move or negotiated with managers for more contact between children and parents. Again, working with tensions and disagreements was a central element of the work. My belief is that this applies across settings, but I return to the argument about the extent or limits of a focus on rights in the final chapter of the book.

The nature of this practice seems a far cry from the lofty ideals of the profession. On the face of it, it does not sound to me as if I was promoting 'social change and development, social cohesion, and the empowerment and liberation of people' (IFSW, 2014). One way of understanding this might be that we are trying to help one person – such as the child – and in doing so we may be in potential conflict with others – such as the parents. This particularly applies when the parents' care is thought to be problematic or abusive. This is, indeed, the fundamental conflict in child and family social work, and similar conflicts can also be found across statutory services, whether that is a conflict between an individual's rights and those of others (for instance, is this person's psychosis so serious that they pose a risk to others?) or for an individual themselves (such as, this person wants to remain in their home but does their level of dementia place them at too great a risk?). Yet these are not the only conflicts. It is crucial to hear and understand the views of children and parents, but we sometimes cannot act on these and often we have to work directly against their wishes (for instance, if they want to return to an abusive situation). We often have difficult conversations within the organisation about resources, for example if a family have no money for food but a manager says they will not authorise a payment. This book argues that such conflicts – which are routine in everyday practice – are only partly about helping. They are more fundamentally about understanding the rights of individuals and working with potentially conflicting rights – such as protection of individuals who may not want protection, or rights to family privacy, or myriad other potential conflicts.

Instead of thinking about social work as a profession defined by helping, thinking about social work as a rights-focused discipline and profession helps to explain why practice is replete with these types of conflicts. It also does other things – providing a broad enough perspective to embrace much or perhaps even all of social work, and allowing us to see the ways in which social work is fundamentally worthwhile even though it is not just about helping people. There have been excellent books written about rights and social work (for example, Lundy, 2011; Ife, 2018; Ife et al, 2022), which I discuss later. However, to simplify their complex arguments, they tend to think that rights are a good thing and social workers should champion and expand them. This book sees rights rather differently. Recognising and expanding rights is an important part of social work, but it is the conflicting nature of rights that is central to understanding statutory social work. The argument is that the rights that social workers work with tend to involve tensions or conflicts. While many public servants provide for rights, for instance by making decisions about benefits or housing eligibility, social workers tend to be involved when such decision-making is particularly fraught. This is most obvious in the arena of safeguarding, whether with children or adults, but it also applies to much of the service and resource provision that workers do. Often we are managing limited resources, and this creates inherent tensions in the work that are not there for a professional deciding whether an individual is eligible for benefits.

The argument of this book is that rights are a core good for society. They protect individuals and support their freedom, yet rights can come into conflict. These tensions can be between rights held by different individuals, between different rights for the same person, or between the beliefs of the individual about what they might need or feel is acceptable and those of society. We therefore need a profession that is able to work with such conflicts. That profession is social work. Our focus on the individual and the social is the essential requirement for such work, because – crucially – rights are where the individual and the social come into contact. Rights are established by society but held by individuals. Working with rights is therefore essentially and irreducibly *social* work. As part of this we need to be able to understand and, yes, help individuals. But we also need to understand the social mandate for the work we do, including the rights we may be working with. And we need to understand the very particular ways in which we can be helpful, because they are very different from counselling. More than anything we need to understand and be able to work constructively with the tensions and conflicts that rights-focused work involves.

Content of the book

To explore the idea of rights-focused social work the book is divided into three parts. Part I provides an introduction to different types of rights and their relevance to social work. The idea of universal rights emerged from the Enlightenment, which is one of the reasons why this book is titled *The Enlightened Social Worker*. Chapter 2 therefore provides a short overview of the Enlightenment tradition, the development of rights and addresses some potential criticisms of such an orientation. It situates social work as necessary for, and enabled by, the creation of liberal democracy, and therefore sees social work as entwined with Enlightenment ideals and ideas. The next chapters in Part I each start with a real case study. The arguments of each chapter are then related to social work with that family to clarify links between theory and practice. Chapter 3 links rights more closely to social work and considers three generations of rights, sometimes referred to as rights to liberty, equality and community. The following chapters consider each of these types of right in more depth. Chapter 4 considers rights to freedom and protection, and in particular examines how and whether we help people change in the context of child protection. It considers issues of choice and coercion in the field of child protection. Chapter 5 turns to rights to resources, sometimes referred to as positive freedoms. Key theories of social need are presented, and it is argued that there is no simple resolution of the issues that arise from these theories – but for that very reason social workers are required in order to manage these tensions. Chapter 6 considers so-called 'third-generation' rights to human connection, and considers love in social work. It argues that rights are best understood within an ethic of love as outlined by bell hooks, and this frames subsequent discussions of theory and practice.

Part I concludes by suggesting that ultimately in working with these tensions we need to use all the emotions, knowledge, skills and values we have as social workers. Part II therefore has the impossible task of introducing the theories we should use in rights-focused practice; the task is impossible because the real answer is that rights-focused practice provides the crucible in which everything we know as social workers is brought together. Yet it seems helpful to consider some of the theoretical orientations that are necessary to work in a rights-focused way. Part II therefore reviews two key traditions for thinking about rights: humanist social work (in Chapter 7) and the social model (in Chapter 8). It is argued that each is essential for approaching rights-focused practice, but that it is the ability to move between a focus on the individual of humanism and the social of the social model which characterises good social work. The conclusion is that social workers need to be able to work with potential tensions between the different traditions and synthesise them for an effective orientation towards rights-focused practice.

The final part of the book concentrates on the practices of rights-focused social work. It has four chapters, the first two on assessment and the next two on direct practice, while recognising and illustrating that the two are intertwined. The first assessment chapter, Chapter 9, argues for assessment as a form of contested theory development. Chapter 10 then outlines and illustrates the nature of formulations, hypotheses and analytic practices that support good assessment work. Chapter 11 focuses on direct practice with individuals and families. It considers how we can apply a rights-focused perspective, undergirded by a love ethic, to understanding need, helping with behaviour change, working with capacity issues and working with conflicting rights. It introduces and elaborates on the concept of 'purposeful dialogue' as a key element of rights-focused practice. Chapter 12 moves beyond the individual to consider rights-focused practice with networks, communities and in society more generally. It considers Family Group Conferences, Contextual Safeguarding and recent academic and policy work to illustrate the role of social workers in moving beyond a focus on the individual.

Of course, social work is not just about balancing rights. A rights-focused perspective also helps us understand how and why social workers do help people, and provides insights into the principles and practices involved in doing so. It allows us to think about assessment, helping and the social work commitment to social justice in different ways. It changes what we understand to be the aims and outcomes we should strive for – and therefore has important implications for policy and for research. This book argues that this approach to rights needs to be delivered in and through relationships, and it puts 'a kind of loving' (Wilson et al, 2003) and a love ethic (hooks, 2002) at the core of social work. It does this because social work needs to combine head and heart, emotions and rationality.

The book develops its view of rights-focused social work as part of a broader Enlightenment tradition that seeks to promote human welfare and wellbeing, to do so through rational inquiry and debate, and that sees rights and democracy as foundational to such a project. That is why it is called *The Enlightened Social Worker*. The conclusion of that chapter, and of the book, is that social work should be proud of the part it has and is playing in making the world a better place. Ultimately, that is both the goal and the achievement of rights-focused social work. The Enlightenment tradition requires social work as an essential profession for a liberal and humane society; knowing that this is the tradition from which social work emerges helps us to understand the purpose and contribution of social work.

2

The Enlightenment, social work and progress

Most of this book is closely related to social work practice. This chapter is somewhat different as it looks at the bigger picture, providing a brief overview of historical context and theoretical issues relating to the development of rights and the need for social work. It argues that social work is best understood as part of a broader 'Enlightenment project'. The Enlightenment provides a constellation of key principles, summarised by the 'Liberty, Equality, Fraternity' slogan from the French Revolution, as well as core ideas that are necessary to make a reality of these principles. These include concepts such as humanism, rationality, democracy and rights that are central to social work, and indeed make it necessary for society to have the profession of social work. Seeing social work as part of a broader Enlightenment project helps to provide a coherent vision of what social work is for, it begins to explain some of the challenges involved in the messy realities of practice, and it allows a description of the essential contribution that social work makes to a humane and caring society that respects the rights of individuals. This key contribution is why social work is an essential and worthwhile activity for any enlightened society.

This chapter starts with a high-level overview of the Enlightenment. It then identifies some key challenges for Enlightenment thinking, including arguments that it has been used as a tool of oppression. In responding to this point, it is suggested that Enlightenment ideals, such as democracy, liberty and individual rights, are achieved through struggle – and our commitment to them entails a commitment to promote these ideals. This also establishes social work as a political activity. This is political with a small 'p': it is not about party politics, but because social workers work to promote rights, and because rights are achieved through political struggle, then social workers need to have an understanding of values, principles and theories related to the politics of the work we do. This idea, that social workers need a critical and political perspective on the work we do, is a recurring theme in the book.

The argument of the chapter, and indeed the book as a whole, then moves on to suggest that individual rights within a democratic society are the best way we currently have of organising society, but that they can and will sometimes be in conflict or tension. Such tensions are often not resolvable, certainly at the general level. For instance, when is parenting so poor that a child should be removed from their family? When should an individual's liberty be restricted because their mental illness might result in them harming others or themself? Instead, we need professionals who are able to understand and work with the tensions and potential conflicts that a rights-based society produces. This provides the foundation for later chapters, which consider rights and social work in more detail – and link rights more closely to actual examples from practice.

The laws and policies that provide the foundation for all statutory work are different ways of framing some of these fundamental questions. While they approach the challenges with specific concepts such as parental responsibility, the paramountcy principle, the right to family privacy or the definition of capacity these are all manifestations of the deeper principles created by the Enlightenment commitment to individual rights – and they produce complex challenges and tensions. It is social workers, more than any other professional group, who need to understand and work with these issues. This chapter starts by considering this broader picture.

What was the Enlightenment?

The Enlightenment is an intellectual movement associated with the 18th century, though its influence remains with us (Herman and Bishop, 2002). It was a revolution in human thinking with consequences that have reverberated down the ages (Porter, 2000). At the heart of the Enlightenment was a belief in reason and rationality and their application to enhancing human welfare (Pinker, 2018). Two important movements preceded and informed it. One was the 'Scientific Revolution' of the 17th century, which saw beliefs based on the Bible or the authority of the church challenged by scientific enquiry. The second was the Reformation. The Reformation led some Christians – who became known collectively as Protestants – to reject the authority of the Pope and emphasise the individual relationship between believer and God. Like the Scientific Revolution, the Reformation challenged the received wisdom and power of the church, and emphasised rational thinking and debate. Together, the Scientific Revolution and the Reformation provided the foundation for the Enlightenment, as they emphasised rationality and individual thinking and challenged received religious orthodoxy. It is hard to overstate the degree to which these three revolutions in human thinking – the Scientific Revolution, the Reformation and the Enlightenment – changed the way we think about knowledge, power and rationality: they created the modern world.

The Enlightenment was a broad movement, that to a large degree provides the 'common sense' within which we continue to operate: it developed a vision of how and what to think that supplanted the previous reliance on religious authority (Porter, 2000). The Enlightenment also provided the foundation for almost all our current academic disciplines, seeing the creation of subjects as diverse as economics and geology. The emphasis on rationality and debate means that there is great diversity and disagreement within the Enlightenment tradition (Pinker, 2018). A repeated theme within this book is that disagreement and dissent is a core part of doing social work: this is in part because it is an inherent part of the Enlightenment tradition. Valuing difference and disagreement flows from valuing individuals and their views and believing in rationality.

Given the sheer variety and heterogeneity of Enlightenment thinking, it is only possible to identify key elements. Here we consider, relatively briefly, four core elements of the Enlightenment. They are a belief in:

- rationality;
- a humanist perspective that puts individual flourishing at the heart of the good society;
- progress; and
- the interrelated ideas of individual rights, democracy and liberty.

The foundational idea for Enlightenment thinking is a belief in the power of rational thinking (Honneth, 1987; Pinker, 2018). This was seen to have allowed strides in scientific progress, and at the heart of the Enlightenment was the idea that we could apply rationality to human affairs. This involved developing disciplines that understood human beings and human society as subjects we can study through rational enquiry and empirical investigation. It also involved a belief that by doing so we could develop better ways of organising and governing society. A belief in rationality also entailed a belief in debate and discussion. The Enlightenment saw an unprecedented flowering of forums for debate – from coffee houses and parliaments to universities and learned societies. A belief that rationality, rather than authority, should be the basis for making decisions entailed a belief that different ideas should be tested through debate and empirical inquiry (Ferrone, 2015).

This inevitably led to consideration of the purpose of society. What goals should we strive for and how might these shape the society we create? Up to the 18th century the answers to these questions had been largely theological – they focused on interpretations of what God might want. Societies were organised to benefit those in power, the Church and Kings or other leaders. Enlightenment thinking developed a different focus. It argued that society should be organised to allow human flourishing. This is the essence of a humanist position – humanists put human welfare and wellbeing at the heart of their thinking and make achieving them the ultimate goal for society.

Of course, it can be argued that we have a long way to go to achieve this, and I explore this point later in this chapter, but nonetheless the ideas of the Enlightenment fuelled the French and American Revolutions as well as more gradual processes of progressive change in most Western countries

(Herman and Bishop, 2002). They provided the intellectual foundation for those who challenged authoritarian power and championed democracy and individual rights (James, 1989). Debate and even war may rage over how to achieve these aims, but the ideologies of both liberal democracy and, later, communism emerged to a large degree from the Enlightenment focus on rational attempts to improve human welfare.

The focus on human welfare led to the development of the concept of individual rights. Rights are a key focus of this book, as it is argued that social work – at least in all statutory settings – is fundamentally about protecting and championing people's rights. The focus on individual rights was closely related to the idea that all humans were of equal worth – a radical idea with revolutionary implications. The motto of the French Revolution, 'liberty, equality, fraternity', remains the pithiest encapsulation of Enlightenment ideals. It highlights that individuals should be free, that all people are of equal worth and – perhaps the most difficult element to achieve – that we should stand together in solidarity. In this book I generally replace the gendered word fraternity with human connection and sometimes solidarity, though each perhaps lacks the emotional bond inherent in fraternity. These ideas fuelled arguments and struggles for rights and democracy across the world, and ultimately created the need for a profession such as social work that could work with rights.

A final Enlightenment idea is important. Most Enlightenment thinkers believed that the values outlined here – rationality, humanism, rights and democracy – would result in progress for human beings. Indeed, more than that, progress is a key test of the Enlightenment project. Enlightenment thinking is designed to promote human flourishing, and can therefore be judged by its success in achieving this. At the end of book I return to consider whether we are making progress and argue that we are, and that social work has had an important role to play in supporting human progress. However, this is to foreshadow the conclusion – there are a lot of other issues to consider before returning to think about the issue of progress. An important starting point is to consider criticisms of Enlightenment thinking, and in doing so to develop a deeper understanding of how we might apply Enlightenment principles in the 21st century.

Criticisms of the Enlightenment

An obvious feature of the Enlightenment is that it was largely produced by middle-class, White, Western, men – and there are powerful arguments that this contributes to key problems and limitations in Enlightenment thinking. Before considering some of these, it is important to note that there have been major contributions to Enlightenment thinking from people with other types of backgrounds. Mary Wollstonecraft provided a powerful early feminist text arguing for the equality of women in 1792 (Wollstonecraft, 2008 [1792]). Black thinkers and activists such as Crummell and Du Bois can be understood as being within the broad Enlightenment tradition (Crummell, 1891; Du Bois, 2015), and Islamic intellectuals were crucial for the Enlightenment both because they preserved and developed thinkers from Ancient Greece during the medieval period and because Islamic advances in science helped generate the Scientific Revolution (Garcia, 2012). Yet it remains true that the Enlightenment was overwhelmingly developed by the most privileged group in society – and the group that remain the most privileged 400 years later – namely: rich, White, Western men. This leads to two powerful sets of criticisms. One is that Enlightenment ideas were used to justify or cover for exploitation. A second is that when the voices of those excluded from the development of Enlightenment thinking – such as women, Black people, non-Western and indigenous communities – are heard, they have very different arguments in relation to key Enlightenment ideas. These crucial and related criticisms have important implications for how we think about the Enlightenment now. The first we consider now, while the second is reviewed later in this chapter.

Enlightenment ideals, oppression and resistance

So, did the Enlightenment facilitate oppression? The most obvious observation is that the Enlightenment ushered in an era of unprecedented exploitation of human beings – and that this exploitation was carried out by the very class of people who developed so-called 'Enlightenment' ideas. Slavery and colonialism, capitalism and the oppression of women all characterised the years following the Enlightenment. On this basis it has been argued that Enlightenment thinking provided a cover or even a rationale for these types of exploitation: they allowed the ruling class to believe themselves 'Enlightened' and this provided a justification for colonising countries seen as less 'advanced' and enslaving groups believed to be less 'civilised' (see Duchet, 1971; Dubois, 2006; Wolff and Cipolloni, 2007 and many others), for treating women as inferior and in particular as less 'rational' and therefore not worthy of the same rights as men (for instance, O'Brien and O'Brien, 2009; Tomaselli, 2017) and for excluding specific groups, such as those without property, from key rights (Wood, 2012).

This criticism of the Enlightenment is powerful and has important consequences, which we turn to later, however on its own it distorts and simplifies the nature of the Enlightenment. Crucially, most of the movements to challenge and fight against these types of oppression have themselves been rooted firmly in Enlightenment ideas (O'Brien and O'Brien, 2009; Wood, 2012). Feminism, anti-colonialism, anti-racism, the French and American Revolutions and most progressive movements have been justified through Enlightenment ideals, such as the fundamental equality and worth of individuals. The most egregious oppressions, such as slavery, colonialism, oppression of women, homophobia or disablism (to name a few) tend to be justified by excluding a group of people from inclusion in the Enlightenment ideals for human beings, generally based on claims that for some reason that group are not of equal worth. These spurious arguments about essential difference and inferiority, which we know by terms such as racism, sexism or disablism, seek to exclude certain groups from the universal Enlightenment ideals. This attempt to create an exception to the principles of all people having equal worth and therefore rights being universal is to some degree a recognition of the power of Enlightenment ideals – those who preach or practice discrimination have to go to considerable lengths to subvert claims for equality. Such attempts have failed or are failing – we have seen an ever-widening recognition of people's equal worth, and racism, sexism and other forms of discrimination have become steadily less acceptable. This is in part because such claims are empirically untrue: the groups or cultures in question are of course *not* 'inferior', and the assumptions that suggest they are can and have been challenged (Rose et al, 1984; Rose and Rose, 2010). However, oppressive ideas have primarily failed not just because they are wrong, but because people have struggled against them. And while there is far to go, and we live a world that is far too unequal, the progress that we have made has come through struggle informed by Enlightenment ideals.

Slavery was not abolished simply because wealthy White men were persuaded by liberal arguments about the equal worth of Black people. There were such figures, people like William Wilberforce and others, however the struggles of slaves, their rebellions and their smaller-scale acts of resistance, as well as the example that figures such as Touissant L'Ouverture, James Somerset and Mary Prince provided once they escaped or overcame slavery made slavery untenable, economically, intellectually and morally (Hart, 1980; James, 1989). The equality of women has been increasingly recognised because of the struggles of women to achieve equality – whether that is suffragettes campaigning for the vote or more recent generations of feminists fighting for equality and highlighting discrimination and oppression. Such fights have also been won or progress made by the extraordinary example of individuals from difficult backgrounds achieving exceptional things. It is hard to justify racism if you encounter the moral and intellectual achievements of Toni Morrison and Maya Angelou, Nelson Mandela and James Baldwin. The same is true for women – how can one justify treating women as anything other than equals if one reads the novels of Austen or observes Marie Curie becoming the only person to be awarded two Nobel Prizes at a time when women were rarely allowed to attend university? Similar patterns can be seen for other struggles for increased rights and equality, such as the civil rights movement in the United States and the United Kingdom, campaigns for equal treatment for gay and lesbian people, recognition of the existence of and need for equality for people who are trans or non-binary, campaigns for rights of disabled people or those with mental health needs, independence from imperial oppression and, as far as I am aware, every other struggle for equality.

All these struggles are founded on the radical Enlightenment ideal that all people are of equal worth and that this should be recognised in the rights they have. Yet this ideal on its own is not enough – this ideal has to be constantly achieved through struggle. In this respect Enlightenment ideals are a call to action that has inspired most movements for human liberation. Sometimes it has been possible for change to happen within the democratic process, with electoral success allowing changes in policies and laws to promote gender, race and disability equality. Sometimes it has required industrial action – with the unions and labour movements key champions of the many benefits associated with the welfare state (Gough, 1979). Many of the movements have embraced non-violence. This contributed to the success of the civil rights movement and some anti-colonial struggles, notably in India. In other instances the struggle has involved violence. Apartheid was overthrown in part through armed resistance. The defeat of fascism was only possible through war for the values of democracy. L'Ouverture's leadership of the slave revolution in Haiti was explicitly intended to claim Enlightenment rights for former slaves, but it required armed struggle (James, 1989).

Of course, there is still far to go, and many examples of groups experiencing discrimination, oppression and unfair treatment. Nonetheless, this history of rights achieved through struggle has profound implications for the arguments within this book. The most important is that the rights we enjoy – and that social workers are fundamentally concerned with – have no objective existence, in the sense that they do not exist independently of the societies that we create as humans. They have been achieved through struggle, both intellectual and physical. This struggle is inspired by values, by Enlightenment values, including the equal worth of each individual and their freedom to live the life they wish to live, but these values are only made real through ongoing struggle. This creates practical and theoretical challenges which are considered throughout this book. Indeed, the argument is that it is precisely because many of these tensions cannot be resolved that we need a profession such as social work, and associated organisations and laws that deal with these conflicts and difficulties. It also means that social work is an inherently political activity. If rights achieved through struggle create the field in which we operate, then social work is always political, because the rights we are working with are often contingent and changing. This is why social workers, more than other professions, can and should wrestle with political and ethical questions – something explored throughout this book.

The invitation to consider social work as part of an Enlightenment project that promotes individual rights, rationality and humanist values does not therefore provide a completed and finished version of how to do social work, because Enlightenment ideas do not promise a resolution to debate and discussion, nor to political struggle. In fact, they do the opposite: they are an invitation to develop ideas, debate and struggle for principles we hold dear. The Enlightenment does not tell us how society should be. Instead, Enlightenment ideals suggest we need constantly to debate and struggle about what sort of society we should live in. The Enlightenment ideal is that endless disputation is both the best way to run society and in itself an aim we should strive towards, because such endless disputation characterises a free society as well as being the best engine for promoting human wellbeing.

To some degree our developing understanding of rights is an exemplar of this. The original rights associated with the Enlightenment were those of classical liberalism and focused on individual freedom. Over time, arguments and struggles resulted in recognition of rights to resources. More recently, there has been growing recognition that rights may be too individualistic and we need to consider rights to connection, community and place (Ife et al, 2022). In the next section and the following chapter the development of these types of rights are outlined and the conundrums and challenges they create are considered. It is argued that the different types of rights generate differing needs for a profession that can handle their intrinsic tensions and conflicts – and that that profession is social work.

The birth of rights: individual freedom and negative rights

The idea of individuals having rights is a relatively new one in human history, with seeds before the Enlightenment. It became widely accepted during the Enlightenment and has been expanded and developed over the centuries since. The idea that rights should be applied universally – that all individuals should have the same basic rights – is even more recent, beginning to be accepted on a wide scale only after the Second World War. Indeed, it is still not accepted in all countries (Ife et al, 2022).

Individual rights are a core element of Enlightenment thinking. They serve two key purposes. The first is to provide a bulwark against the power of the state or other concentrations of power (Mill, 1989 [1859]; Lee, 2015). While Enlightenment thinkers believe in democracy, there was also a keen appreciation of the 'tyranny of the majority'. As experienced in the English Civil War and the French, Russian and other revolutions, once a group has power and believes they can use it, even if they believe or say it is for the general good, abuse of that power is almost always close behind. Enlightenment thinking created the idea of liberal democracy. The name liberal democracy captures well the Enlightenment solution to this abuse of power. There was a belief in democracy, but there are also inalienable individual rights that protect the individual from abuse of power – these are the liberal element. In protecting the rights of individuals, rights also protect democracy itself, because they curtail the unfettered use of power (Mill, 1989 [1859]). Thus, for instance, rights to free speech, assembly and political organisation are not only a good thing for individuals, they protect democracy itself.

The first generation of rights: negative freedom and liberty

The classic articulation of the liberal ideal for rights is that each individual should be allowed to do what they wish, provided it does not hurt someone else. As the declaration of the French Revolution put it: 'Liberty consists in the freedom to do everything which injures no one else' (Declaration of the Rights of Man, 1789). Similarly, J.S. Mill stated: 'The only purpose for which power can be rightfully exercised over any member of a civilized community, against his will, is to prevent harm to others' (Mill, 1989 [1859]). This is known as the 'harm principle'. While we may debate exceptions to this principle, the broad idea that liberty should only be restricted when others are harmed, remains a central idea within a liberal society.

Classic liberal accounts of rights based on the harm principle tend to focus on minimising constraints on individual freedom. This is known as 'negative freedom'. Classic negative freedoms are the right to fair trial, the right to free expression and the right to vote. While the state needs to provide protection for the nation (for instance, through the military) and for individuals (for instance, through effective policing), what it provides beyond that should be kept to a minimum, and it should not limit people's freedom.

This liberal account of negative freedom has, even within its own terms, some challenges that lead to a need for the involvement of social workers. An obvious one, that even the strongest proponent of a liberal position would recognise, is that not everybody has the capacity to exercise such freedom. Members of some groups are particularly likely to have actual or potential limits to their capacity to exercise such freedoms. This might include children, people with serious mental illness, learning difficulties or dementia. If we are to make a reality of the harm principle as a basis for our society, we need to ensure that people with potentially limited capacity to exercise their individual freedom have their rights protected – including rights to not be abused and rights to have their views taken seriously. To a large degree the creation of contemporary child and family social work in the United Kingdom and other liberal democracies has been developed to deal with this challenge. Similar issues exist in relation to working with adults. An issue that links the disparate groups of people that social workers work with is that they often have issues relating to decision-making capacity. That is a key reason we need social workers and others who can sensitively and thoughtfully work with the complexities that this creates.

These are issues from within the liberal paradigm of rights. In other words, even a staunch proponent of minimal state provision would recognise that not all people have the capacity to exercise freedom and that this creates challenges for a liberal vision of rights. However, rights are generally considered to be much broader than just rights to negative freedoms and the next two sections outline other types of rights.

The second generation of rights: positive freedom, needs and equality

There have been a second powerful set of criticisms of this minimalist approach to rights, namely arguments that without resources people are not able to exercise key rights and that society therefore needs to provide resources that allow people to exercise their freedoms (see, for instance, Sen, 1985; Doyal and Gough, 1991; Plant, 2019). This is an argument for more than the absence of constraint, it requires society to provide services or resources, and it is therefore an argument for a conception of 'positive freedom' and the positive rights needed to provide for such freedoms (Berlin, 2017 [1967]). There is therefore a sense in which it is an argument for at least some level of equality within a society.

This approach to rights is sometimes called 'second-generation' rights, as it emerged much later than the original narrow focus of negative rights (Ife et al, 2022). Through the 20th century there was an increased emphasis on the resources that people needed in order to be free. This led to the development of second-generation rights, particularly in the period after the Second World War. This period saw the idea of rights expanded from negative freedoms to include rights to resources needed to be free. This is most famously captured in the 1948 United Nations Universal Declaration of Human Rights, which added to traditional negative freedoms such positive rights as, for example, the right to rest and leisure (Article 24), an adequate standard of living (Article 25) and to education (Article 26). In parallel, most Western countries developed welfare states that made a reality of many of these rights.

Yet here, too, there are tensions and complexities in applying rights to some individuals and groups. In general, we tend to provide rights either universally (for instance, roads or education) or in a targeted way (for instance, benefits). Yet, again, people without capacity may not be able to make use of such rights. For most such people, members of their family will have responsibility for meeting their needs, and we usually allow such relationships to meet needs. Yet sometimes this is not possible. Again, in such circumstances there may be different views about what is needed and what should be provided, and once again social workers tend to be at the heart of such discussions. This is the focus of Chapter 4.

The approach to rights outlined thus far arises directly from Enlightenment thinking, and it is a central part of the Enlightenment project that seeks to establish a rational basis for society based on principles of mutual respect, individual autonomy and human thriving. A key challenge to the Enlightenment approach is that it individualises the idea of rights, and in doing so contributes to an individualised account of the individual within society. This individualised focus ignores our need for connection, community and place. These are sometimes called the 'third generation' of rights (Ife, 2018).

Criticisms of individualised rights and the development of the third generation of rights

It was noted earlier that one of the key criticisms of Enlightenment thinking is that it was developed by privileged groups, specifically White, Western men – people like me, in fact. When the voices of others, such as women or those from different cultural backgrounds, are heard then different ideas about rights emerge. This section considers what we can learn from such arguments, for our understanding of rights and of rights-focused social work.

Feminist critics have argued that the rational individual at the heart of classic rights theorising is a typically masculine construct, with a tendency to be overly individualistic (Pritchard-Jones, 2018). One element of this is to argue that rationality is a problematic concept – for instance because it marginalises emotions (Lloyd, 2017). It is also argued that individual rights focus on the idea of the independent and decision-making individual, but that human beings are intrinsically and irreducibly interdependent (Fine and Glendinning, 2005; Pritchard-Jones, 2018). Feminist scholars have also highlighted that both first- and second-generation approaches to rights tend to have an uncritical view of institutions such as the state and the family and they lack analysis of the way that they can operate as sites of oppression within a patriarchal system (Binion, 1995; Greer, 1971).

From a different starting point, non-Western criticisms of rights have also focused on the individualised nature of classic liberal rights and argued that this approach fails to see people in their context. This has been argued by Japanese, African and first nation Australian theorists (for example, Christie, 2003; Ihara, 2004; Hunt, 2008; and see Sen, 1999 and Mende, 2021 for excellent discussions). Ife and others provides an insightful discussion of key arguments with applications for social work (Ife et al, 2022; and see Skegg, 2005). What these critiques share is a sense that we are humans in relationships, that our obligations towards one another are part of what make us who we are, and that great care needs to be taken in distilling rights out of this complexity and ascribing them to individuals. Some theorists place particular emphasis on physical place as constituting identity (for example, Carmalt, 2007). Others argue that seeing individuals as individuals is problematic, and that we can only make sense of ourselves and our lives in and through relationships within communities (see, for instance, Featherstone et al, 2018). This being the case, individual rights are argued to be a partial and potentially problematic approach.

These are not just theoretical issues: such approaches have provided important practical challenges to current social work practice. For instance, they have been used to question the tendency to see children as individuals, and to argue that children, and indeed all humans, are intrinsically part of a network of relationships. Family is a core element of this. Such a vision of children provides a powerful argument against removing children from their wider family. A practical example is the adaptation of Maori traditions in an effort to find alternatives to child removal and the resulting development of Family Group Conferences. Family Group Conferences allow wider family to make decisions about how to keep a child who is considered to be at risk safe and to help them.

Feminist criticisms of individualised rationality and liberty have been particularly helpful in understanding how relationships and resources can influence 'freedom'. For instance, lack of options may keep women in abusive relationships, and coercive control can also limit the psychological freedom of those who have been abused.

A response to these criticisms: social work and third-generation rights

Three specific points can to be made in response to these criticisms. The first is that it is untrue to equate the development of rights discourse solely with White, Western men (Mende, 2021). This was largely true of the initial Enlightenment development of negative freedoms and classic Liberalism, where writers such as Locke, Hume, Kant and others were all from this privileged group – because only this group were allowed to participate meaningfully in the production and reproduction of knowledge at this time. However, since then other voices have been influential in developing thinking about rights, and in particular second-generation positive rights. This is most obvious in relation to the voice of women. Eleanor Roosevelt was chairperson of the committee that drafted the 1948 United Nations Universal Declaration of Human Rights. Women have influenced the development of ideas about rights in myriad other ways, including important contributions from social workers, such as Jane Addams, who established social work in the United States, fought for the rights of women, children and others and won the Nobel Prize in 1931, and Leymah Gbowee, another social worker who won a Nobel Prize for peace activism and fighting for women's rights in 2011. Many other women have influenced our developing understanding and practices in relation to rights, including for instance Nussbaum (2007) and Boserup (1970). Writers and activists from non-Western backgrounds have also had a substantial influence on our understanding of rights in recent decades, such as Sen's key work on capabilities – which explicitly embraces a cross-cultural perspective (Sen, 1999).

Second, it is possible to disagree with, or at least question, some of the criticisms that are made (Sen, 1999). For instance, it is true that an excessive focus on individual rights can lose the sense of family and community, and an emphasis on the individual may be more a feature of Western thinking than some other cultures. Yet losing a focus on individual rights altogether is potentially dangerous – much abuse of women and children, of people with disabilities, or gay people or other groups, was made possible in part because we considered family or other collective grouping to be more important than individuals. When individuals and their rights get subsumed into something bigger – whether that be family, community or state – there is a danger that the rights of some are reduced and there is the possibility of those with less power being abused. Indeed, it is more than a possibility, it seems to be an almost universal phenomenon. Individual rights act as a protection against abuses that happen in social institutions, including informal institutions such as families and neighbourhoods.

Third, there is also a danger in an uncritical approach to non-Western cultures, simplistically painting them as having solely positive attributes linked to connection and community (Sen, 1999). In most cultures – maybe all cultures – there has been mistreatment of specific groups and of individuals. It is therefore naïve and inaccurate to describe non-Western cultures in a simplistically positive way. The danger is, again, that we may extol the virtues of a specific culture's focus on family, tribe or community without also having a critical appreciation of the ways that power and control work in all human societies and organisations.

Nonetheless, the criticism that an excessive focus on individuals and their rights can lead us to underestimate our fundamental need for human connection is true. A society where we are all free to do what we want but have no connections and responsibilities to one another would be an empty and unsatisfying place to live. Taken together these criticisms, revisions and new ideas have therefore developed what is sometimes call the 'third generation' of rights, which place more emphasis on environment, place and relationship (Ife et al, 2022). This emphasis on human connection and community can be seen as emphasising rights related to solidarity. While there are various examples of proposals to enshrine such rights, for instance by protecting certain communities or lands that may be significant to particular groups, it is generally accepted that there are fewer examples of successful enactments of third-generation rights. It is possible, though, that there are examples of rights to solidarity or at least connection in some social work legislation, as discussed in Chapter 6.

This book places rights to human connection, and in particular to loving relationships and communities, as a core aim of social work. It therefore argues that the third generation of rights are crucial for the work we do. Yet it argues that such a commitment is far from straightforward. Like working with other types of rights, working to promote loving relationships creates challenges that require a professional practice characterised by kindness, respectfulness and wisdom, but that is also able to work with contradictions, conflicts and tensions.

Towards rights-focused social work

The argument of this book is that a rights-based democracy is the best form of society we currently have, but that the rights to protect individuals inevitably produce tensions and difficulties. This has led to the creation of a profession that, more than any other, works with these issues. In particular, social work – and especially statutory social work in the United Kingdom – tends to work with people where capacity to exercise their freedom may be limited. This produces many tensions that social workers need to understand and be able to work constructively with. Social work is therefore essential for protecting and promoting the rights of individuals and it is also essential if we are to have a society that takes the rights of people, and particularly those who may not be able easily to exercise their own rights, seriously.

In the next four chapters I consider different elements of rights-focused social work. Each of the chapters starts with a family that I worked with or knew very well, and uses that as a case study to explore in greater detail issues about what rights are and how we might work with them in social work. Ultimately, the argument of the book is that social work is essential and worthwhile because it champions individual freedom, social equality and equity and human connection. In doing so it provides an essential service for those we work with, but also for society more generally. In doing their work each day social workers are building a society we can all be proud of, one that is founded on the core principles of the Enlightenment and that when done well makes a positive difference to innumerable people.

3

On rights and social work

The last chapter dealt with ideas that may seem rather removed from the everyday practice of social work. To try to keep ideas about rights related to social work practice this chapter and each of the others in Part I starts with a real family to explore what rights-focused social work means in practice. The case study for this chapter seeks to illustrate how social workers work with rights and the tensions they create. Rights and social work and the legal basis for thinking about rights are then considered and related back to the case study.

A case study of rights-focused practice

The case study is of a family of two children, who we will call Ted (aged six) and Cara (aged eight). Ted and Cara had been in care for almost two years. About six months ago they moved to live with long-term foster carers, with the plan being for them to stay permanently while having regular contact with their mother and father. Their mother and father now live separately, and each has serious mental health problems. Shortly after the children moved they got a new social worker, Rosa. Rosa visited Ted and Cara several times and got to know them and their foster carers, as well as talking to their school, health professionals and the previous foster carers. In the first few weeks her main focus was making sure that the children were settling in and that the new carers were coping. She helped the children understand what was happening and why, and that being in care was not their fault and that it was not the plan for them to go back to living with either their mother or father. She talked to the foster carers and arranged practical help for them during quite a challenging period while they took on two young children.

Rosa also arranged some practical things for the children, like ensuring the children got the dental treatment they needed and had eye tests. She talked to the parents about these issues and made sure they were happy. She tried her best to arrange regular contact with both parents, something that proved fairly easy with the mother but difficult with the father. Rosa did not give up, she kept meeting the father and eventually arranged regular video meetings. Rosa also talked to the parents about what was happening and for bigger decisions she checked what their opinion was before taking action. This was true for two important areas Rosa was involved with.

One of these was to sort out the citizenship of the children. The parents were not originally from the United Kingdom and as a result the children's status in the country was unclear. This required a lot of form-filling and some legal help but was ultimately formalised to give the children the right to remain in the United Kingdom and, at a later point, apply for citizenship.

A second issue was schooling. The children were being driven back to the school they had always gone to, near their mother's house. The current and the previous foster carers felt that the children would benefit from moving to the local school. It would allow the children to make local friends, it meant they could walk to and from school and it would lessen the potential for either parent to disrupt care for the children by turning up when they were experiencing mental health problems. Against this, it would mean another change for the children. Rosa talked with the parents, both of whom were happy about the proposed move, partly because they recognised that the new school had a better academic reputation. She talked to the children about school, and they told her they were happy where they were. She did not ask them about moving to a new school, as she felt that they were not old enough to make an informed decision. She also felt that if they were aware of the possibility of moving then what might be quite a protracted process – that might not end in them changing school – would be unsettling. She talked to the foster carers and the school to get a sense of how the children were doing in school. The foster carers felt that while the children were used to their current school, and felt at home there, they did not seem to have many friends and were possibly not achieving their academic potential. The foster carers felt that if these were their own children they would move them to the local school, and therefore as children in care they should get the same opportunities.

On balance Rosa believed that the children should move, and her manager agreed. Rosa therefore applied for Ted and Cara to move school. According to the law and national policy guidance, children in care should get priority and therefore arranging the change of school should have been fairly straightforward. However, the local authority had a different policy. This involved all school applications being reviewed in a meeting of senior managers and a decision being made. This group decided the children should not be moved as the school they were at was 'adequate' and they also argued that because the current school was under-subscribed it would be problematic for the local authority for children to leave it for a school that had a waiting list.

Rosa was unhappy with this decision. She wrote to the chair of the meeting explaining the ways in which it did not meet legal requirements. She complained to a senior manager within children's social care about the process. Eventually the decision was overturned and the children were sent to their local school – where they settled quickly and thrived. This happened in part because it became obvious that the way that the local authority were making such decisions did not follow the legal requirements, and seemed to be as much about keeping numbers up in under-subscribed schools as it was about meeting the needs of individual children. As a result of this case, the council changed its policy to recognise the special rights children in care have and to make meeting those rights the primary issue to be considered in decision-making.

Rights and the case study

It is worth reflecting on this example. Rosa did a great job of rights-focused social work – but the sorts of issues that Rosa was dealing with are bread-and-butter social work issues. So, for instance, what were the rights Rosa was concerned with? At the highest level Ted and Cara were in care because they have a right to be protected. Rosa was working hard to ensure they had a positive care experience by ensuring they received the services and help they needed, including sorting out immigration status, schooling and the dentist. In doing so, she upheld other rights. She got to know the children well and she had a strong sense of their views on important issues – because children have a right to have their views understood and taken into account. She worked hard to involve both parents in key decisions, because she knows they continue to have parental responsibility and therefore a right to be involved in important decisions. She also knows how important they are to the children and wants to support that ongoing relationship.

It is worth noting that this rights-focused work often involved some level of conflict. The obvious conflict is the disagreement about choice of school, where Rosa championed the rights of the children, and indeed their parents and their foster carers, all of whom have legitimate input into decisions about schools for children. But there were other tensions that may be less obvious. The children did not want to move school. Rosa knew this but decided that on balance a change of school would be the right thing for the children. This is an example of her considering the capacity of the children to make a fully informed decision. There were lower-level tensions about what should happen that Rosa worked with. The father being inconsistent about contact needed to be worked with carefully, because it was upsetting for the children when he did not turn up but keeping him actively involved was important both for the children's long-term welfare and because as a parent he, as well as the children, have rights to connection.

A focus on rights helps us understand the constant tensions and conflicts that social workers struggle with. As noted at the start of the book, trying to understand why so much of social work is characterised by such tensions was a key motivation for writing this book and most of the chapters deal with actual or potential conflicts. Some of the case studies deal with some of the most obvious tensions, for instance when there are issues of child protection. Yet that is merely one example of the types of tensions workers encounter. In this case study, and in much social work practice, the potential conflict may be with organisational decisions, such as the one that was made about schooling. A focus on rights helps us understand that the social work role is to a large degree to work with and seek to resolve such conflicts.

In a relatively short period of time Rosa made a positive difference to the lives of Ted and Cara that may last a lifetime. This has not been primarily through her relationship with the children, though this is warm and trusting, but through the things she has done for them 'behind the scenes'. She has played a key role in settling them into a new, permanent foster family; she has ensured the parents remain actively involved; she has sorted out various issues, including their legal status in the country; and she has arranged for them to go to a local school which is likely to be a good fit for them. It might be possible to see some of this work through the lens of relationship-based practice. Certainly Rosa made relationships with multiple people, not least the children. Relationship-based approaches to social work can help us understand the complexity of some of this relationship work. Yet these were not in any sense therapeutic relationships. Rather, they were relationships for a purpose. What was that purpose? Much that Rosa did was to make things better for the children, however not everything she did was done for that purpose. The work that Rosa did to understand the perspective of the children or to involve the parents in decisions was not done solely to 'improve outcomes', rather it was to ensure the rights of all those involved were upheld.

A rights-focused approach to social work has several advantages in helping us understand what social work is, beyond explaining the tension so often present in the role. One is that it allows us to value both outcomes and process. For instance, getting to know Ted and Cara and their parents is not important merely to improve their 'outcomes', it is important in its own right, because they have a right to their perspectives being understood and taken into account – even if the decision made is ultimately at odds with their view. A focus on rights therefore values all the aspects of the role. Much social work theory focuses on direct practice – the way we work directly with children and adults, our relationships and communication skills. Yet the everyday experience of social work is that there is more to the role. As can be seen from the case study, Rosa did much of her best social work while sorting out immigration status or challenging local authority decisions about schooling. The children barely knew this work was happening. It is work that is unglamorous and often unappreciated, carried out through emails and form-filling in the background, yet in this example – and myriad others every day – this type of work changes lives.

Another benefit of a rights-focused perspective is that, at the highest level, it allows us to marry the individual and the social in our work. Social work should combine helping individuals with a broader social justice perspective. Rights are socially created but they apply to individuals. They therefore intrinsically require us to work with both levels together, the individual and the broader social level. A focus on rights makes the political nature of social work evident, while also focusing on the individuals who the rights apply to. This dual nature is what makes a profession that values both social justice and individual experiences – a profession such as social work – necessary for rights-focused work.

Many of these ideas are returned to later in the book. In this chapter we explore the idea of rights and of different types of rights further. The next section considers social work as a rights-focused profession. We then return to the case study of Rosa, Ted and Cara, and link the work of Rosa to this developing understanding of rights. This sets the scene for the next three chapters, which consider social work and rights-focused practice in relation to rights to liberty, equality and connection or love respectively.

Social work and human rights

Chapter 2 provided a brief overview of different types of rights. It is now appropriate to consider the relationship between rights and social work further. The 1988 International Federation of Social Work (IFSW) Policy Statement on Human Rights stated that 'social work has, from its conception, been a human rights profession, having as its basic tenet the intrinsic value of every human being and as one of its main aims the promotion of equitable social structures, which can offer people security and development while upholding their dignity' (IFSW, 2001). Despite this assertion that social work has always been a human rights profession it is not until the 2000 international definition of social work that there is explicit reference to human rights (Androff, 2015). In its final line it states that 'principles of human rights and social justice are fundamental to social work' (IFSW, 2001). The revised and most recent definition of social work from 2014 also includes reference to human rights: 'principles of social justice, human rights, collective responsibility and respect for diversities are central to social work' (IFSW, 2014).

A focus on rights can also be found in key documents about social work in the United Kingdom. The British Association of Social Work (BASW) Code of Ethics has three parts, focused on human rights, social justice and professional integrity. The section on human rights starts with the following statement: 'Social work is based on respect for the inherent worth and dignity of all people as expressed in the United Nations Universal Declaration of Human Rights (1948), other related UN declarations and the European

Convention on Human Rights and the conventions derived from those declarations' (BASW, 2021a).

So, a commitment to human rights is seen as fundamental to social work and it is enshrined in professional definitions and values. These are supported by international declarations, such as the United Nations Declaration and the European Convention. They are also explicit or implicit in the laws, policies and procedures that guide statutory social work practice in the United Kingdom. Statutory social work is practice defined and empowered by laws, and the bulk of social workers for adults and children in the United Kingdom work in statutory settings. These laws are the basis for rights within the jurisdiction that we practice in. There are separate laws for different countries, and within countries there is usually different legislation for different groups, for instance children, people with a serious mental illness, those in need because of disability and so on. For example, a social worker working in children's services in England would need to know and understand the 1989 Children Act, which is still the most important piece of legislation, but they would also need to be aware of more recent legislation, such as the Children and Families Act 2014 and the Children and Social Work Act 2017. They would also need to have knowledge of the key policies that are intended to guide those delivering the legislation, such as Working Together, 2018. Finally, they should understand local policies and practices.

Taken together this combination of professional values, international definitions of human rights and national legal and policy documents provide the framework which social workers need in order to practice in a rights-informed way. Yet the reason we need social workers, or at least the primary reason social workers are employed in the United Kingdom, is because the rights enshrined in these different sources are so often in conflict or tension. This is in part because they are working with and representing people who may not have full capacity to make decisions. It can also be related to the nature of the needs that workers are working with, as discussed in Chapter 5. This creates a wide variety of rights that may be in conflict, or at least tension.

Rights in social work practice

As well as the definitions of social work that mention human rights, academics have written about rights and social work. These texts tend to focus on rights as a good thing, and as something that social workers should promote (for instance Androff, 2015; Ife, 2018; Ife et al, 2022). The distinctive focus of this book is that it moves beyond arguing that human rights are important to suggest that workers are often involved when rights are in actual or potential conflict. We may, for instance, be promoting some rights, but overruling others. This leads to questions about how to work with such tensions. The book is therefore largely an attempt to answer the following question: If much of social work is about working with rights that are in potential conflict, what are the implications for how we think about and do social work?

The previous chapter outlined three types of rights: rights to individual freedoms; rights to having our needs met or positive freedom; and rights to human connection and community. For some of these rights when people do not have or might not have full capacity to act for themselves it creates conflicts and challenges that cannot be resolved with general laws or overarching policies. It requires professionals and processes that allow us to work with competing rights. The same is true for some rights to resources that social workers are often involved in assessing access to, for instance for older people, those with disability or other groups social workers become involved in creating what should be bespoke packages of care. This involves understanding and working with the needs of individuals, while realising that these may be at odds with the resources made available by society for these issues. These are examples of the sort of rights-focused work that requires professionals who are willing to wrestle with the practical challenges, tensions and conflicts created by different types of rights. Those professionals are, more than any other group, social workers. And in doing this complicated, conflict-infused work, they are often in practice doing the practical working out of what may appear to be theoretical arguments. So, for instance, the argument that children have a right to protection but that parents should have considerable freedom to parent as they wish to needs to be resolved for each child and family. Social workers are therefore practical philosophers, working through complicated ethical challenges created by a rights-based liberal democracy on a person-by-person basis.

This perhaps becomes clearer if we return to the example of Rosa, Ted and Cara from the start of the chapter. Rosa is protecting the negative freedoms of several people through her work. The fact that Ted and Cara are in care is to protect them from harm, and resolving their immigration status gives them rights to live and work in the United Kingdom and travel abroad that are independent of resources. The ongoing involvement and contact with their parents protects the rights of the parents as well as the children. Rosa also supported the positive freedoms of the children, providing education and dental care. At a more fundamental level, the decision to place the children in foster care was to meet their needs – both their negative right to protection from harm and their positive right to the resources they need. Yet this is not the only way positive freedoms were supported. Before Rosa's involvement, Ted and Cara's mother fled domestic abuse by the father and lived in a refuge. The social worker at the time helped them get a flat, arranged payments when benefits were slow to come through and also sorted out regular deliveries from the food bank. These were all actions designed to help meet the needs of the children and their mother, and to help her look after them. Rosa's work is also full of connection and relationships, in other words support for third-generation rights. She works to keep the children in touch with their parents, and to support their relationship with the current and previous foster carers. She thinks carefully about the new school and its ability to meet not just the educational needs of the children but also to build their sense of community and their local friendships. In doing so Rosa and previous social workers are demonstrating a practice that is concerned with all three 'generations' of rights – she is protecting individual freedoms, she is ensuring people have the resources they need and she is building connections and relationships. She is also striving to do all this in ways that respect rights and manage potential conflicts or tensions between rights. In other words she is treating rights not just as an outcome but also as informing the process of her work. Her work is inspired by a commitment to liberty, equality and solidarity – even if she would not have articulated it as such. In a nutshell, she is doing rights-focused social work. And this chapter is written in part to thank her, and the thousands of other social workers striving to protect rights every day.

This chapter has provided an overview of rights and social work. It has applied the idea of rights to liberty, equality and connection in social work settings. It has been argued that each of these creates conflicts and tensions, and that social work is particularly characterised by work around these tensions. Yet it has raised questions that need to be answered, about the types of challenges created by rights-focused practice and their implications for how we think about and practice social work. The next three chapters consider each of the basic types of right, the liberty, equality and connection of rights, and consider their implications for social work in theory and practice in greater depth.

4

Liberty, helping and protection

Chapter 2 introduced the 'harm principle' at the heart of liberal democracy. This chapter focuses on the consequences of the fact that not everybody can exercise the ideal freedom imagined within a liberal approach to rights. The case study, the example of practice later in the chapter and much of the discussion focuses on the area of child protection, but the issues covered seem likely to apply to a broad range of statutory work. The chapter starts with a consideration of capacity issues. It then explores helping in social work, and argues that where protection is involved it is more useful to conceptualise practice in relation to rights. The idea of helpful rights-focused practice is then developed through the rest of the chapter, with focus on a ladder of restrictions of rights, which I call the 'ladder of consequences', that informs much contemporary practice. What good – and not-so-good – practice might look like when working with such a 'ladder of consequences' is then unpacked.

Rights and capacity issues

It has been noted that social workers in the United Kingdom often work with groups where there may be questions about decision-making capacity, such as children, people with learning difficulties, mental illness or other issues that may impact on capacity for rational action. The fact that people within these groups do not have full capacity to make decisions means that somebody needs to act on their behalf. Often this somebody is not a professional. For children and many adults it may be a parent, a member of their family or a partner. Historically such people had full responsibility for people who did not have capacity. Parents had almost complete power over their children, husbands over their wives and family members could have individuals sectioned (Marland, 2013; Fox Harding, 2015). Over time it has been recognised that, while families usually want the best for family members, they can also be sites of abuse or oppression (Fox Harding, 2015). We have therefore created protections for individuals from potential abuses within the institution of the family, such as those within the Mental Capacity Act 2005 or the Children Act 1989. Social workers are the primary profession involved in such work, though with policies and laws that allow and require others to be involved, including where needed the oversight of courts.

Issues related to capacity create conundrums for a liberal society, and social workers are a key profession who have to work with these dilemmas. Berrick (2018) summarises some of these in relation to child and family services, and characterises them collectively as the 'impossible imperative', because society wishes social workers to achieve often conflicting objectives, such as keeping children in their birth family *and* protecting them from harm or helping parents *and* protecting children. These are the types of potentially conflicting imperatives that social workers have to work with; the need for someone to work with such issues is why we need statutory social work.

The first challenge, because it is the one that leads us to be involved in subsequent ones, is assessing whether the person we are working with has the capacity to make their own decisions and take responsibility for them. Capacity is rarely a binary decision. It is more like a spectrum, and indeed a multidimensional spectrum with cognitive, emotional, material, physical and other dimensions of capacity to be considered. Assessments of capacity also need to take into account the nature of the decisions that are being considered. For instance, a severely learning disabled adult might have capacity to choose what food they have for breakfast but not to choose not to eat if they are not able to understand the consequences of not eating. Social workers should be constantly working to understand the capacity of those they work with and whether it creates limits to the ability of people to make their own decisions. This is certainly true for children, many of whom have limited capacity to make decisions. So, the first challenge in working with the limits of liberty is assessing capacity.

Where an individual does have compromised capacity then the 'impossible imperatives' that Berrick writes about begin to come into play. An obvious one is that we seek to promote parental freedom to bring up their children as they wish to, but recognise that there need to be limits to this. In doing so we are promoting the 'harm principle', that people should be free to act as they wish provided they do not harm others. The Supreme Court summarised this principle, saying: 'The responsibility of parents to bring up their children as they see fit, within limits, is an essential part of respect for family life in a western democracy' (United Kingdom Supreme Court, 2016, Case 51). Much of the work of children's social work in the United Kingdom is about these two little words 'within limits'. Decisions about the limits of this freedom are complicated. As a liberal society we allow a wide degree of variety in parenting, yet we also set some limits to this. Where we do feel protective action needs to be taken, we need to offer parents clarity about what is happening, why it is happening and where possible offer them opportunities to change. Where a decision is taken that parents cannot care for a child, there are further complicated decisions to be made involving different sets of rights. We seek to keep children within the wider family where that is possible, and to keep children in contact with their parents. Yet each of these imperatives needs to be balanced against others that may sometimes work in a different direction, such as what the child wants or what we feel is in their best interests. Similar considerations apply to social work with other groups with limited capacity for decision making, such as individuals with acute and serious mental illness or substantial learning difficulties.

These tensions and conflicts are the bread and butter of statutory social work. They also provide the framework for the work we do, as well as the reason we need social workers in a liberal and humane society. These are genuine challenges, and a good society is one that seeks to approach them in wise, kind and transparent ways.

On rights and helping

This chapter considers work with people, the idea of helping, the question of whether we can make people change and how rights-focused practice should take individual liberty, helping and change seriously. A key point is that while social workers use many of the skills of counselling, the way that they work with people is different in fundamental ways. In particular, it requires us to be clear about concerns and consequences in a way that differs substantially from a therapeutic encounter. This chapter therefore outlines some key principles for rights-focused practice in children's services, which I hope it might be possible to apply to other settings where social workers work with ideas of liberty, harm and protection.

I became a social worker to help children and their families, and insofar as I had theories about how to help people I mostly thought that I might help by providing practical support and being a listening and caring person. In working in children's services I did provide some practical help – I was keen on writing to charities to get money for families, and I became adept at knowing what was needed to support benefits and housing applications. I also tried to be a listening and caring person. Yet the experience of working in child and family social work changed profoundly my understanding of what I was doing, because neither social support nor caring help seemed to be at the heart of the role.

One factor that influenced my thinking and my practice was that the problems I was dealing with, particularly as I became more experienced and worked with only serious issues, did not seem likely to be changed by a bit of practical support and a caring professional. These families often involved some combination of entrenched drug or alcohol issues, histories of abuse and trauma, current domestic abuse, mental health problems, learning difficulties and grinding poverty. These issues often wore down the parents, and many did not seem ready, willing or able to change. In such circumstances it seemed that stronger medicine than 'relationship-based practice' or radical perspectives were needed. What was needed was a way to work with serious and entrenched issues, and in particular to do so with families which were at best ambivalent and at worst actively hostile to the involvement of social workers. Yet there seemed a still deeper issue. Reflecting back on what I was doing I do not think it is best understood as helping people, or if it is helping people it is not doing so in the way conventionally described in the social work textbooks I am familiar with. Something else seemed to be going on. To capture and discuss some of these issues further the case study for this chapter is a family I worked with.

The Mancini family

The eldest child, Ricky, was three and the mother – Kay – was five months pregnant. When I was allocated the family I read about a long history of serious heroin and crack-cocaine problems. The parents had moved many times, and there were incidents of serious violence towards Kay from the children's father, Kyle. Two weeks ago there had been a phone call to the previous social worker when Kay went to pick up Ricky from nursery – she was heavily under the influence of drugs and literally had a syringe hanging from her arm when she tried to pick him up. The worker arranged for Ricky to go and live with his grandmother. She also arranged to pass the family over to me – as she was about to go on maternity leave. We did a handover visit to the Kyle and Kay during which we talked about a child protection case conference and made it clear that if Ricky came back to live with them we would apply for an Emergency Protection Order. Kyle was so unhappy with this that he picked up a baseball bat, went into the bathroom next door and very loudly smashed it up, while we sat there wondering whether to make a run for it or to sit tight. We did the latter, and eventually left after he returned much calmer (though he had communicated some very important information to us through his actions). You can imagine that we had rather different emotions as the previous social worker handed the family over to me … in my imagination, despite her being in the late stages of pregnancy, she skipped down the path, while I trudged with a heavy heart. How on earth was I going to work with the Mancini family?

This is obviously a very serious family situation. For Kyle and Kay their drug addiction was so strong at that stage that neither of them seemed able to overcome it. Of course, that created a problem that we were working with – because from the perspective of children's social care, and indeed from that of our society more generally, they needed to either change or lose their children. It was not acceptable for them to continue to look after Ricky, nor a new baby, in this way. The tools I came into social work with – providing practical help and a caring relationship – did not seem up to the task of creating change for these families.

Figure 4.1: The ladder of consequences

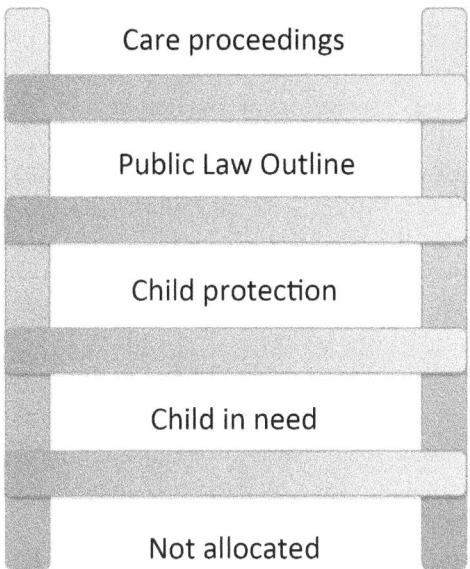

This was not just a challenge I faced as an individual social worker. It was and is an institutional challenge faced by child protection services wherever they exist. The institutional response to this challenge has, I think, three key elements.

First, there is the need to *protect* children. This is obviously the priority, with working with parents for change being a secondary issue. Protection is achieved through a ladder of protective interventions (see Figure 4.1) – with more involvement where there is more protection required. This involvement may be more frequent visits or more interagency surveillance, through to protective removal of children. Sometimes, for instance in an emergency situation, families move up the ladder very quickly. For others there is a more methodical process of moving up and down levels of seriousness.

The second purpose of the ladder, however, is to provide an escalating stair of *consequences* for changing or not changing. Each of these steps can be seen as placing more restrictions on family life and increasing the danger of the ultimate sanctions, which include removing children but extend beyond that, with considerations about how permanent a removal is and how much contact is allowed also being effectively 'sanctions' for parents, even if this is not the basis upon which decisions are made. It is, in effect, the institutionalised crystallisation of the balancing of rights to protection and the right to parental freedoms that is carried out in children's social care. The more serious the concerns for the child, the more rights of parents are overruled.

Figure 4.1 outlines some of these steps. Step zero is no allocation. A family may receive help from other services, or not need any. Step one is simply allocation for help. This might not seem a restriction, in that 'child in need' work is voluntary. Sometimes it is offered in this purely voluntary manner, but actually allocation as 'child in need' is often provided as an alternative to 'child protection', either before or after escalation to that level. While a parent may choose not to cooperate they run the risk of a move to the next step: child protection. Child protection work involves more visits, more information sharing and it is not voluntary, in that not cooperating is very likely to lead to the next step, which is some sort of legal action. Prior to legal involvement the Public Law Outline states that a letter needs to be sent to parents and a plan to avoid the need for legal involvement has to be set out. This can be thought of as drinking in the last chance saloon for parents – if change does not happen here, then legal action is the next step. The steps beyond this can take various forms, but a typical one might be to apply to court for an interim care order. Beyond that there is a full care order and there is the possibility of adoption or permanent placement elsewhere, as well as issues about how much contact and whether it is supervised. Taken together these provide a ladder of increasingly serious involvement in family life in order to protect children.

The third purpose of the ladder is that social workers in children's services use this ladder as a way of creating change, or at least opportunities for change. Much of my work as a social worker was managing movement up and down the ladder of consequences. This was true for me, and it is still the everyday reality of social work. So, in practice, workers are explaining what may happen if parents or carers do not change, agreeing plans and reviewing whether they have been achieved. This is difficult work – but it is also essential. What would our society be if children like Ricky were just allowed to be abused and neglected? On the other hand, we would not want a society that just removed children without exploring the potential for avoiding this and for return – and therefore the possibility of change. My point here is that it is reasonable and right that we have a series of steps related to concerns, that we escalate up them as needed to protect children and that parents are aware of these steps and the consequences of different types of action. This is part of rights-focused practice, being clear with parents and others when their rights are being overridden. That is the uncomfortable nature of the work, like the interview I did with Kyle, Ricky's father, explaining that Ricky could not return to him at the moment. A key issue, however, is how social workers should undertake the very difficult practice that working with concerns and consequences involves.

To a large degree in the 1990s social workers were left to get on with this challenging work. Reviews into child deaths in the 1980s, such as those of Jasmine Beckford, Kimberley Carlisle and others, repeatedly emphasised that social workers needed to be able to challenge parents (Parton, 1985, 2014; Brent, 1987; Greenwich, 1987). The concept of being 'child centred' was coined, and in part this emphasised the idea that we needed to say difficult things to parents. This has been emphasised in subsequent reviews, where the importance of appropriate challenge has been raised in various ways (Laming, 2003; Haringey, 2010). Yet, how to do this difficult task? Guidance was sparse on this, and subsequent research suggests practice is often carried out in a rather authoritarian and unhelpful way (Featherstone et al, 2014b; Parton, 2014; Rogowski, 2015; Sheehan, 2022).

The comparative lack of guidance for this incredibly difficult type of conversation has contributed to the proliferation in recent decades of frameworks for practice. Approaches such as Signs of Safety, systemic practice or Motivational Interviewing all seek to apply principles and practices from counselling to the difficult conversations required in child protection (Turnell and Edwards, 1999; Goodman et al, 2011; Forrester et al, 2012). In a similar vein, restorative practice, which has a more explicit origin and focus on the complexities of social control, leans heavily on therapeutic practices for how to do such work (Williams et al, 2022). In practice I think these therapeutic type approaches have more similarities than differences, with each focusing on how to build a trusting relationship and ways of supporting change. For the rest of this chapter I want to unpick the ethics and implicit theories involved in using therapeutic methods – developed largely to help people who want to be helped – with people who have not asked for help, such as many parents involved in child protection. This is largely because I think they have much to offer rights-focused social work but that the very different nature of these conversations needs to be understood.

So, in summary, social work practice, at least in the area of child protection, is fundamentally shaped by a ladder of consequences. This framework provides opportunities for social workers to try to help people, but to do so we primarily rely on counselling type skills. As noted in Chapter 1, this can create a sense of a mismatch between the nature of practice as it actually is and the aspirations that are sometimes suggested for social workers. This mismatch can make it difficult to know how we might appropriately apply, say, motivational interviewing or systemic practice when we need to have a very difficult conversation. For instance, what would be the appropriate response to Kyle smashing up the bathroom? A reflective statement or a circular question would not be called for. This leads many practitioners to feel the therapeutic or counselling style methods they are taught are of limited usefulness, and many have said to me they do not use them for the tougher child protection type conversations.

Quite a lot of this book, and a fair bit of a previous one I wrote with David Wilkins and Charlotte Whittaker (Forrester et al, 2021), focuses on the practice involved in such difficult conversations. In the next section

I want to think through the theoretical and ethical issues involved in using the ladder of consequences as a framework for not just protection and being explicit about consequences, but also as a way of helping people change.

The ladder of consequences and parental change

My experience of working with this framework was that it performed two key functions in relation to parental change. First, it sometimes did contribute to creating change. Parents with serious problems would see the possibility of losing children, or less serious consequences such as a child protection conference, and that would be a prompt for them to make changes in their lives. Second, even where it did not create change, when done properly (more of which later), it provided people with the *opportunity* to change. This is ethically important in its own right, even when change does not happen — providing opportunities is part of rights-focused practice and is essential for a humane society. The ladder of consequences should provide parents with clarity about how serious the situation is, the need for change and what will happen if they do not change. Even if parents do not or cannot change, offering them the opportunity to do so is in its own right a good thing — it is what we would want for our own families or those we love. If we take the drastic step of removing a child from his or her parents we should be confident they have been given every reasonable opportunity to prevent that happening.

This is a very different type of change to the type most commonly considered in social work texts, where the focus is often on helping people who want to be helped. What are the theories of change that we might apply here? The ladder provides powerful extrinsic motivations to change behaviour, because it sets out serious consequences. This is very different to most social work theory on helping people, which is about identifying people's intrinsic goals and supporting them. In fact, the differentiation between intrinsic and extrinsic motivation is not as straightforward as it might seem. For instance, it is worth considering the literature on court-mandated treatment for substance misuse. In general, research has found court-ordered treatment is as effective or even more effective than voluntary treatment (see Miller and Flaherty, 2000; Carey et al, 2016; Hachtel et al, 2019, though see also Werb et al, 2016). Many therapists had said these would not work because people need to want to change — at most they would produce some superficial change that would not last (Potter-Efron and Potter-Efron, 1986). In a similar way, systemic therapists see 'first order' change, often in response to immediate impetuses, as unlikely to last compared to deeper and more holistic 'second order' change (Hoffman, 1985). Qualitative research shed light on the perhaps surprising finding that court-mandated treatment seemed so effective. People referred for therapy as part of a court order usually felt that they had a problem. Indeed, for many the court order provided help that they already wanted (for example, Stevens et al, 2006). For others, being in court and being sentenced served as something of a wakeup call – it increased their intrinsic motivation to change. This was why court-mandated treatment worked: most of those worked with actually wanted to change, or to be more accurate they felt a mixture of motivations including some sense of wanting to change.

This points to the difficulty in separating intrinsic and external motivations. In fact, most of our 'intrinsic' motivations are probably external motivations that have been internalised. Imagine, for instance, that you are drinking very heavily with a group of friends on a regular basis. You enjoy the drinking and the good times you have together. It would appear that your intrinsic motivations are to keep drinking – and they probably are to begin with. But let's imagine that problems begin to pile up. You notice that you are putting on weight and becoming unfit. At a medical appointment, your doctor notes that if you continue your current direction of travel you will have serious health problems. Your partner starts to become upset that you are out all the time and that you seem to think your drinking is more important than they are. You start to have arguments all the time and a happy, loving relationship becomes fraught and difficult. Your work has also begun to notice. You have been warned about your lateness, and you know there are rumours about you drinking in the office. You used to be a popular member of the team, but you now have the nagging sense you are something of a 'problem'. By now your intrinsic motivations are mixed. You still enjoy the drinking and socialising, but you can also see that it causes you a lot of other problems and you are wondering whether you should do something about it.

This is the classic position of ambivalence so often found in relation to behaviour change – and is a situation discussed more further on in this chapter and in later chapters. Here, I want to make a more specific point, which is that our motivations are rarely solely intrinsic or extrinsic. It is more that external things, like the views of others about our behaviour, impinge on us, and sometimes we internalise them. That is why court-ordered treatment for drug or alcohol problems often worked – most of the individuals already had significant intrinsic and extrinsic motivation to change. The same is likely to be true for parents involved in child protection: it is not as simple as them having intrinsic or extrinsic motivations to change, but more that the ladder of consequences may or may not be consistent with the changes they feel they want to make or feel able to make in their lives. Put another way, good social work involves being clear about consequences, but it also requires us to identify and work with intrinsic motivations that people may have, as well as understanding the individual and structural barriers to change that may exist.

So how can we work around change in protection? The ethics of social work

Once someone is involved on the ladder, how should we work with them? First, there are two ways we should *not* work with them. One of these is to think that we can *force* people to behave in certain ways. The ladder has consequences, but parents do not have to behave in ways that avoid those consequences. Parents or others may not be able to change or they may choose not to, but we cannot and should not think or act as if we can *make* them change. The second is that we should not use therapeutic approaches to manipulate people. Using counselling-style methods without clarity about what is happening is unethical, and also unlikely to be helpful.

The most important feature of good practice in working with the ladder of consequences is to be clear and transparent. Where we need to use authority, we need to be clear why we are concerned, what our hopes or expectations are and what the consequences might be if they are not met. An unexpected finding in research I did with colleagues was that these features of practice were more important in predicting positive outcomes for families than the caring and empathic elements I have always valued (Forrester et al, 2019). Yet there is a danger that this result suggests a false dichotomy. The heart of good practice is to be able to be clear about authority and consequences, but to be able to combine this with empathic and caring approaches – and in an analysis we did we found the two are correlated, which means that in effect workers who are good at authority are also good at empathy and relationship building (Forrester et al, 2020). Caring skills, such as empathy and collaboration, are important for two reasons. One is that ethically as a society this is how we would like this difficult work to be undertaken: if a social worker visited your family you would want them to be clear about concerns *and* be caring. This is an inherent good, regardless of whether it creates change. Combining the care and control elements of social work is the heart of good, rights-focused practice. The second reason is that these empathic and caring approaches maximise the likelihood of people changing. It is worth unpicking some of the complexity around this.

How should we work with the ladder of consequences?

My own interest in therapeutic approaches, such as Motivational Interviewing, arose in part because I began to feel that I was not helping families except when the concerns were most serious. For these families, the consequences sometimes led to change, and where they did not the protection of children – children like Ricky and his sister when she was born – was undoubtedly a positive outcome. For other families I rarely felt I was particularly helpful in creating change. My concern about whether

Table 4.1: Worker responses to parents

The client's comment	The worker's response
A 23-year-old father telephones you and says: 'I'm not going to be able to keep my appointment at the child protection conference tomorrow; we just learned that my dad has cancer.'	'The conference is important for you to attend. Unfortunately we can't postpone it. If you can make it to the conference it would be greatly appreciated. I hope things work out for your father.'
A 32-year-old woman says: 'Last night Joe came home drunk again, and kicked in the TV set while the kids were still watching it, and then he knocked me down. He scared us all half to death.'	'What did you do with the children? Did you call the police?'

social workers made a difference was reinforced by findings from my research studies. In the first study, which focused on families where parents had drug or alcohol issues, we found that the bulk of social workers felt powerless, with many sharing similar experiences to my own: they felt that they were often just waiting for something to go wrong, without a sense of how they could actively help parents with alcohol or drug issues, or indeed a variety of other problems (Forrester and Harwin, 2011).

Subsequent studies I have done have focused on trying to improve practice. Yet the findings from them about how social workers talk to parents have often raised questions and possible concerns. The most obvious problem, the one I was conscious of first, was that there was a pervasive lack of empathy and care in the work – particularly where there were serious child protection issues. Consider the responses to the prompts in Table 4.1. Social workers were given the prompt on the left and asked how they would respond (see Forrester et al, 2008). On the right are some fairly typical responses. It is worth taking a moment to think how you might respond and what you think of the responses provided.

I have used these prompts many times in presentations and training to get practitioners thinking about how we should talk to people. I never fail to be surprised by the variety of responses that they produce. In broad terms, non-social workers and students, particularly towards the beginning of their course, tend to be horrified. They point out that these responses lack empathy and care. They highlight the difficult experiences the person is describing and suggest showing that we understand and care is crucial, and is missing from the social work responses. So they might suggest responses such as 'I am really sorry to hear that. How are you feeling?' for the first one and 'That sounds frightening, tell me more about what happened ...' for the second.

Yet the response from groups of experienced social workers is often more varied. For instance, in a recent session they expressed scepticism about whether the father did in fact have cancer and said their response might be

'I'm sorry to hear that, but we can't move the case conference. Maybe you can tell me what you would like said to the conference on your behalf?' For the second one there is usually more sympathy, but workers are still keen to know how the children are and whether they had been kept safe.

The key issue here is not that one response is right and another wrong. A more fundamental issue is that the differences in responses highlight the complexities of the social work role. On the one hand, unlike many professionals, we are not there primarily to help the person we are talking to. There is the need to protect children, including raising concerns and exploring their safety. On the other hand, we can and should find ways of responding that are caring and empathic. The challenge is therefore to combine the control and care functions of the role.

In this regard these types of responses are not just a feature of research and training – we have consistently found fairly similar patterns of practice in genuine conversations. Across multiple studies colleagues and I have recorded and analysed over 800 meetings between social workers and parents, plus over 400 meetings between social workers and actors (called 'simulated clients'). Overall, we have tended to find normal practice, that is practice without some attempt to work using a specific framework, is fairly low in empathy and high in confrontation (see Bostock et al, 2017; Forrester et al, 2017, 2018). It is something that if they heard it most people outside social work would consider to be fairly uncaring practice. To bring that to life here is a brief excerpt from a fairly typical interview. It is taken from Whittaker (forthcoming) who is reanalysing data from Forrester et al (2018). The context is that the mother had been seriously injured by the child's father to the extent that they had to go to accident and emergency (A&E). The mother has just explained that she did not call the police during the attack as she was fearful that the violence would escalate and that she has no intention of resuming the relationship:

Worker: I'm just really concerned that if you resume the relationship, you know, you're going to be putting yourself at serious risk and you're going to be putting your child at serious risk as well because it's not something you're able to predict really, you understand?

Parent: You can't predict how somebody is when they're drunk … at all. … I have ended it. I don't want to go back there …

Worker: Because, from the information shared by the GP … I just find it concerning, you understand, given that … given that you've ended the relationship before and you have resumed it again, you understand. So, what has changed now, because if he should come back next week, next

	month, when we close this case. Then if he comes back and says to you …
Parent:	I understand what you're saying.
Worker:	What you have to bear in mind is, you know, I've told you, if you put yourself and the child at risk again, you understand, if we're not able to. … What has happened now has demonstrated that you are not able to protect yourself and [child], you understand, because you didn't call the police when you're supposed to. You even went as far as not telling the professionals at A&E the truth when you were at the emergency service.
Parent:	I don't want to go back there though. Never again. That's why I'm selling and moving on. I haven't told him I'm moving, I haven't told him where. … It's just easier … not to have any involvement any more. He wasn't a good dad to [Child] anyway, so … I'm not losing out on anything for [child]. I'm too interested in starting my own career to bother about relationships.
Worker:	So what I expect you to do is contact Women's Aid. They offer counselling, they offer legal advice as well. So whatever support you feel you need, they can always advise on how to go about it and, also, they will help you process the injunction and … you have to report it to the police and they will give you a criminal reference you understand.

There is a lot going on in this relatively short excerpt. It is a good example of the way that social workers often hold mothers responsible for protecting children from abusive men, rather than addressing the perpetrators of the abuse (Hester, 2011; Featherstone, 2023). This is an issue that we found frequently in our recordings, and it is similar to the responses found in Table 4.1. The social worker constructs the mother as potentially not adequately protecting herself or her child. They cite the failure to contact appropriate professionals. They then tell the mother what to do – to contact Women's Aid, to use the legal help and counselling they provide, to get an injunction and to report it to the police. There is no discussion of this – these are the expectations that the social worker has of the mother if she is to be deemed protective. Here I want to consider two questions in relation to this excerpt, and the more general pattern of practice we have found this exemplifies. First, why do social workers talk to people like this? Second, how should they actually talk with people – what would be a better way of talking? I then bring that back to implications for thinking and practising in a rights-focused way.

Why do social workers talk to people like this?

I think there are two broad reasons why social workers practice like this. One is that these are inherently incredibly difficult conversations to have. In everyday life we spend a great deal of time avoiding conflict and confrontation. We would almost never say to someone we knew well that their care for their child is not good enough – it would be the sort of thing that might end even very close relationships. Yet this is in essence the sort of conversation that social workers need to have about child protection issues all the time. It is hard to think of a more difficult thing to talk about. These conversations are freighted with the burden of stigma, shame, power and consequences that makes them perhaps the most difficult conversations it is possible to have in any setting with anyone (see, for instance, Gibson, 2015, 2016, 2020). So, the first reason that practice is not as we might want it to be is that this is an area that is inherently exceptionally difficult.

The second reason is that not only do we not support workers to practice in ways we might recognise as 'good practice' but many features of the system deliberately tend to create a rather authoritarian and uncaring version of practice. One issue is that there is a lack of support for having these difficult conversations. Until recently there were few frameworks for practice: social workers were largely expected to just get on with it. They were often not properly trained or supervised to have such difficult conversations. Studies I have been involved with have shown that intensive training and helpful supervision each make a big positive difference to the quality of practice (Bostock et al, 2017; Forrester et al, 2017, 2019), but these have been relatively rare in children's services in England and Wales until comparatively recently.

Yet it is more fundamental than saying there is a lack of support for good practice; in fact, many of our organisational practices across children's services might have been designed to produce the sort of practice identified in the excerpt above. For instance, Wilkins et al (2017) describe an approach to supervision that at heart involved managers telling social workers what they had to do. This is worse than not providing workers with support, because often the tasks given to social workers are likely to be ones that parents may be resistant to. For instance, in the previous excerpt it is easy to imagine that the supervisor has said to the social worker 'You must tell the mother to go to Legal Aid, get counselling and an injunction and tell the police if the father gets in touch'. If that is what happened, the social worker is just dutifully carrying out these instructions. We do not know that the supervisor said this – but that is perhaps not the main point, as it is because supervisors definitely *tend* to say things like this that practitioners internalise this as the way that parents should to be talked to (see Wilkins et al, 2020).

Supervision is just one part of this picture. Workers will pick up the importance of challenging parents and the lists of actions expected of parents (particularly mothers) from a wide variety of sources. They are found in child protection case conferences and the plans that they agree, in informal chats about families between workers, and in policies and practices across the organisation. They will be inculcated into student social workers and newly qualified staff as part of their on-the-job learning in placement. These values and expectations have been driven by government policies, including, above all else, high profile child death inquiries. These have an enormous impact on the nature of children's services. The most significant in recent years has been the inquiry into the death of Peter Connelly. It makes clear statements about practices that they feel would have prevented Peter's death:

> What was required was an authoritative approach to the family, with a very tight grip on the intervention. Ms A needed to be challenged and confronted about her poor parenting and generally neglectful approach to the home. Clear targets should have been set with short timescales, particularly in respect of the way she turned the older children out for school, and her upkeep of the home. (Haringey, 2010: 39)

Of course, we cannot know whether such an approach would have protected Peter. I personally doubt it, but that is not the point. The issue is the way in which powerful injunctions to a specific form of practice influence what social workers and others do with parents in these difficult conversations. To some degree, the social worker saying to the mother in the excerpt that she needs to carry out a series of actions can be considered a demonstration of the version of 'good practice' identified in this hugely influential report. This has echoes of Treby's work, in which supervision had a largely surveillance function, with managers giving workers lists of tasks to do (Treby, 2022). This surveillance approach was then reflected in the practice of social workers, who either carried out the tasks they had been given (such as checking the fridge for food) or passed them on to parents (such as saying you should go to counselling).

We are faced, then, with a double challenge. Child protection conversations are inherently very difficult. We have also created a system that reproduces a form of practice that often focuses on telling people what to do. While this is probably better than one alternative – namely not letting people know about concerns, perhaps because raising them is just too difficult – it is a sort of authoritarianism that is undesirable on multiple levels. The most important test of this is that it is not how we would like to be talked to by a social worker if they had concerns about our parenting.

How should social workers talk with people?

A substantial part of this book considers this question in some detail, and here I just want to outline two key elements of good communication that flow from the previous discussion. The first is that social workers need to be able to talk to people about concerns and consequences. As already noted, these are difficult conversations. Rights-focused social work involves being able to be clear about concerns but also able to elicit from people their views, listen carefully to them and create a genuine dialogue about the concerns. This is challenging work. It involves an ability to both listen and talk in ways that are respectful, caring and authoritative. Surprisingly, perhaps, there has been comparatively little attention to how such conversations should be carried out, with much writing and most teaching focusing on counselling type communication skills (see Social Care Institute for Excellence, 2004; Dinham, 2006; Reith-Hall and Montgomery, 2022). These are essential for social work, but they need to be adapted to this very different type of conversation.

The second fundamental element of good communication in social work is that workers should be able to have helpful conversations about change. Change can take multiple forms. It may be working to change social circumstances. For instance, for the Mancini family I worked hard to get them out of temporary accommodation and into a flat. It may be about supporting change from other people. For instance, in the earlier excerpt, the onus should perhaps at least in part be to address the father's abusive behaviour, and this requires an attempt to work with him and not just the mother. Even if the main focus of the work is with the mother, seeking to engage in a respectful partnership with her rather than telling her what to do is likely to be crucial. Finally, we sometimes have to help people change their behaviour. For instance, in the Mancini family I had many conversations with both Kyle and Kay about their drug use. In general, such conversations are characterised by a mixture of emotions, thoughts and motivations. A powerful motivation may be to reduce or get rid of social work involvement – to move down or off the ladder of consequences. For the Mancinis it was to get their children back. Social workers need the skills to work with these complicated conversations in ways that help people decide what they will do.

We are, in many ways, just beginning as a profession to wrestle with how to do this work well. I hope that this book will be useful in providing a framework for thinking about the nature of such practices, and the ways they differ from the predominantly therapeutic approaches they have been developed from. In later chapters I consider some of the key elements of good practice for this sort of rights-focused work. What is important in such conversations, whatever theories or practice frameworks they are informed by, is that they are able to engage with the messy and complicated mixture of feelings about change that people may have, and that in doing so they do not lose clarity about the concerns and consequences involved in rights-focused work. I find two complementary ways of thinking about this helpful.

The first is that ultimately in helping people we are trying to maximise their individual freedom. For almost all of us there is a gap between the person we would like to be and the person we actually are; the way we would like to behave and the way we actually behave; the parent we are and the parent we want to be. For those we work with, and particularly parents, this gap can be very substantial. The Mancinis were, for instance, very aware that they were not being the parents they wished to be. The key point here is that in helping people by talking with them we should not be focused primarily on creating behaviour change; such a focus runs the risk that we treat parents as merely a means to an end, something that Kant defines as the essence of unethical treatment (Plant, 2009). A focus on changing the behaviour of parents becomes unethical if it is solely to help children. This is ultimately a form of manipulation, and it is a form of manipulation or even coercion that we see constantly in social work practice – where plans and expectations are too often drawn up by professionals and then imposed on parents. Rather, when we are working with parents or others we should be helping them to be as conscious and clear about whether and how they would like to change, including exploring and making sense of the mess of intrinsic and extrinsic motivations that characterise the internal life of every human being, and including those created by the consequences of our concerns, as captured in the ladder of consequences. Such a process enhances individual choice and freedom. It is therefore the very antithesis of *making* people change, or manipulating people. Instead, it involves working with the feelings people have about their behaviour and seeking to enhance their ability to be the person or the parent they want to be.

The second, related, way of thinking about this is that when we come into practice we often focus on the needs of the parents and miss those of the child. As we become more experienced we are able to focus more on the child and raise concerns about them. However, excellent practice moves beyond just focusing on either parent or child: it focuses on both parent *and* child (Forrester et al, 2008). It recognises that both are potentially vulnerable, that both have rights, and that both are intrinsically and inherently worthy of respect. The highest level of good practice is therefore both child and parent focused – and able to keep both in mind and take both seriously. This is the heart of good practice in child protection – and similar considerations inform all safeguarding or protection work. In summary, then, good practice in the area of child protection involves protection, clarity about concerns and consequences, and an ability to help people explore what their motivations are and what action they would like to take to achieve their goals.

Conclusion

It seems important to end by reflecting on the Mancini family. When the baby – called Rachel – was born we took her into care. There followed weeks of working with the parents to try to give them time with Rachel and opportunities to change. Despite our best efforts they were not able to stop using drugs, and ultimately Ricky and Rachel were placed separately within the wider family. In the end Kay left Kyle, and she was able to address her drug use and eventually returned to live near the wider family and see Rachel and Ricky regularly. Kyle was not able to stop using drugs and sadly died of an overdose. As Ricky and Rachel entered middle childhood they were loved and cared for and seemed happy and secure. I hope this continued into adulthood, and I think of them often.

The work with the Mancini family illustrates the practice issues discussed throughout this chapter. The children were protected. The parents were given a clear sense of our concerns, and we facilitated opportunities for them to respond to them and have their children back. I doubt that my practice in helping the parents was particularly skilled, but I do think it was respectful and that we – children's services – made a genuine effort to give the parents opportunities to change. When that was not possible we were able to keep the children in the wider family. In doing so we illustrated a rights-focused approach, protecting children not able to protect themselves, providing opportunities for parents and seeking to support changes that the parents aspired to.

This chapter has considered individual freedom and limitations related to capacity. It has then examined at length the implications of such issues for how we work with people, for ideas of change and helping in the context of rights-focused practice. The next chapter considers a different set of challenges relating to rights. It explores the resources needed to be free, the contested and complex concept of need, and how social workers can approach the complicated process of understanding and assessing need.

5

Social work, positive freedom and need

This chapter considers social need and assessments for services or resources. These are sometimes considered rights to 'positive freedoms' and are part of the second generation of rights, which arose during the 20th century and were manifested in the development of welfare states in some countries. It might be thought that providing for need is less fraught with conflict and tension than other elements of social work, yet social workers are typically employed when there are such tensions. This is particularly true in statutory settings. The chapter spends some time considering different approaches to the idea of need and the ways in which they create challenges and conflicts. It concludes with a high-level overview of the types of knowledge that social workers need in order to work with such tensions.

As with the other chapters in this part of the book we start with a case study, so that the more abstract elements of the argument can be linked back to the realities of practice. For this chapter the focus of the case study is a family I worked with but it is also perhaps me, and my practice in relation to providing services to children defined as 'in need' under the 1989 Children Act.

Social work with children in need: a case study

The case study is of a time when I lobbied for more money. I worked with Jenny and her children Mikey and Charlie, who were nine and ten. Jenny was a loving mother but had a very serious alcohol problem. She was also quite an unusual person to work with because she was very honest. For whatever reason, and a psychiatrist later suggested it might be alcohol-inflicted brain damage, she rarely told lies, even when doing so would have made her life easier. We had frequent reports that the boys were wandering the estate and that they were begging neighbours for food and they were missing a lot of school. Later, Mikey came into care and Charlie went to live elsewhere in the family. At this stage I was working to keep the family together.

One Friday I visited Jenny and she told me that she had no money to feed the boys over the weekend. She showed me the empty fridge and cupboards. I went back to my manager and asked for some money, maybe £20. He was reluctant to authorise it. He pointed out that she had received her benefits. There was no specific reason for the lack of money and he repeated the mantra of the service: 'We are not a benefits agency.' There was a general ethos that if we started to give money too readily families would consider it a supplement to their benefits. My argument was probably as simple as 'but what will the children eat?'. Eventually, being at heart a kind manager, he authorised the payment and I took it around.

On the Monday I went round with some level of anxiety about how the family had coped over the weekend. I met Jenny in high spirits. She looked different, with her hair dyed blonde, cut and styled. When I asked her how she had paid for that she told me she had used the £20 I had given her, and had borrowed food from friends and family.

This tale is not told in order to suggest that not giving families money is the right thing to do. In fact, Jenny lived in significant poverty and having money to get her hair done is probably a perfectly reasonable need. On the other hand my manager was of the view that Jenny's lack of money was because she was spending it on alcohol, and that this was not acceptable. Some of the complexity involved in this social work decision is picked out later in the chapter.

Social work and social need

This type of work is relatively mundane and everyday – similar issues are being worked with across the country, and in all the groups that social workers work with. I certainly did not consider that I was theorising the nature of the good society or the nature of need, yet I am going to argue that that is exactly what I was doing. Through discussions with my manager we were doing two things. We were working through the complicated relationship between what people say they need, what they actually need and what society is willing to provide for in relation to their needs. These are, in fact, deep philosophical waters. They involve assumptions about what people need, and therefore what it is to be human, and what we should provide for one another, and therefore what sort of society we should live in. The second thing we were doing – without realising it – is that we were not just thinking about the practice involved with such issues, we were actually creating the answers. What did Jenny and her children need? What is our society's response to those perceived needs? In answering these questions in practice we contributed, in a tiny way, to creating the sort of society we live in. The answer, in this instance at this time, was one that gave Jenny the benefit of the doubt and provided her with some money so that she and her children could eat.

It is because so many of the issues that social workers work with have these bigger implications and contexts that there is an emphasis on the social in our training. I was once asked by a senior civil servant "Why does everyone go on about social justice in social work education?" The answer is that all our work, including apparently small-scale decisions such as providing or not providing money for Jenny and her children, takes place at the intersection of the individual and the social – in the case study Jenny's individual perspective on her and her children's felt needs and what society is prepared to provide for. They are about social needs, which are about rights and therefore about social justice. This chapter explores these issues by considering the idea of human need in general and social need in particular. This explores some debates that may seem theoretical, but that ultimately provide insights into key features of social work.

Social work, equality, positive rights and social need

In talking about the resources we agree to provide as a society for people to have some level of positive freedom we are considering a key concept for social work and social policy, namely the idea of 'social need'. Social needs are the needs people have that society should provide for. They therefore have two elements: they are things we need *and* they are things that we collectively agree to provide. They might include universal resources (such as education or roads) or targeted ones (such as benefits or social housing). In this context social workers constantly assess the needs of children and adults, as well as trying to provide for some social needs. Their duties to do so are set out in key legislation. As for negative freedoms there are specific groups of people that social workers tend to be involved with. In the United Kingdom this includes the needs of some children, older people, people with disabilities and people with mental health issues. It is again often groups of people where there may be limitations in capacity to exercise individual freedom that are more likely to require the involvement of social workers. Here we explore the nature of social need in order to understand what the specific role of social workers tends to be in relation to it, why some groups and needs tend to require social workers and what the implications are for developing a rights-focused approach to social work.

Individual and social need

There are enormous practical and theoretical problems with assessing what people need and where appropriate providing for those needs. In a thoughtful series of essays on this topic, Ignatieff (1984) explores what need is and how we can know what the needs of others are. He does not come to any conclusions, but he asks important questions: can we know what our own needs are? Given how difficult that is, how can we know what the needs of other people are? On what basis can we seek to assess the needs of others? In public services, how can we balance the need for everyone to be treated equally, with the fact that each person is unique? And how can we make sure that services are respectful and listen to the views of those they work with, while making them aware we sometimes will not (and should not) act on those views – not least because people may not always know what is best for them?

Ultimately Ignatieff concludes that any theory of need is 'a language of the common good' (1984: 194). As such it incorporates, whether explicitly or implicitly, conceptualisations of what it is to be human, what a good life for an individual involves, and what a good society is or should be. These are some of the biggest questions philosophers can ask, and they are at the heart of social work – whether we realise it or not. Of course, the busy practitioner trying to get a payment for a taxi for a family to get their children to an appointment, or me when I was trying to get Jenny money for the weekend for her children (or perhaps for her haircut), does not dwell on what their vision of human nature or a good society is. Rather, they are constructing the answer in practice through their actions. For instance, they are in practice answering the question 'Do we in this society, or at least in this bit of this society at this time, provide taxi fares in these circumstances?'. They are also working on beliefs about individual agency in specific contexts, for instance, can this father with three children under five get his children to the hospital without a taxi?

There is a profound sense in which social workers are often working as practical philosophers, seeking to understand what people need to thrive and what society considers they can and should be provided with. Usually this 'philosophical' work is not seen as philosophical – it may manifest itself as making a case that a service should or should not be provided. Yet implicit in such arguments are always claims about what humans need, and what needs society should provide for. It is worth considering these arguments here as they help us understand the nature and purpose of social work and human rights.

The question of what people need is hotly debated because the conclusions have profound implications for the sort of society we should create. In broad terms, the idea of objective need has been central to more left-wing political positions, because objective needs provide the basis for collective provision, and therefore a more substantive idea of social need. The pithiest example of this is Marx's slogan 'from each according to his ability, to each according to his need', which captures the essence of the communist position. This has long been critiqued by right-wing theorists, who question whether there is such a thing as objective need, and, where they acknowledge such needs, they tend to emphasise them at a minimal level (Hayek, 1945; Nozick, 1974). Theorists on the right tend to emphasise the negative freedoms discussed in previous chapters – such as freedom of speech, freedom to pursue one's own economic wellbeing – and minimise collective or state provision for positive needs. They tend to see taking money away from people through taxation as a limitation on individual freedom and therefore something to be kept to a minimum (Nozick, 1974). In a nutshell, historically the right tends to emphasise freedom from the state, while the left tends to argue for the state to provide what people need to be free.

This historical pattern changed to some degree in the latter half of the 20th century, when criticism of objective need from a broadly left-wing perspective increased. Movements such as those led by people using services, feminists, anti-racists, disability activists and others argued that 'objective' conceptions of need tended to be framed by the dominant groups in society, and that they tended to ignore the views of the less powerful about what they needed (Lewis, 1997; Oliver and Barnes, 2012). Often such criticisms centred on problems with the creation of a monolithic state to provide for need, and emphasised the potential abuses created by such provision. For instance, feminist scholars identified the ways in which state benefit provisions were based on and reinforced patriarchal roles for women (in the home) and men (working outside the home) (Lewis, 1997; Pascall, 1997); mental health service survivors organised and critiqued the medicalised, expert-driven ways in which services were provided (Croft and Beresford, 1992).

This created something of a crisis on the left. Was it possible to articulate a vision of need that embraced diversity, and that therefore did not result in a prescriptive view of need in which the state or the professional knew best? Key theorists approached this challenge in different ways, including Sen, Plant, and Doyal and Gough. While there are differences in their formulations, there are substantial similarities in their resolution of the difficulty. All of them argue that society needs to provide the resources necessary to allow individuals to pursue their own vision of a good life. Whether this is conceptualised as 'positive freedom' (Plant, 1998, 2019), 'capabilities' (Sen, 1985, 1999) or 'health and autonomy' (Doyal and Gough, 1984, 1991), they share the idea that people should have what they need to pursue the goals and priorities that they define for themselves. This social democrat vision of need is essentially using liberal arguments, and particularly the harm principle, to argue that people should be free to do what they wish provided they do not harm others but adding to it that individuals need appropriate resources to exercise these freedoms. This is the classic argument for 'positive freedom', that is the resources to exercise freedom. In this formulation, social needs are not defined by a shared, single sense of what a good society should look like – as one might find in nationalist or religious or communist visions. Rather, a good society here is defined as one in which individuals are free to pursue their own vision of a good life. As such, the potential abuses of an authoritarian state are – at least in theory – avoided, and the needs of different groups and individuals can be met as they wish.

This is a neat philosophical resolution of the problems confronting the concept of objective need. It allows those on the left to unite around an idea of need as freedom, and it includes an inherent critique of the failed experiment of communism (on the grounds that this relied on an authoritarian view of need as defined by the state). Yet, as outlined by Sheppard in a key argument, there are substantial problems with it (Sheppard, 1995). These problems ultimately create the necessity for social workers, and define much of the social work role, so it is worth outlining and reflecting on them.

The first problem is that while providing to each according to their own vision of freedom is neat, in practice there are problems in delivering such a vision. As Ignatieff notes, King Lear's expectations of a retinue of a hundred knights may be what he believes a king needs, but it is difficult to justify this as a need that society, or even his daughters, should meet. At the level of society, we need to make decisions about the resources we provide for needs, even if we define needs as what people require to have a degree of freedom or self-determination. Contemporary politics is to a large degree a debate about the extent to which our resources should be pooled (primarily through tax) and provided collectively or allowed to remain with individuals. We do not need to engage in this debate here, but merely recognise that the outcome at any one time will define the level of social need that we provide for. Social need, in other words, is what we acknowledge that we provide collectively to one another – the needs we collectively acknowledge of strangers. It is therefore characterised by political debate and struggle, and while it is never resolved, decisions for current provision are made through political processes.

A key contribution from Sheppard is that he argues that considerations such as these mean there is no such thing as an objective definition of *social* need. Even if we can agree that individual needs might be objective, societies agree collectively the needs that they will meet – the social needs. While Sheppard does not dwell on it, this 'agreement' is rarely simply a matter of debate and consensus. It is more likely to be characterised by dispute, struggle and, in democracies, by success at the ballot box. Thus, for instance, in the United Kingdom we pride ourselves on the National Health Service, while in the United States they have made a political choice for individuals to be responsible for their own health care.

Crucially, Sheppard goes on to argue that while socially agreed needs are not objective, they can for many purposes be treated *as if* they were. In other words, social workers are assessing what individuals consider that they need against the resources, policies and laws that society creates to ration the provision of services. He argues that in a democracy this is an acceptable basis for the provision of social need, and for the role of social workers. This is a helpful contribution to our understanding of need.

Sheppard's argument that social need can be treated *as if* it is objective is helpful because social need as provided by society is in fact what social workers (and others) have to work with. If there is not some agreed provision, then the capacity for social workers to provide for a need is limited or non-existent. Yet there are problems with Sheppard's formulation. Most importantly, it is overly prescriptive. Treating social need as if it were objective simply recreates the problems that were critiqued by feminists, service users and others: it produces the potential problems of top-down, disempowering, professionally controlled provision that were created by a reliance on objective need.

If social needs are treated as if they are objective there is also no room for challenge of society's provisions. What if one thinks that society should be providing for a need? What if one's understanding of real need means that one thinks there is a strong case for providing for something? What if one's values as a social worker mean that you are opposed to a specific policy or the lack of certain provision or a particular decision?

The argument of this book is that these challenges are irreducible and that they are part of the rationale for the social work profession. In providing for social needs – in providing for positive freedom rights – we have to be able to take seriously three types of need: subjective, objective and social. To be clear these are:

- *Subjective need* – what we feel we need. For instance, Jenny perhaps genuinely felt that she needed money to get through the weekend. This is her truth and part of social work is to understand this truth.
- *Objective need* – what a person needs in order to have a degree of autonomy. This is the definition of freedom provided by Sen (1999), Doyal and Gough (1989) and others. Using evidence applied to specific individual situations we can make judgements about what people really need. This is akin to what Bradshaw (1972) calls 'normative' need, which can be decided by experts based on evidence. As discussed further in the chapters on how social workers do assessments, needs – like many other important things – are real, but we can never completely objectively understand them. So there is a truth, even if we can never wholly know it. Prosaically, maybe Jenny did not need money to feed the children, because she managed to feed them without using it.
- *Social need* – the needs that society agrees collectively to provide for. Whatever our assessment of objective needs, we as a society agree what needs will be met and to what level. This is defined in part by law and policy, but is also shaped by local practices and individual workers and managers. Unlike benefit payments, social work assessment of social need tends to involve complicated considerations. For instance, the reason that my manager was reluctant to make a payment for Jenny was not that

she did not need money. It was more that because almost everyone we worked with needed money the service very strictly rationed financial support. One element of this was also making judgements about why additional money was needed above benefit payments, and this in turn involved decisions about issues such as whether money might be spent on alcohol or whether it would be spent on the children.

Each of these types of knowledge about need is vitally important. Each requires social workers to engage with specific types of perspectives about needs, such as the client's view, the legal mandate and our knowledge of child development. The skills we need of social workers require an ability to bring these different types of knowledge into a dialogue with one another, but a dialogue that can be resolved for each person or situation we work with. This is a particular type of purposeful dialogue that is at the heart of this book's arguments, and considered at length in Part III.

Social work, social needs and rights

Social needs are rights. They are the resources that we as a society agree we should provide for one another. Some are provided on a universal basis and others are delivered in a fairly uniform way. Of interest to us are the rights to resources that social workers tend to work with.

Social workers can be involved in providing for social needs in a variety of different settings. For instance, a social worker working in a domestic abuse refuge is helping provide for social needs, in that the refuge is funded to provide for collective need. This is true even if the refuge is a charity, as society agrees some social needs should be funded through charities. However, many social workers are employed through local government to provide for needs that are defined by law and policy, that is, they are in statutory roles. This type of provision is typically characterised by the presence of one or more of four key features. One is the type of capacity issue discussed earlier. Often social workers are working with groups where capacity for responsible decision-making cannot be assumed. The arguments around this for negative freedoms also apply to the social needs that people in such groups may have. Social workers are often making judgements about whether people know what is best for them – a position that is fraught with difficulty and the potential for paternalistic practice.

The second is they are often areas of need where there are likely to be conflicts between subjective, objective and social needs. This is primarily created by rationing. Of course social needs are always rationed, however in many fields this rationing is based primarily on considering objective needs. For instance, benefits are delivered according to a standard definition of eligibility and medical provision by the decision of medical staff and the level of provision. In contrast, social work services typically place the views of clients as a central element. This means the potential tensions between subjective, objective and social need are a core element of practice – it is often why we need social workers to assess need. Social work is involved with bespoke provision, and the client's view is always therefore important. Yet for this very reason there may be tensions between the client's perspective, the resources available or professional knowledge about objective needs.

Third, the needs social workers assess and provide for are holistic. They tend to consider the person as a whole, and can therefore relate to any element of their wellbeing rather than a specific dimension, such as educational or health provision.

Fourth, social workers usually work with individuals in the context of their families and communities. Their assessments and interventions are not therefore solely with individuals but, rather, have to take into account varied perspectives, including potentially conflicting ideas about need and the rights of different parties. For all four of these reasons a rights-focused perspective is useful for understanding the nature of this work.

The uncomfortable nature of social work

The argument of this chapter, and indeed of this book, is that these different perspectives on what people need and what should be provided are constantly in tension. While we may be tempted by Sheppard's suggestion that social needs be treated as if they are objective – and in fact often provision is provided as if this were the case – the truth is that there are constant tensions between the different perspectives on need, and therefore the rights of the people we work with. For instance, consider the case study of Jenny, Mikey and Charlie. There is no doubt that Jenny felt she and her family were in need. I think they probably were really in need – certainly the cupboards were bare. What is more open to question is whether society felt they were in *social* need, that is whether they needed money, or indeed food. For most people the answer would probably be 'no'. I think the general public would feel that if benefit money was spent on alcohol or a haircut instead of food there would be little sense that they should be provided with more money. The difference in Jenny's situation was that the lack of money might have been harmful to her children. Again, it is because children do not have capacity to take responsibility for their own safety and welfare that I was involved. Yet I was also negotiating a tension between supporting Jenny to parent them, and recognising that she was not always able to do so. Similar tensions exist across the work of social workers in all statutory settings, where there can be differences between what people think they need, what the social workers believe they need and what society is willing to provide.

Social workers are not unique in having to negotiate such dilemmas, but they are the main profession that we expect to do so. There are no easy resolutions to these issues. We cannot rely solely on what clients feel they need, nor objective evidence about need, nor what society agrees to provide. Instead, social workers need to be able to negotiate between the three understandings of need – and often between multiple people's perspectives. Once again, we need social workers who are comfortable with this potentially uncomfortable work. To do it they need skills and values that allow them to explore and understand the perspective of those they work with. In the case study example this would include Jenny, Mikey and Charlie. They need to have a strong understanding of the social scientific basis for thinking about what objective needs there are. In the case study example this may seem relatively straightforward – in that children need food. However, my manager was exercised by other considerations. Both Mikey and Charlie seemed to be physically thriving, so he felt that Jenny and her family were actually very able at providing them with food. He also understood alcohol addiction and felt, probably rightly, that some or all of the money would be spent on alcohol. This illustrates that to do this work social workers need to understand people and society. Finally, workers need to understand the social mandate that they work within. What does the law and local policy say about needs? What are the expectations for provision, the spaces for advocacy, and what are the limits? This applied in my advocacy for a small amount of money for Jenny, but could equally be a worker exploring respite breaks for a family with a child with very severe disability or seeking adjustments to a home to help an older man return from hospital.

The contested nature of this work requires theories and practices that allow us to work with conflict and where possible resolve tensions. It requires social workers who are comfortable with the often uncomfortable nature of this work. And it demonstrates that social workers are often 'practical philosophers', working through complicated ideas and beliefs and evidence about what individuals need and society is willing to provide on a case-by-case basis. How we might think about and practice in such circumstances is considered in depth in Parts II and III. Before that, Part I concludes with a chapter on how we work to promote connection. It argues for the importance of love and places a love ethic at the heart of rights-focused practice.

6

Human connection, community and love

This chapter starts by considering the 'third generation' of rights introduced in Chapters 1 and 2. These are rights to connection and to community and can be loosely related to the 'fraternity' or 'solidarity' element of the call from the French Revolution for 'liberty, equality, fraternity'. This chapter relates them to the fundamental human need for love and how we promote that for those we work with. It then turns to consider love in the social work relationship, and argues for social work to be built on a foundation of love. Arguments here are founded on the inspirational work of bell hooks and her ethic of love (hooks, 2000, 2001, 2002). It is suggested that rights-focused practice needs to be done in a loving way, but the chapter also explores the limits of this type of love. This includes examples of times when love is not enough and the challenges involved in a loving social work. One of the conclusions of the chapter is that the tensions involved in a loving approach to rights make a profession such as social work necessary. They cannot be resolved, they are irreducible, and therefore we need wise, kind and compassionate professionals to constantly wrestle with them. Those professions are not solely social workers – but for social workers this sort of loving approach to rights-focused practice is central.

The chapter starts with a real family that I worked with. Reflections on working with this family start the discussion about love and connection, and experiences in working with them inform the chapter throughout.

The Williams family

The Williams family were literally one of the first cases I was allocated as a newly qualified worker. Sitting on my desk on my first day was a pile of thick files, and on top of that pile was the Williams family file. The children were Marie, aged eight, and Nell, aged six. Their mother, Jenny, was a long-term heroin user. There had been referrals to children's services over the years but in general Jenny was considered fairly stable, she seemed to use mainly methadone on prescription, and Marie and Nell were doing well. They went to school regularly, there were no concerns, they were well dressed and in recent years there had been no new referrals. Ed was the father of Nell but not Marie. He had used heroin but seemed to have stopped and was believed to provide a lot of the care and stability in the household; or, at least until recently it was thought that he had.

I picked up the file in September. In June, Jenny had contacted the police because Marie had disclosed to Jenny that Ed had sexually abused her. Jenny had immediately thrown Ed out and had fully cooperated with the investigation. She was upset and very angry. During this process Jenny disclosed that she had been sexually abused by her own father, and this fuelled her desire to protect her own children. Jenny seemed to be doing everything she could to protect the girls. However, as I read the file and contacted the school and the police, some concerns began to emerge. There had been two police notifications of Ed hanging around the family property during the summer. The police officer I talked to felt that it was possible Jenny was letting Ed back into the home, though she did not have any evidence for this – it was just a 'hunch'. More concretely the girls were not in school and nobody knew where they were.

My first task was obviously to find the family. I visited over 20 times, announced and unannounced. I peered through windows and letterboxes. I tried to phone Jenny and also tried to contact members of her family. I visited her parents' house in Essex. Nobody answered the door, but suddenly a snarling Alsatian came running at me and I had to back away, holding my bag up to protect myself and scrambling over a wall to safety. Eventually, our concerns became so great that we started care proceedings. To my astonishment, on the day we went to court, as we were about to go into the courtroom, Jenny turned up with Marie and Nell – all looking well turned out and expressing amazement that we had started care proceedings.

I had my first meeting with Jenny in a side room at the court. She was angry and upset that I had started care proceedings. I tried to explain why we were worried. Quite quickly she moved from anger to sobbing tears, explaining that she could not cope, admitting she had gone back to live with her parents with the girls – in part to get away from Ed but also to get away from the drugs that surrounded their Peckham flat. She maintained that she protected the girls from her father. Eventually, we agreed that the girls should come into care for a while, and that this would allow Jenny and me to work together. I emphasised that the last thing I wanted to do was permanently separate the family, while trying to be clear about my concerns.

There followed six months of intensive work with the family. In particular, I got to know Jenny well. I met Ed, and heard his side of things. He was subsequently convicted for sexually abusing both girls – sitting with the girls and Jenny at the criminal court when we learnt that he had finally pleaded guilty was one of the most satisfying parts of working with the family. Most of all I got to know Marie and Nell really well. They went to live with a foster carer about an hour away. Budgets were tight, then as now, and after a few weeks my manager would not fund taxis for them to stay at the same school – he felt they should move to the local school. I wanted to keep the continuity with their current school as long as eventually returning home was the plan. So for many weeks I set off at 7am and spent 90 minutes driving the girls to school through thick London traffic; at least my manager agreed to fund their taxis home from school or contact.

There were many more events and adventures in working with the family. Jenny had multiple problems, including an abusive childhood and an ongoing addiction, but, by her own admission, her biggest was that she hated not being in a relationship. As a result, she had a series of relationships which were problematic, many of which were abusive. I think today the girls would probably have remained in care. What actually happened is that they returned home. Eventually things stabilised, and when I moved to a different office we closed the case. I know there were subsequent referrals relating to domestic abuse, and I know the girls spent a short period back in care. I do not know what happened as they moved into their teenage years, and I do not know for sure whether keeping the family together was the right decision. I hope it was. For this chapter the focus is not whether the right decisions were made. Instead, I want to talk about the family, and my feelings about them. Like all the children and many of the adults I worked with I felt what I started to call 'a kind of loving' towards them (Wilson et al, 2003). I was certainly not dispassionately making decisions about their lives and trying to help them. Quite the opposite, I was passionately engaged. In this chapter I want to unpack what that involves and consider the relationship between rights and love.

What's love got to do with it?

The recent independent reviews in both England and Scotland called for services for children and families to be founded on love, and to strive to ensure children are loved (The Promise, 2021; Independent Review of Children's Social Care, 2022). No doubt this is because in both reviews the voices of children and adults who had been in care spoke powerfully about the importance of love. Love is not mentioned in the primary legislation governing child or adult social work services in any of the UK countries. I am also not aware of it being mentioned in the official guidance or in key policies. Instead, what tends to feature are the needs of children and adults, including their need to sometimes be protected, and therefore their rights to specific services or interventions.

My experience is that social work assessment and teaching is also largely devoid of a focus on love. We are obsessed with 'attachment', despite the weak relationship between attachment patterns in childhood and outcomes in adulthood (for example, Sutton, 2019). Indeed, experts have suggested we should stop using the term unless we have no alternative (White et al, 2019; Wilkins, 2020; Forslund et al, 2022). It persists, I think, because it provides a way we can talk about love without seeming too emotional – too vague and lacking in scientific rigour. When we say there is a strong or positive attachment between a parent and a child what we usually mean is that they love each other.[1] It is almost as if we have to smuggle love into social work under the guise of attachment. Similarly, we write about stability and permanence and consistency as important – yet these are mainly important insofar as they provide and sustain love. A permanent, stable place to live where there is no love is unlikely to be what a child needs.

Maybe love seems too vague, too hard to define, too emotional for us to write about it directly. Maybe it is tarnished by popular culture's obsession with romantic love. So we do everything we can to write about relationships and their importance without being clear that what matters, what we all yearn for, what we all need, is to love and be loved. Yet, because love is our most fundamental need, it cannot be written out of the story. Whatever language we use, and however much we dress it up in psychological camouflage, the human need for love means that ensuring those we work with are loved is a core element of social work.

This is not quite the same as the third-generation argument for rights to connection, and for communities and even for places to have rights. It is more true to say that our involvement with people and groups that may not be able to meet their own needs – people like children, those with serious mental illness or learning difficulty – means we need to think about the core human needs. And the most fundamental need we all have is to be loved and to be in loving relationship. This starts with the newborn baby. Only our ability to elicit love keeps any of us alive from the moment of our birth, because people who love us provide for our needs. In this respect Maslow's hierarchy is perhaps misleading. More fundamental for all of us than any other need is to be loved, because once we are loved then others will help ensure our needs are met (Maslow, 1943).

It is not just in infancy that our need for love is fundamental. As we grow up and embark on life's journey, the need to love and be loved is the most important need we have. That is why there are infinite examples of humans sacrificing their own needs, safety or even their lives to help those who they love. The core of human success as a species is our profoundly social nature, and love is what makes that possible.

---

[1] In theory attachment is different from love, for instance indicating an ability to attune and meet a child's needs, however that nuance is in my opinion rarely the reason we talk about attachment rather than love in social work.

So, love is fundamental. But what is love? And how do social workers work to promote loving relationships? Indeed, how do they use and experience love in the work they – we – do? The next sections consider each of these in turn before thinking about love as a right and the limits of love.

What is love?

C.S. Lewis wrote a famous long essay, *The four loves*, on the philosophy and theology of love (Lewis, 1960). It is a good starting place for thinking about love. Lewis makes the point that the word 'love' in the Ancient Greek version of the Bible actually refers to four different words. This suggests that we have an impoverished vocabulary for thinking and talking about love. In Greek three of the words refer to love in specific relationships – romantic/erotic love, friendship, and love between a child and parent. Each of these is a type of 'need love', in that we need the other. When the Bible refers to the type of love God has for us or we are meant to have for one another a different word is used – *agape*. *Agape* is, in the Christian tradition, not about meeting our needs but about doing what is best for others. *Agape* means genuinely wanting the best for others. It is a feeling, in that *agape* connects us with God and God is love, and an action, because it is something we do.

C.S. Lewis' argument is that the other types of love can be good or bad, and that the degree to which they are a good love is decided by whether they are also combined with *agape*. When we love others and genuinely want the best for them, then these are manifestations of God's grace. *Agape* makes all other loves, and indeed all other actions, good. When we love without genuinely wanting the best for the other, then the other types of love become distortions of real love. They become about our needs, not those of the other. They may be love, but they are not a good love.

This is a Christian perspective on love, but as an atheist I can see its usefulness in helping us think about what love is. In particular, the emphasis on the importance of genuinely wanting the best for the other person, not just at a rational level but an emotional level, is a useful way of thinking about love.

A more recent visionary and thinker about love is bell hooks. In her trilogy on love hooks defines love, and in a series of linked essays hooks argues that love is the fundamental and most important need for human flourishing, and that it should provide the foundation for our personal relationships, our relationship with our self and our political action (hooks, 2000, 2001, 2002). hooks notes that love is both a noun (a thing we feel) and a verb (something we do). She is more interested in it as a verb, as actions. And as actions she argues that love is something we can decide to do or not do. For hooks love is 'the will to nurture our own and another's spiritual growth' (2000: 6). hooks is at pains to define the spiritual as referring to that which is most important and sacred, and not necessarily in reference to religious faith. Crucially, as love is about action then our decision to live in loving ways creates an ethic of love – a set of principles and practices to guide us in loving action. She goes on to outline the key elements of love and loving action and concludes that '[w]hen we are loving we openly and honestly express care, affection, responsibility, respect, commitment, and trust' (2000: 14). These are the key elements of love, they need to be present for this to be genuine, unselfish love. They complement and extend the insights of C.S. Lewis. This is a wonderful and profound definition of love. What use might it be for social work?

Social work and loving relationships

Given the central importance of love to humans, it is unsurprising that so much of our work is in fact focused on sustaining and cherishing loving relationships, or establishing and supporting new ones. The most obvious place to start is with the family, the foundation of love for most of us, but social workers seek to keep loving relationships around the people we work with in the form of friends, school and community whenever we can.

In my work with the Williams family I think I was driven by a desire to keep the loving relationships that existed around the girls. This included lots of contact with their mother, but also at a school that had been a source of stability and nurture through a difficult childhood and where both of them had friends that were important to them. This is perhaps the bread and butter of social work – even when the concerns are serious, social workers usually work hard to keep children in their families and in touch with those who love them. Indeed, as discussed in what follows, sometimes we are criticised for doing this too much.

Of course, that is not always possible, and when we cannot do it we seek to nurture new loving relationships around the child. This might be finding someone in the wider family who can care for them. It might involve long-term foster care, in which case we would seek to provide an alternative family to care for and love the child while sustaining their contact with their birth family. Finally, in rare instances children need to be placed into an alternative family permanently, for instance to be adopted. Here we seek to find a positive alternative family to love them.

The eminent child psychologist Urie Bronfenbrenner was apparently asked what he had learnt in 40 years studying the needs of children. After some thought he replied 'every kid needs one person who is irrationally crazy about them' (Brendtro, 2006). This is a wonderful quote, and a pithy summary of the love children – and all of us – need. Ensuring every child has at least one person – and ideally several – who are crazy about them should be at the heart of the children's social care system.

Social workers and love

It is relatively uncontentious to suggest children need to be loved and that therefore social workers should be supporting loving relationships. A less frequently discussed issue is whether social workers can and should love the people they work with. As a result, I am not sure we have the vocabulary to talk about our feelings for the children and parents we work with. The language of transference and counter-transference from psychodynamic theory is one of the rare contributions to our understanding of the emotions produced in working with people. It identifies that clients may feel strong emotions towards their counsellor, perhaps transferring emotions they might feel towards their parents – whether that be love, idealisation or troubled and negative feelings. Later, it was realised that counsellors also have strong emotions about clients, and that these may be linked to their earlier experiences. This was the idea of counter-transference. In psychodynamic therapy transference and counter-transference are still fundamental to treatment, allowing the exploration and working through of issues from the client's past. They also contribute to the importance of clinical supervision, to provide a safe space for the counsellor to explore their strong emotions about those they worked with.

The lack of a similar safe space to talk through the emotional content of the work is one of the biggest problems we face in contemporary social work. It is hard to imagine a field of work more likely to generate strong emotional reactions than working with families where there are concerns about abuse and neglect. Yet research suggests that what is strikingly absent from conventional supervision is any talk of emotions (Wilkins et al, 2017, 2022). Instead, there is a focus on the practical, such as tasks to be completed. Similar issues seem to pervade social work across various settings (Ingram, 2015). On a personal level, some years ago I was providing consultations to workers to support the use of Motivational Interviewing (MI). The format was that workers talked to me fortnightly, in a confidential discussion aimed at skill development with no line management accountability. I had thought we would be discussing the skills of MI and how to use them. Yet for the first month what I actually encountered was what felt like a tsunami of emotions. Workers would share their anxieties and their fears, they told me they disliked a mother or feared a father but that they were afraid that to say so would sound unprofessional. They also found it hard to talk about positive emotions, how much they liked a child or how they felt for a parent who was struggling but trying their best. Before we could begin to think about how to work with a family we had to unpick the strong, often overwhelming, emotions that workers were carrying.

How strange that we have created a system that tries to pretend these strong emotions do not exist. We expect this work, fraught with anxiety and love, fear and tenderness, to be carried out without giving workers the emotional support they need to understand their own emotions and look after themselves. In such a context, is it any wonder that we find talking about love difficult?

This reluctance to talk of love in the social work relationship is replicated in the literature. There are some exceptions, for instance Bilson has considered Maturana's work on love (Bilson, 2007), Morley and Ife (2002) have argued for a 'love of humanity' to underlie social work, and Tanner (2020) has explored compassion as a sort of love-in-practice. Of most direct relevance Godden (2017) has identified the potential for bell hooks' work to inform social work. Yet what is striking is how rare these articles are. They are very much the exception.

A kind of loving

If I reflect on my work with the Williams family, I think I experienced a kind of loving towards Marie and Nell, and towards Jenny. I believe, without having the words to talk about it, that I was striving for the sort of love ethic that bell hooks outlines, in that I tried to make sure my work was founded on care, affection, responsibility, respect, commitment and trust. I felt love as both a noun and a verb. I was doing love – a loving social work – but I also experienced powerful emotions.

I want to argue that this sort of love is found constantly in social work, that it is, in fact, essential for good work, and that we need to find better ways of talking, thinking and practising in loving ways. This is because love is both a need and a right for all humans. It is a need in a way that has been described in this chapter. We all need love, it is the most fundamental of human needs, and therefore any profession that seeks to meet people's needs has to provide for loving relationships. In addition, love is a foundation for practice. It describes how we can and should relate to those we work with. In this respect, love is the foundation of rights-focused practice.

Up to now this book has concentrated on different types of rights and how to work when they may conflict. In Chapter 4 it began to consider the practices of working with people in respectful ways that create dialogue. This chapter takes the argument a step further. When working with the rights of people it is not just what we do, it is the way that we do it that is important. As the song goes, 'Tain't what you do, it's the way that you do it'. Here the question is, in upholding people's rights, including working when rights are in tension or conflict, how should we work with people? The answer to this question is, at least in part, 'in loving ways'. This is for two reasons.

First, it is because this is how society wants rights-focused social work to be undertaken. If you or I had a social worker, we would want one who worked with an ethic of love. This test – 'what would I want from a social worker?' – is a good one to apply to any question about what good practice is. This is supported by the research on what people want from their worker, which includes many of the key features of loving action as defined by hooks, such as being honest, reliable, caring and wanting the best for the person (McLeod, 2010; Bennett et al, 2011; Beresford, 2012; Baginsky, 2023).

In choosing social work, a profession with a focus on social justice and helping people in difficult situations, to carry out the challenging task of working with rights that may be in conflict, what is clear is that society wants this work done in a caring, wise and thoughtful way. Social work may often fail to achieve this ideal, but it is reasonable to conclude that society wants this work to be carried out with kindness, compassion and love. Rights-focused social work carried out through a love ethic is therefore something society seeks, even if they might not use the word love. In practising in loving ways we help create the sort of society we want to see, the sort of society most of us came into social work for – one informed by an ethic of love.

Second, love makes a difference. There is an enormous literature on what works in helping people and why (see Roth and Fonaghy, 2006). In my view, if you unpack effective ways of helping they almost always rely on a caring, reliable, kind and compassionate helper. Loving practice is what provides the foundation for helping, because most of us recognise and respond to people who genuinely care. In fact, the practice framework you use is probably less important than really wanting the best for the people you work with. An example of this arose in some training I did on MI. MI emphasises avoiding telling people what to do, and instead trying to elicit from people their own motivations. A team manager said to me she was struggling with MI. She said, in her brusque, no-nonsense manner: "I love working with young couples with drug problems. I sit them down and say 'Look, I know and you know you're using drugs. Let's cut the crap and talk about it. I'm not leaving here until you're honest with me'." By her own account, and that of people in her team, this worked really well – parents loved her. The question is: why did this approach work? There is no textbook that would suggest this is how you should practice. While it does have the advantage of honesty and transparency it could easily be abusive and uncaring. My guess is that the key is that the young parents knew that this social worker really cared. As she said, she loved working with them. This allowed her to establish a caring and honest relationship in ways that no textbook would say were right. Ultimately, her work was informed by a love ethic. I think for most of us the technical skills a helper has are far less important than the fact that they really care. Indeed, often the skills within a method are ways of showing we care, for instance through deep listening.

So, rights-focused social work involves applying a love ethic to the complicated world of working with rights and needs. Yet, there are challenges and contradictions in doing such work. In the next section I explore some of these and make the argument that the difficulty of resolving some of these issues is precisely why we need social workers to wrestle with them.

Complications in applying a love ethic to rights-focused practice

It is comparatively easy to write idealistically about love in social work. Yet in practice working in a loving way is complicated and full of challenges. In this section two are considered: professional boundaries and apparently unloveable people.

Love and professional boundaries

Love becomes more complicated when we consider the relationship between social worker and those we work with. As I said earlier, I loved Marie and Nell and Jenny. Yet there were limits to this love. It was boundaried, as professional relationships have to be. Professional boundaries are a central part of being a professional; they are one of the things that differentiate the professional from the personal. The boundaries can be temporal, for instance not being available out of hours, and spatial, such as not living near those we work with. Most importantly, they are emotional and intellectual. We need to be able to step back from those we work with, to be able to distance as well as engage with people.

This is partly a matter of self-care – the social worker who never stops thinking about or feeling for the people they work with is unlikely to last long. We need time in our non-work roles to recharge and this gives us the energy needed to do the job. At a more important level, the reality of the job is that we are professionals and this is different to friends and family. In part, boundaries provide us with the ability to step back and consider what is happening for a child or family. This is crucial for the decision-making elements of the job; becoming overly invested in keeping children at home because of the feelings one has for the mother, or in protecting the child because of our strong feelings about abuse, would be potentially dangerous. Most importantly, boundaries allow us to be honest about the nature of the relationship we have. It is loving and caring, it should be undergirded by an ethic of love, but it is a professional relationship and as such it has limits. These include the temporal, spatial and personal (emotional and intellectual).

Boundaries do not prevent us from doing social work undergirded by an ethic of love: they are what allow us to do so. They allow us to do the complicated work of rights-focused social work in a loving and caring way by providing limits. These limits allow us to look after ourselves, and they allow us to step back and reflect on our own feelings and emotions and how they are impacting on our work. Boundaries allow us to be loving professionals.

What about unloveable people and actions?

Not everybody we work with is easy to love, and it is a misunderstanding of an ethic of love to think they need to be. Take the example of the Williams family. I had strongly negative feelings about Ed, because I absolutely believed the girls' accounts and, without going into details, they sickened me. When I met him I felt that he tried to manipulate me into thinking that Jenny could not be trusted and that she had convinced Marie to make a disclosure of sexual abuse as a way of getting him out of the house. It was nonetheless necessary to talk with him, to find out his account of what had happened, to get a sense of his plans and motivations.

There is something in human nature that often seems to want to punish people who have done bad things. For instance, there are frequently examples of vigilantes taking direct action against sexual abusers. This response is not confined to sexual abusers. Some parts of the general population have very negative and punishing attitudes towards swathes of people, including anyone who has committed a crime, immigrants, drug or alcohol users, those with mental health issues, people who behave antisocially, people on benefits … the list seems endless. Social work as a profession emphasises the very opposite. It places a heavy emphasis on a critical approach to understanding such issues, and a commitment to social justice and inclusion is at the heart of any vision of social work (see Chapters 8 and 12 for more on this). At the level of working with individuals, we stress the idea of being 'non-judgemental', which also tries to promote the opposite of this punitive approach. Yet what does it mean to be 'non-judgemental' with someone like Ed who has sexually abused children? And how can an ethic of love help us understand better what is involved in working with such issues?

The first point to make is that there is a difference between condemning an action and condemning a person. It was, at least in theory, possible for me to utterly condemn Ed's actions without condemning him as a person. Put another way, despite the very bad, in fact I would say evil, things he had done, that does not mean he is not capable of doing good things, and nor does it mean he is incapable of changing. Condemning actions rather than people allows us to keep working with individuals. It allows us to be able to retain some element of hope.

Yet in this regard the role of a social worker, at least in the context of child protection and other protective roles, is more difficult than that of a counsellor. While a counsellor, like a social worker, can condemn the behaviour but not the person, and seek out the potential for good in the person they are working with, a difference is that the social worker often also has to make recommendations about the future. These need to be based on balanced predictions about the consequences of different actions. So, for instance, I was strongly opposed to Ed having any contact with the girls. Yet this was not a condemnation of Ed as a person, it was an appraisal of what was likely to be best for the girls. This is really what being non-judgemental means. We judge behaviours, and we make judgements about future behaviours, but we do not judge people as a whole.

The ethic of love offers a second insight into how we respond to people who do evil. That is to differentiate between love as a feeling and love as a series of behaviours. I personally felt revulsion towards Ed, and also quite a lot of anger. In preparing to meet him I took quite a lot of time trying to get into the right mindset. I am not sure whether I achieved my aim or not, but I tried to treat him in a respectful and caring way despite his behaviour. This is the heart of an ethic of love. In fact, being loving toward those we feel love for is the easy part. The challenge is to provide kindness and compassion to those whose behaviour makes them hard to love. I think this is a core element of social work, because I think rights-focused practice needs to be undergirded by an ethic of love.

Implications of an ethic of love for social work

Of course, I think many people we work with would feel uncomfortable with the idea that social workers should be loving towards them, in the same way that I do not feel I need my doctor or my children's teachers to love me. Yet this is a misunderstanding of the nature of the love ethic. People do not usually want their social worker to feel the emotions of love, but they probably do want the actions that go with a loving practice. They want a social worker who is caring, reliable, kind and honest; the sort of practitioner that is described by an ethic of love. And I would like all professionals who work with me to be like this (in fact, in an ideal world everyone would be loving to each other …).

A love ethic also has implications beyond the way we practice as a social worker. This chapter started by focusing on our rights to human connection and community. It then moved to focus on the love ethic and its implications for how we practise rights-focused social work. This also relates to third-generation rights to connection and community. If we believe that loving relationships are fundamental and foundational for human flourishing, then in working with rights we need to work to promote such connections. That is why a love ethic provides a foundation for not only how we practise but also how we understand the rights and needs of those we work with.

The sort of practice written about in this chapter, loving practice, is hard work. Previous chapters have highlighted the intellectual challenges involved in social work, and the high level of skill it requires. In developing the idea of a love ethic, this chapter has focused more on the emotional challenges of the work. This is difficult, complicated and often very draining work.

That is why we need social workers willing to wrestle with the challenges that it involves, as well as organisations able to support it.

There is nothing simple or easy about social work. It is intellectually challenging, technically complicated and emotionally complex work. Yet it is essential, not only for the people we work with but also to create a good society. It protects the rights of those who cannot exercise their own rights, it works with some of the most complicated ethical issues in contemporary society and it should strive to do so in ways that are respectful and loving. As such, social work is essential for any good society, for any society that respects individual liberty and connection, inclusion and love. In doing social work we are creating together the sort of society that we want to be part of. That, for me, is why a love ethic is a foundation upon which to build social work – and, indeed, live a life.

PART II
Theories for rights-focused practice

7

Humanist social work

The chapter outlines the characteristic foci of a humanist orientation, including an emphasis on human potential, individual choice and the conditions for good living.[1] Key theorists such as Maslow, Rogers and Erickson are introduced as well as practice methods such as person-centred counselling (PCC), solution-focused practice and Motivational Interviewing (MI). The strengths and limitations of the orientation and its practices are then discussed. It is argued that humanist approaches provide crucial insights and helpful ways of working and that they are a particularly good fit for rights-focused practice, but that they downplay the social element – and that this is particularly problematic for social work and for a focus on rights. This provides the context for the next chapter, which introduces the social model and then argues that a combination of humanist approaches and the social model provide a strong foundation for rights-focused social work.

History of humanist psychology and social work

The humanist tradition in psychology and social work is a family of theories and ideas that are direct descendents of Enlightenment thinking (McLeod, 2003). In that context it was an orientation that put human flourishing, rather than the needs of God or kings or nations, as the goal for a good society. The humanist orientation arose in psychology after the Second World War. Up to that point two contrasting movements had dominated the discipline. The first was the psychoanalytic approach. Psychoanalysis places a heavy emphasis on the formative experiences of the early years, it explores conflicts within the psyche that are produced during this period and has an elaborate set of explanations for how we develop our personalities. Psychoanalysis invented what we would understand as counselling, in which talking with a therapist is considered to be something that can be helpful. We take this for granted today, but at the time this was a revolutionary idea. In classic psychoanalysis the therapist analyses the client's unconscious and subconscious motivations

---

[1] Humanism can also be used to refer to an atheist belief system which emphasises the importance of human flourishing in the absence of God. For current purposes the two uses are unconnected.

and conflicts and helps them to achieve self-awareness, and therefore, it is hoped, some element of insight and perhaps control over their lives.

The main rival to psychoanalysis in psychology in the first half of the 20th century was behaviourism. Behaviourism arose from animal studies that demonstrated the power of rewards and punishments in shaping behaviour. This insight was then applied to the study of humans, where it was found that we, too, can have our behaviour shaped by rewards and punishments. Behaviourism places a heavy emphasis on the application of the scientific method to understanding humans, and in contrast to psychoanalysis paid no regard to internal introspection or subjective experiences. These were not considered amenable to scientific study and therefore not the proper focus of psychology.

The utterly different theoretical understandings, methodological preferences and practical applications of psychoanalysis and behaviourism in studying and helping human beings made psychology, and social work, highly contested disciplines through the first half of the 20th century. To a large degree humanism arose as a response to these conflicts, as a new way of thinking about human beings and how to help them. It emerged as a 'third force' in psychology after the Second World War, founded on a set of key assumptions (McLeod, 2003). Of these, probably the most important was the belief that people have free will. Personal agency is the term used to capture the fact that we all have choices to make and that we live with their consequences. This stands in direct contrast to the overtly deterministic foundations of behaviourism (which in its pure form believes all our behaviours are determined through patterns of reward and punishment). Psychoanalysis has a more complicated relationship with free will, but emphasises the central importance of early experiences and therefore places less emphasis on it than a humanist perspective.

Humanists also believe that people tend to be good, and are therefore motivated to make themselves and the wider world a better place. Humanism emphasises the worth of individuals, the importance of their values and their ability to solve problems, their creativity and their ability to help one another. Humanism is thus an unabashedly optimistic view of what it is to be human, in which human desires to 'self-actualise', or be the best we can be, are fundamental. To explore humanism in greater depth we now turn to consider briefly the contribution of key figures who created humanist thinking. Most of these figures are men and all are White, a fact that reflects the limited opportunities for women or Black people to become senior figures at this time.

Abraham Maslow

Abraham Maslow is widely regarded as the founder of humanist psychology (McLeod, 2003). He formulated the idea of a 'third force' and articulated many of the key beliefs of a humanist orientation (see Maslow, 1943, 1968). The contribution that Maslow is best remembered for is his 'hierarchy of needs' (Maslow, 1943). In fact, what Maslow was trying to do was to develop a typology of what motivates us as human beings. Maslow was seeking an alternative to the Freudian focus on fundamental drives (specifically, sex and death) or the behaviourist emphasis on external factors shaping our behaviour. Instead, he made two fundamental arguments in developing his famous triangle of human needs. The first was that humans have a variety of different motivations that drive us. Some of these are relatively basic needs, for instance we need to eat, sleep and breathe. However, human behaviour can be motivated by other needs. Maslow identifies that, beyond the basic physiological needs and need for safety, we need self-esteem and a sense of belonging and much of our behaviour can be related to these needs. However, he felt that not all human behaviour could be explained by these motivations. Great art, scientific breakthroughs or altruistic sacrifices cannot be explained without identifying additional motivations. He therefore introduces the idea that humans are also motivated to be the best we can be, to achieve our maximum potential. He called this the motivation to 'self-actualise'.

The second argument was that these human needs could be loosely placed in order. Anyone who has choked on food will know that one immediately prioritises breathing over everything else. In a similar way Maslow suggests that these human needs can be put into the order in which we tend to prioritise them. Of course, this ordering is not absolute – sometimes we can choose to sacrifice, for instance, our safety for what we perceive to be the greater good, or even for a sense of belonging. That is compatible with Maslow's position – he believed in human free will and his triangle is simply an attempt to show the way we tend to prioritise our different needs. The more fundamental contribution this makes is that it creates a picture of human beings as having multiple needs and therefore motivations – a picture in contrast to that of behaviourism or psychoanalysis. A key purpose of the hierarchy is also to help us understand that lower-level needs usually need to be met before we can consider higher-level needs. This is particularly helpful from a social work perspective, where we need to understand that often basic needs must be met before we can consider other types of change.

One final comment on Maslow's hierarchy is of relevance. As is typical of humanists it is inherently an optimistic view of human beings. The ultimate *telos* or purpose for which we strive is 'self-actualisation', that is fully being the best we can be. This may involve making great art or science or being a wonderful grandmother or grandfather. This is a different view of what people strive for than Freud or others might picture, where human drives for sex or power are fundamental. This does raise questions about where the darker elements of human behaviour come from. Maslow would perhaps respond by suggesting that these reflect unmet needs in individuals. For now it is sufficient to note that this is an explicitly positive view of human nature.

Carl Rogers

A second foundational thinker for humanist psychology was Carl Rogers (McLeod, 2003). Rogers' key contribution was to build on the theoretical insights of Maslow and other important theorists, such as Eric Erickson, and develop a practice for how to help people based on humanist principles (Rogers, 1942, 1946, 1951, 1959). This practice became known as client- or person-centred counselling. Client-centred counselling or therapy has been enormously influential, providing the foundation and inspiration for many of the ways of helping individuals that inform social work, including basic communication skills taught on many social work courses and specific ways of working, such as MI and solution-focused practice (Miller and Rollnick, 2012; Knight, 2013).

   A key influence on the development of Rogers' theories was his experience with social work as the director of the Society for the Prevention of Cruelty to Children in Rochester, New York in the 1930s (Kirschenbaum, 2003). This brought him into contact with a key social work theorist: Jessie Taft (Murphy et al, 2013). Taft was a leading exponent of the ideas of Alfred Adler, and her interpretation of these contributed to the development of a 'functionalist' vision of social work that stood in opposition to the Freudian orientation that dominated US social work at the time. Adler, and Taft's nascent functionalism, placed an emphasis on the 'here and now' and how the helping relationship could help the individual function in the present, with less attention paid to early childhood issues. This was a key shift for Rogers in developing his ideas and his practice.

   Rogers went on to incorporate key tenets of humanist thinking in developing a theory and practice of PCC. At its heart, Rogerian theory, in common with Maslow and others, saw humans as actively involved in making sense of our lives, having some degree of control or free will over our actions and as being motivated by multiple factors, rather than just one or two core drives. Like Maslow, he emphasised the positive factors that drive us as human beings. Crucially, he felt counselling worked if certain conditions were met. The most important of these was that people did not feel threatened (Rogers, 1942, 1951). At the heart of PCC was therefore developing an orientation towards people, with accompanying skills, that allow us to build non-threatening helping relationships with people who are being counselled. This involved the idea of 'unconditional positive regard' – which is the sense that we value the person in and for themselves, whatever their behaviours. Unconditional positive regard is similar to key elements of a love ethic, and certainly Rogers' ideas are a good fit with many of bell hooks' arguments. He also developed a set of skills designed to help the practitioners develop such relationships (Rogers, 1951). These included the use of open questions and the importance of reflections, in which the therapist attempts to offer back to the person being counselled their understanding of the person's point of view (which might be their thoughts, emotions, values or other factors they are trying to offer). We return to these crucial skills in Part III, when we consider direct practice and rights-focused social work.

These two elements – building a warm, non-judgemental relationship and offering back to people the counsellor's understanding of their situation – are the heart of PCC. In PCC individuals are understood to have the resources to make sense of their own lives and make changes if they wish to. In contrast to the Freudian orthodoxy of the time, those receiving help are both the experts on their lives and the people who can, if they choose to, make the changes they need. The purpose of counselling is therefore to facilitate a process of self reflection in the context of a warm and non-judgemental relationship. These ideas are fundamental to much of the approach to practice which is outlined in Part III of this book, where the details of practice approaches are examined with real examples. In this chapter the focus remains on the development of a humanist approach and its application into social work.

Humanist helping

Humanism is still an influential perspective in psychology, but in the academic discipline it has receded in importance, with more emphasis on the scientific method in recent decades. In contrast, humanist approaches have been hugely influential in the development of counselling and related approaches to helping people. Rogerian listening skills provide the foundation for most counselling approaches today.

In part these developments have been driven by the results of research. Despite intellectually dominating psychology, counselling and social work for the best part of a century, Freudian approaches were rarely able to show robust evidence that they help people – here 'robust evidence' means a trial with a valid comparison group, such as a randomised controlled trial (Eysenck, 1994). More recently there is some evidence of the positive impact that some versions of psychodynamic approaches can have (Roth and Fonagy, 2006). Nonetheless, historically the lack of evidence opened up psychoanalysis to criticism and strengthened the arguments for alternative approaches.

Behaviourist methods have extensive evidence of their ability to shape the behaviour of both animals and humans, yet on their own they are of limited usefulness for the majority of problems that people feel they need professional help with. Behaviourist approaches pay little attention to the helping relationship, and their ability to shape behaviour seems to be strongest when combined with more human-centred, and indeed humanist, approaches. The best known example of this is perhaps cognitive behavioural therapy (CBT). CBT is probably the most widely offered form of psychological help. It combines insights from behaviourism with a focus on internal cognitions and a humanist emphasis on building a helping relationship. It is therefore an example of an approach that combines what were previously framed as competing schools of thought. There is an extensive evidence base that it can help people with a variety of problems (Roth and Fonagy, 2006).

Humanist approaches to helping have prospered both in combination with others and in their purer form. CBT is one example of a combined approach, but elements of humanist helping can be found in many therapies. Humanist approaches also remain in a purer form, with therapies such as MI, compassion-focused therapy and solution-focused practice being firmly humanist in their orientation and values. The enduring popularity of humanist orientations to helping is founded on three elements. It is worth considering each of these.

Values and beliefs

Humanist approaches emphasise the capacity of the individual to change. They therefore focus on strengths and building confidence and are client-centred, in that the client is the expert on their world and change needs to come from them. Humanist approaches place a heavy emphasis on building a trusting and collaborative relationship and exploring the client's perspective and motivations. This is reflected in core values of the humanist orientation. These include a non-judgemental orientation and some version of what Rogers characterised as 'unconditional positive regard'. Unconditional positive regard involves always valuing the person worked with. Being non-judgemental can mean literally not judging a person's actions. Most of the time this positive view of the person worked with is an important and uncontroversial element of counselling, for instance, even though a client may be drinking too much, as a counsellor we can be metaphorically 'in their corner', recognising the positive elements of their character and the reasons why they may drink. There are sometimes more difficult challenges, for instance how we work with someone who has done something very unacceptable, for example sexually abusing a child. In such circumstances a non-judgemental view would relate to the person not the behaviour. A humanist counsellor could be clear that what was done was wrong without condemning the person as a whole. It is perhaps a secular version of the idea that we condemn the sin, not the sinner. It is probably not a coincidence that key humanist helpers, such as Carl Rogers or William R. Miller (the creator of MI), had very religious backgrounds.

Practices

These values are manifested in the practices of humanist counselling. Rogers emphasised the importance of non-directive listening. This involves listening deeply to the individual and seeking to develop an understanding of their perceptions and to share that understanding with them. This involves appropriate body language; open questions that give the person listened to the power to shape the conversation; and reflections, or reflective statements, that offer the helper's understanding of what the individual is feeling or thinking. Reflections are in effect a hypothesis about what is going on for the person. They serve three key functions. One is that they show people that deep listening and understanding has been happening: hearing back what one feels or thinks is a powerful therapeutic experience in itself. Second, they offer the opportunity to correct, adapt or challenge the understanding offered. In essence, reflections offer a feedback loop, because they share the understanding of the counsellor explicitly. In contrast other key elements of listening, such as questions, are based on an assumed understanding of what somebody is experiencing – we ask a question because we *think* we understand and want to know more. In contrast, we provide a reflection when we want to share what we think we understand and in doing so we offer the opportunity for correction. As such, reflections provide a crucial feedback loop to improve our understanding as a helper. Finally, they encourage further exploration. The most common response to a reflection is more exploration and greater depth. Indeed, reflections keep us with the issues being brought up, while questions tend to move the conversation on to new topics. This final element – the sense that the client should be able to control the conversation – is a central feature of PCC. The idea is that the client is able to resolve their own problems, that they have the seeds for their own solutions within. The helper's job is to offer something like a mirror for the client, albeit a warm and caring one, to help them towards self-awareness and, if they choose it, to change. This is the non-directive element of PCC. In Chapter 11 the use of these skills to allow rights-focused dialogue is discussed.

Evidence

Early evidence for PCC was promising, though in the context of little rigorous evaluation of therapeutic methods (Weston, 2011). A more recent review found that PCC approaches on their own tend to work, but less well than some comparison treatments (Yao and Kabir, 2023). This is likely to be because they provide a good foundation for helping people, but benefit from more focus on ways people might change, such as those provided by CBT or MI.

Later developments in humanist helping

Rogerian PCC counselling is relatively rarely practised in its pure form today. In particular, it is rare for a counsellor to take a wholly non-directive approach. Usually counsellors shape the conversation in ways that are intended to be more helpful. Interestingly, there is a recording of Rogers practising PCC, and careful analysis suggests that he is in fact influencing the conversation, for instance through selective attention, in ways he no doubt believes will make it more helpful (Edwards et al, 1982). For instance, Rogers is strategically giving attention to certain elements of the client's account, while paying less to other parts. This notwithstanding, the values and skills of PCC have been fundamental in the development of a new generation of counselling approaches. One of the most direct descendants of PCC is MI. William R. Miller, the originator of MI, is clear that MI developed directly from his use of PCC, and believes most of what makes MI effective is the PCC skills and values. The skills and values of MI form a core element of this book, and it is therefore worth considering the development of MI here before returning to the practices of MI in Chapter 11.

The origin of MI was Miller's reflections on his practice, which he set out in a key paper published in 1983 (Miller, 1983). In contrast to much of addiction treatment at that time, which often had a very confrontational approach, Miller applied the skills and values of PCC into his work. As a result he felt that he rarely encountered the 'resistance' from clients that others felt was endemic to working with alcohol and drug problems. Instead he seemed able to build helping relationships with people. However, through the process of trying to explain what he was doing and why he was doing it Miller recognised that while founded on the principles of PCC, he was not being non-directive. In fact, he was actively trying to help people overcome their problems with alcohol by managing the conversation in certain ways. Miller tried to understand the way he used the skills and values of PCC in a directive and strategic way. With his long-time collaborator, Stephen Rollnick, the idea of ambivalence about change was developed as a central element of MI (Miller and Rollnick, 2012). At its simplest, people may feel both positively and negatively about a problem behaviour and about change. For instance, to give a personal example, I may know that I should exercise more, but find it hard to get up in the morning and go for a run. MI uses PCC skills and values to explore with people whether there is a difference between their current behaviour and how they would like to behave, and if there is it helps them to make a plan to do things differently. Of course, this is a simplistic overview and the practices are hard to master, yet at heart it is as simple as that.

MI has been enormously influential, particularly in the field of alcohol treatment where it has consistently been shown to be an effective way of helping people – often with rather brief interventions. Its success in that setting has led to numerous studies exploring and developing the approach in other settings. So, for instance, Rollnick has applied MI ideas to the work of GPs, schools and sports coaches, among others (Miller and Rollnick, 2012). In doing so he, Miller and others have expanded the approach so that it can be used in longer-term counselling, in brief interventions or as a more general way of communicating with people about behaviours that they or others find to be a problem. There is extensive evidence that MI makes a difference, for instance there are systematic reviews in relation to working with offenders (McMurran, 2009), reducing alcohol problems in young adults (Foxcroft et al, 2016) or use in health settings (Ruback et al, 2005; Lundahl et al, 2013). I unpack the practices of MI and think about their applicability to social work in Chapter 11.

MI is just one example of a humanist approach that has developed out of the work of Rogers and others. We saw earlier how humanist methods influenced the development of CBT. They have also been fundamental to other developments in counselling. Compassion-focused therapy seeks to help people be more compassionate towards themselves and others (Gilbert, 2009). It grows directly out of the humanist tradition. For other approaches to helping the humanist influence is obvious, though it is often mixed with multiple other influences. Solution-focused practice, in its various guises, owes something to both the functionalist perspective considered earlier and the humanist orientation (Murphy et al, 2013). Restorative practice was developed as a response to crime but has subsequently incorporated ideas and values from humanist psychology (Hopkins, 2015). The list could go on. It is probably true to say that the humanist orientation provides a foundational set of values and practices for most contemporary counselling.

Humanism and social work

Unsurprisingly, humanism has been enormously influential in social work. Reviews of what social work skills are taught to students found they were predominantly those associated with non-directive, person-centred listening – though as the authors note, relatively little attention is then paid to how we might apply these skills into the specific practice of social work (Social Care Institute for Excellence, 2004). In child and family social work many of the most popular current frameworks for practice are founded on humanist principles. For instance, Signs of Safety adapts solution-focused practice for child protection work (Turnell and Edwards, 1999), MI is incorporated as a communication style in the Family Safeguarding Model and the adaptation of restorative practice for work with children and families has required the inclusion of many humanist practices for working with individuals (Williams et al, 2022).

Humanism has found a ready home in social work because many of its values fit well with those of the profession. The respectful and person-centred orientation is consistent with fundamental social work values, such as client self-determination. The practices provide a strong introduction to listening and to helping people and therefore are well placed to provide a foundation for social work.

Yet there are challenges for a humanist orientation in social work. Two are particularly important – and interlinked. The first is that there is a danger that a humanist orientation misses the social, in other words that in focusing on working with individuals it fails to take account of the social factors that influence and impact on people. The second is that it does not sufficiently consider the social work role per se, developed as it was as a psychological orientation and a counselling approach. In fact, social work happens at the intersection of the personal and the social. To incorporate humanism into social work practice therefore requires not just an understanding of the individual but also a more broadly political perspective. The next chapter considers how we might address these issues by introducing the social model and then seeking to synthesise it with a humanist approach to helping individuals with the more social perspective offered through the social model. Indeed, this whole book can be seen as an attempt to achieve such a synthesis.

Yet a humanist orientation provides a strong starting point for thinking about rights-focused practice. Its respectful and hopeful orientation, combined with an excellent account of how to listen deeply and key elements involved in helping individuals, provides both values and practices that are consistent with rights-focused social work – and particularly the sort of rights-focused work based on a love ethic argued for in this book. These ideas are further explored in Part III, where attention turns to how they need to be adapted for social work, but first we turn to address the lack of a social element in humanist social work.

8

The social model

This chapter offers a contrasting approach to thinking about the issues which social workers typically work with by introducing the social model. The chapter starts by describing the medical model, and then provides an introduction to the development of the social model in relation to disability issues, before exploring the application of the model to other areas such as mental health and alcohol or drug problems. More recent arguments for the social model to be used in child and family work are introduced. The chapter then seeks to synthesise humanist approaches and the social model. Rights-focused practice is argued to provide a space where the social and the individual, the humanist and the social model, can fruitfully interact to inform social work theory and practice.

What is the medical model?

The social model is generally understood in opposition to the medical model. At its simplest the medical model tends to focus on two steps – diagnosis and treatment. Diagnosis involves identifying a defined illness or impairment. This is conceptualised as within the individual, and therefore treatment tends to focus on the individual. For disability the medical treatment might involve providing aids or medication that minimise the limitations created by an impairment. In the area of mental health, the diagnosis of a specific condition, such as schizophrenia or depression, can be followed by a treatment for the individual, which might be medication or therapy or a combination of both. It is worth noting that there is the danger of an overly simplistic characterisation of the medical model here. Oates recounts Heifer asking a class what the medical model is. There was a long pause before one brave student put up their hand and said: 'I don't know what it is, but I know that it's bad' (Oates, 1996: 3). In fact, doctors and others with a medical orientation often approach the issues they deal with in a very sophisticated way. Public health and epidemiology have provided huge amounts of evidence about the ways in which social factors influence health, as well as proposing social reforms to address such issues (see, for instance, Marmot, 2020). Even those using a broadly medical model, for instance in working with an individual, often recognise and try to address social issues.

It is nonetheless true that the predominant approach to clinical practice for mental health issues, learning difficulties, disabilities, and alcohol and drug problems has tended to emphasise diagnosing an issue or 'illness' and providing an individual treatment. The social model is an attempt to develop a radically different understanding of the issues being looked at and how we should respond to them.

Development of the social model

The social model was first developed by disability rights campaigners and fundamentally arose from political struggle (Oliver and Barnes, 2012). It has subsequently been adapted and applied to a variety of issues, including many of the areas that social workers engage with. While social work existed before the social model was articulated, the model provides a way of thinking critically about issues and how to respond to them that is particularly characteristic of and helpful for social work.

The development of the social model in relation to disability

The social model was created by disability rights activists in the 1970s and 1980s (Oliver, 1984). They started by criticising the concept of 'handicap' – the term commonly applied to disabilities at the time. A handicap in common parlance is 'a circumstance that makes progress or success difficult' (*Oxford English Dictionary*). They argued that equating disabilities with handicaps meant that the disability was seen as the cause of the problem. In fact, they argued, there is a difference between an impairment, a disability and a handicap (see Susser, 1990; Oliver, 2017). An impairment is a physical limitation or problem, which can be related to an illness (for instance, difficulty breathing due to severe asthma) or injury (for instance, a leg amputation as a result of a road accident will impair movement). A disability is the functional limitation that the impairment produces. For instance, an amputated leg limits movement in various ways; breathing difficulties may make exercise impossible. The crucial issue is that the degree to which a disability becomes a handicap is often portrayed as solely a product of the level of disability (the functional limitation created by an impairment), yet in fact it is an interaction between the nature of the disability and the way that society is organised. An oft-used example is that of somebody who uses a wheelchair. Their disability may mean they cannot walk, however it is society that makes decisions about how it builds pavements and buses and buildings, and therefore the experience of living with this disability. These physical structures can be arranged to minimise or maximise the actual level of handicap experienced by somebody with a disability: we can have a society that makes it easy or impossible for people who use wheelchairs to travel and access buildings. And it is not just the physical environment that shapes the relationship between disability and handicap, society makes decisions about employment rights, availability of benefits, organisation of healthcare and many other factors that influence whether a disability becomes a handicap – whether it prevents somebody from doing something. For instance, do we provide high quality wheelchairs, appropriate medicines or additional help such as signers or carers for those who need it? These resources can decide whether a disability becomes a handicap.

While the wheelchair image is simple to grasp, the analysis can be applied to any type of disability. What types of adjustments do we need to ensure that people with, for instance, impaired vision or hearing can participate in society? Or those with illnesses such as epilepsy, or those with learning difficulties? Powerful campaigns by disability rights campaigners have transformed our approach to disability since the introduction of the social model: transport and buildings have duties of accessibility, and there are laws to protect the rights of people with disabilities, such as the duty of employers to make reasonable adjustments. Of course there is much still to be done and there is strong evidence that people with disabilities experience structural and personal discrimination in myriad ways (Maroto and Pettinicchio, 2014). Disabled activists and their allies still perform a crucial role in identifying and pushing back at these barriers and inequities. The key point for the current argument is that the social model provided a new way of conceptualising this struggle, and a powerful way of reframing the nature of disability, turning it from an individualised, medical issue to an issue of social justice.

The social model was subsequently extended to apply to mental health issues (Mulvany, 2000; Beresford et al, 2016), and then to apply to other issues (for example, Goodley, 2001) with recent interest in applying it to the area of family support and child protection (Featherstone et al, 2018). These applications of the model are considered later in the chapter. It is worth first unpacking further the key ideas that inform the social model. The core elements of the social model emerged from the process of struggle. They are linked to arguments and struggles going back to the 1960s or earlier, which became more focused and more powerful as the disability rights movement organised more effectively in the 1970s and beyond. An influential crystallisation of them was in the work of Michael Oliver (Oliver, 1984; Oliver and Barnes, 2012). In a key work, *The politics of disability*, he presented a version of the model that has four key elements. The first and probably most fundamental is that those directly affected by an issue should have power and voice in defining the nature of the issues and the solutions they wish to have. This was the essence of the struggles of disability rights activists and the social model emerged from this fundamental call for a change of perspective – instead of 'experts' defining the problem, those directly needing services should be allowed to define both the problem and the solutions they needed. In doing so campaigners explicitly learnt from contemporaneous struggles, such as those for civil rights, the feminist movement and the anti-apartheid struggle. They drew parallels with these groups and asked for similar rights, fundamentally to Enlightenment principles such as equality and equity.

The second crucial insight from the model is that we need to have a critical view about how social problems are defined. This is indissolubly linked to the first point: when left to professionals, handicap was seen as residing within the person. It took disability rights campaigners to reframe this and underline the social construction of handicap. This turned the problem on its head – instead of seeing the individual disabled person as needing help, it required a reappraisal of society so that we can seek to include those with varied abilities. These two insights are the most fundamental contributions of the social model for social work. Social work by its nature deals with 'social problems'; social workers work with issues that society sees as causing problems both for individuals and for society more generally. The specific contribution of the social model is to emphasise that we should start with a critical view of the 'problem' we are dealing with. Who is this a problem for? Who defines the nature of the problem and the way we respond? Crucially, it then emphasises those directly experiencing the 'problem' as best placed to define the nature of the issue. And as we can see with the example of disability, this can lead to a radical reimagining of both the nature of the 'problem' and the way we should respond to it.

There are two further elements of the social model that are crucial both for applying it to disability and more generally for using it within social work. The first is that, as the name suggests, the social model tends to place a focus on understanding the social causes of 'problems'. This is not just about how the problem is defined, as discussed earlier, but also about how a problem is created. For instance, social causes of handicap may include a lack of adequate benefits, a failure to provide housing or transport or a lack of work opportunities for those with disabilities. So powerful have these arguments become that we rarely use the term handicap today. People have disabilities, and it is society's job to ensure that they do not become handicapped. In other areas, discussed later, the social causes of a 'problem' are crucially important. For instance, research has emphasised the key role of poverty in increasing the likelihood of children coming into care (Bywaters et al, 2016) and there is extensive research exploring the over-representation of Black people in the more coercive elements of the psychiatric system (for example, Bhui, 2001).

The final element of the model relates to this point: because many of the problems have social causes, we need to seek social solutions. Medical science has made enormous advances that provide real benefits for many people with disabilities, however it says little about how we can enable and empower people by changing society. This was the contribution that the disability rights movement made – and in doing so they provided a model that we can apply across a multitude of social issues.

Key groups influenced by the social model included people with learning difficulties, mental health issues, or drug and alcohol problems. Service user movements and activists took insights from disability rights campaigns and applied them to mental health and other areas. Most importantly, like disability activists, many organised politically and fought for different ways of thinking about and responding to issues. This allowed them to ask key questions, such as: Who defines emotional difficulties or unusual behaviour as a mental illness? Who decides what help people might need? This in turn led to academic arguments and political campaigns for a move away from a medical model of psychiatric problems towards one where those who used services had control over the services as well as more say in the help that they received as individuals. As touched upon in Chapter 3, the organisation and campaigning of those who received services led to fundamental questions about who has power – and who should have power – in delivering services (see Beresford and Croft, 2002).

The social model and child and family social work

In recent years there has been a concerted attempt to develop and apply a social model to working with children and families. A key text here is Featherstone et al (2018) and earlier work by the same group of authors (Featherstone et al, 2014a). Featherstone and colleagues start by critiquing the current child protection system. They marshal a welter of quantitative and qualitative evidence that child protection can be a difficult, unhelpful and sometimes abusive experience for parents. They highlight recent work by Bywaters and others that has established the strong link between inequality and children being subject to a child protection plan or entering care (Bywaters et al, 2016). They also emphasise the importance of other inequalities, such as those relating to race and gender, and the way these intersect with poverty to place particular groups at higher risk of entering care (Bywaters et al, 2017). The work of Bilson and others has also established the ever increasing numbers of children being drawn into child protection processes and entering care (Bilson and Martin, 2017).

Featherstone et al argue that the child protection system as it is currently delivered does not work: it draws large and increasing numbers of families into investigations that are rarely helpful, the experience is often difficult for parents and others and there is limited evidence that it protects children at serious risk of harm. They also argue that the current system also serves to individualise social problems. For instance, poverty is largely marginalised in work with families, and domestic abuse is responded to not as a gender issue but as a risk that mothers should protect children from (Featherstone and Peckover, 2007). In doing this, social workers all too often reinforce gender inequalities rather than challenging them. In response to these problems, Featherstone et al suggest a social model may provide a better way of understanding and responding to child abuse. For instance, rather than looking at the child as an individual separate from their family or community, children – indeed all humans – can be understood as existing in relationships and therefore embedded within families and communities. The option of removing children in such circumstances always does wider harm, and the child protection mantra to 'focus on the child' can serve to disguise the wider harms that child protection can do by individualising the child rather than seeing them as essentially relational.

Of course the essence of the social model is that it is produced by those who experience a service, and this vision for child protection is proposed by academics. For this reason these author/activists have placed an emphasis on working closely with those with direct lived experience of services. This includes organisations such as the Family Rights Group and projects working with women who have experienced domestic abuse or those who have had children removed (Featherstone et al, 2011). Beyond this group there has been more emphasis on working with people with experience of care or child protection, and there are examples of innovative use of peer advocacy, inclusive approaches such as Family Group Conferences or work with parents who were in care to produce a Charter for other care-experienced parents (Burford, 2017; Roberts, 2021). These are all hopefully symptoms of the beginnings of a shift in our understanding of whose voices should be heard in thinking about child protection.

This work applying the social model demonstrates the richness of the approach as a way of critiquing and potentially changing how we understand and respond to the social problem of child abuse. This work is ongoing, and who knows what placing the voices of those directly affected at the centre of our thinking and actions might achieve in the future? It provides an example of the strength of the social model as applied to any type of social problem, and more specifically the contribution that it can make to social work. Yet the social model is not without criticisms and limitations, and it is important to consider these before thinking through how the social model can be used in rights-focused practice.

Limitations of the social model

As noted by various authors the social model is not in fact a model. A model is a simplified account of something more complicated. The social model is a critique of the medical model but, unlike the medical model, it has not articulated a specific, simplified way of understanding issues. Rather, the social model is a set of arguments that have facilitated political struggle, academic analysis and critical professional practice.

The social model has been critiqued for three particular issues. First, there are different versions of the social model and there may be a lack of consensus about what it involves. For instance, Owens (2015) describes distinct Scandinavian, North American and UK versions, with each version of the social model shaped by the national welfare regime that it was critiquing. In essence, the issue here is that the social model may be clearer and more useful as a way of critiquing current provision than as a model for what should be provided instead. Second, in seeking to create conditions for solidarity and action by defining people with a disability (or other oppressed groups) as a group, the social model pays less attention to differences within the group. For instance, the focus on oppression becomes a defining issue for membership of the category of 'disabled', with less attention paid to variations in experiences of oppression and no interest in those who may not experience oppression. This is related to the final critique, which is that the focus on the social and political means the social model can have less to say about subjective experiences. For instance, it does not focus on the embodied and lived experience of disability (Owens, 2015).

This is related to a pragmatic limitation, which is important for our purposes. The social model is not focused on individual practice. It provides a useful critique of an individualised form of practice, without providing detailed guidance on how social workers should work with individuals without replicating the medical model. The social model provides an *orientation* for practice, which emphasises questioning the presentation of a specific issue as a social problem, understanding the perspective of the person with a 'problem' and in general providing a user-centred type of help. These are fundamental questions of orientation which inform this book, but they do not provide detail for how social workers or others should do this when working with individuals or families. More importantly, they do not wrestle with some of the complexities that this may involve. For instance, what are the implications of the social model for working with a family where the concerns for a child are so great that you, as a social worker, think that they need to come into care? In a nutshell, precisely because the social model is critical of an individualised approach to practice it provides little guidance for how to conduct practice with individuals.

The social model, rights and social work

Central to the social model has always been a focus on rights. Indeed, the social model can be summarised as a move from treatment to rights. This includes rights to individual liberty, positive rights to resources and connection rights for individuals, as discussed in Part I. As such, a social model provides a foundation for a rights-focused orientation in social work. It points us to the importance of thinking about rights, it emphasises the voice of those we work with and it illustrates the role of political struggle in achieving and expanding the rights that individuals can have. While it therefore has relatively little to say about individual practice, if we want social workers to practice in a social model informed way then we need to consider how the principles of the social model can be applied into practice.

As outlined in Part I, rights-focused practice involves working with potential conflicts about rights. One of the key contributions a social model makes is to enable and require critical thinking about the rights that we are working with. It leads us to question what rights people have, and what rights they should have. Social workers are not simply the administrators of state-sanctioned rights. We should be champions for the rights that those we work with should have. This is not a straightforward position for a professional. At its simplest this means we should be questioning whether the existing rights of those we work with are being upheld. The case study in Chapter 3 is an example of this, with the social worker championing the right of the children to move school. This sort of micro-level organisational struggle is an everyday part of practice for rights-focused social workers.

Many academics have argued that the nature of social work requires us to be involved in political struggle to help those we work with (see Bailey and Brake, 1975 for the classic exposition). For a rights-focused social worker there are dilemmas created by this. Much of this book works on the assumption that in a liberal democracy the rights we uphold and work with are broadly ones we are happy to support, and that social workers then become involved in making sure they are applied in humane and equitable ways. Yet, what of situations when that is not the case? Social workers have been involved in many activities that are not acceptable from a rights-focused perspective. At the extreme, social workers were employed in Nazi Germany (Barney and Dalton, 2006), however more recently and closer to home social workers have been implicated in massive denials of rights such as the removal of aboriginal children from their families in Australia or the transportation of children from the United Kingdom to Canada (Maylea, 2021). These human rights violations underline the fact that social workers must be guided by a higher ethical framework. As noted in Chapter 2, the limitation of Sheppard's conceptualisation of social workers is that it provides no freedom for a critical view of existing policies. Social workers should not be simply administering current social policies, but should have a critical perspective on the policies they are implementing.

To some degree this is true for other professionals working for the state. We know that outcomes in education, health, crime and other areas are profoundly influenced by social structures. It is therefore legitimate for teachers, doctors, nurses and others to have a critical view of the way that their areas of work are affected by social policies and government action. And, indeed, they often do. Public health is a field related to medicine which focuses on social influences on health, and the professional bodies and leading individuals within the professions of medicine, nursing and teaching often have critical perspectives on government policy. It is obvious that social work should have at least as much to say about the social factors that influence the experiences and outcomes for the people we work with, as well as our ability to do the jobs the state has asked for us. Yet there is a strong tendency in social work literature to argue that social workers should do more than this, that we should be campaigners. A classic, if extreme, version of this can be found in the 'Case Con Manifesto' of the 1970s, which concludes:

> The problems of our 'clients' are rooted in the society in which they live, not in supposed individual inadequacies. Until this society, based on private ownership, profit and the needs of a minority ruling class, is replaced by a workers' state, based on the interests of the vast majority of the population, the fundamental causes of social problems will remain. It is therefore our aim to join the struggle for this workers' state. (Brake and Bailey, 1975, Appendix One)

Such arguments are not just historical. As noted in Chapter 1, Maylea has recently called for the end of the social work profession because we are too often accommodating to the inhumane practices of the state. Dominelli (2017) has persuasively argued for social workers to be politically active. So, should social workers be political activists? Is this more true for social workers than other professions? And if it is, why is that the case and what are the limits, if any, to that activism?

The argument that social workers should be – as part of their professional role – politically active in the way set out by Case Con is not one I find convincing. When I was a social work student I read Lena Dominelli's *Anti-racist social work* (2017). She had a case study in which a family originally from Bangladesh came to social services because they were experiencing poverty. This was in part as a result of sending money back to Bangladesh to provide for children who still lived there. Dominelli argued that not only should a social worker seek to ensure that the family had all the entitlements available to them (a position that any worker would agree with), but that in addition anti-racist practice should involve recognising that this was a broader issue, helping local families organise and campaigning for children abroad to be eligible for child benefit. I brought this example to my practice educator in a local authority children's services department, who said that this type of political action would not be allowed in the placement as it is not what social workers are employed to do. Indeed, she was clear that if I undertook such action during work time I would fail my placement.

The fundamental problem is that a child and family social worker in a local authority is a role with a job description that does not include political activism. Put bluntly, it is unrealistic and naïve to suggest that the state should employ people in order to overthrow it. Indeed, given that nobody would employ them to overthrow the state, the radical social work argument leads to the conclusion that one should become an activist, rather than believing that social workers are themselves activists in this way. And there is a path into politics that many social workers have taken, from Clement Attlee to Mark Drakeford.

It might therefore be possible to conclude that social workers should carry out the tasks ascribed to them by policy and law, with some limited room for critical positioning in a way similar to other professions. This is probably the everyday experience of most workers. Yet this too is not sufficient. There is something different about social work compared to other professions, and that difference is fundamentally linked to the rights-based nature of the social work task. For the professions mentioned, to a large degree the quality of service they would like to deliver can be defined by the profession. Thus, doctors, nurses and teachers can each describe the nature of excellent medicine, nursing or education. From that foundation they can criticise either the provision of services to deliver the ideal, or policies that influence outcomes negatively. This is to some degree true for social work as well. However, the challenge for social work – at least in the United Kingdom and many other countries with welfare states – is that to a large degree the state defines the social work role, at least in the statutory settings that most work in. This is because social work is a rights-focused profession. The way in which the government defines the rights of individuals we work with is therefore central, indeed it is definitional, in deciding what the social work role is. While the government has influence on elements of other professional roles, these are peripheral compared to the way it centrally defines the social work role. At its simplest, if we did not have government legislation to protect individuals and provide for social needs, we would not have statutory social work. A consequence of this is that social work is inherently more political than most professions. Put another way, the rights-focused nature of social work means that it is constantly working at the intersection of the individual and the social.

The specific tension occurs when we believe that a policy or law is inconsistent with our professional values or knowledge. To give another personal example, in the mid-1990s I was a senior practitioner in inner London when the government removed the right of asylum seekers to receive benefits, yet local authorities retained responsibilities to provide for children, without having been prepared for such an eventuality. By accident I became the manager for a service providing a version of benefits via payments under Section 17 of the 1989 Children Act for over 350 families.

This was probably the most unpleasant job I have ever done, and it was certainly the one that most challenged my professional ethics. It involved a level of policing and sometimes denying people payments that I found very uncomfortable. I did not participate in political campaigning during work hours, as that was not what I was employed to do. Instead I lobbied within the organisation for better provision – for instance to give 100 per cent of benefits, not 80 per cent as advised by the government – and I tried to work across local authorities to lobby for better help for asylum-seeking families; and I did my best with the services we had.

While this example illustrates the difficulty in the idea of social worker as activist, it also highlights the limitations in the Sheppard argument. Sheppard argues that social needs can be treated *as if* they were objective. In this example that would have required me to simply accept the clearly discriminatory and racist government policy and treat it as if people seeking asylum had lower levels of need than other people. This is at odds with social work principles and is just empirically wrong – if anything, their needs are greater for various reasons.

This leaves me, and in my opinion social work as a profession, in a difficult situation. On the one hand, we are not employed to be political activists and whatever activism we do is therefore in our own time. On the other hand, we cannot simply accept and enact unjust or unfair policies. We have a professional duty to resist, and to stand up for the principles and higher-level rights – such as those in the UN Convention – that we believe in.

The conclusion I draw is that it is not possible to resolve this tension: it is an irreducible and necessary part of the social work role. Indeed, to go further, having professionals who can work with such tensions around rights is a core part of having a humane and liberal society. We need professionals who protect rights, and who therefore feel uncomfortable and can challenge when rights are not upheld. Social workers perform this key role for society. As such, we often find ourselves wrestling with difficult dilemmas, both in working with individuals and in responding to policies that in our professional opinion are unjust.

This sense of social workers as having to work with uncomfortable and often unresolvable dilemmas is a recurring theme of this book. It is tempting to try to resolve the dichotomies at the heart of social work, particularly in practice but also in some academic texts, by focusing on just one, for instance by saying we work with individuals *or* that we believe in political action; to say we focus on the child *or* the parent; to accept the voice of the client *or* to prioritise that of the professional. In fact social work is rarely about 'either/or' positions, rather it operates in the often uncomfortable spaces between. It works with the tensions and difficulties that this involves, and while it seeks to resolve them when possible, often it requires us to be able to be comfortable with being uncomfortable, to recognise that a mature approach to both human nature and society means that we need to work with conflicting and difficult imperatives.

Rights, humanist approaches and the social model

This ability to work with potentially conflicting imperatives or understandings also applies to the social model. Humanist social work and the social model have some complementary elements, such as a profound respect for individuals. Yet they are also at odds in important ways, such as the focus on the individual and the social. The argument of this chapter, and indeed this book, is not that these tensions can be resolved, at least in any simple way. Rather, the argument is that the social model and humanist social work provide perspectives and tools that help us inhabit the difficult terrain of conflicts and tensions relating to rights that has been outlined throughout this book. In particular, humanist approaches to helping people were designed with counselling in mind, but they can provide many of the tools we need to work in a rights-focused way with individuals. The social model was developed to support the struggle for rights, but it can help us be critical of individualised perspectives, including that within a humanist orientation. The social model provides a critical perspective on the issues we are working with and the services we provide, and humanist approaches provide tools for managing some of the tensions that this critical perspective creates.

The key point is that in doing social work we are not using either tradition for the purpose for which it was developed. It therefore helps that both approaches are part of a higher-level Enlightenment tradition. They therefore share some key features, including a focus on human welfare and wellbeing, respect for individuals and their perspectives and a commitment to rationality and debate and empirical inquiry. These elements make them compatible with a different purpose, namely working with human rights in the ways outlined in Part I. As noted throughout Part I, rights sit at the intersection of the individual and the social. Humanist approaches help us work with individuals in respectful and humane ways. The social model ensures that we do not become so focused on the individual that we fail to be critical about the issues we are working with or the social factors that may be contributing to them. As such the two traditions provide a strong foundation for us to think about the practices involved in rights-focused social work. What is needed are practices that are built upon and consistent with these orientations, but that allow social workers to engage with the messy uncertainties, the complexities and discomforts that are an essential feature of rights-focused practice. These are the focus of Part III.

PART III
Rights-focused practice

9

Assessment as theory development

Rights-focused practice requires an ability to synthesise different types of knowledge from varied sources. In particular, as noted in Chapter 5, three types of knowledge are crucial:

1. *Subjective perspectives*: the views of those we work with, including children, parents, carers and professionals.
2. *Objective evidence*: our professional view, including more objective and normative evidence and more factual information from various sources.
3. *Society's view*: of what is acceptable and can be provided as expressed in law, policy, procedures and resourcing.

Assessment in social work is therefore a complicated undertaking. It involves gathering, combining and seeking to understand different types of evidence in order to ensure the rights of all those involved are understood and worked with. This chapter argues that many approaches to assessment are too simplistic to support this type of complexity. How we might helpfully think about assessment, particularly when working with a rights-focused approach, is then the focus of the chapter. The aim is to provide a theory of and for assessment, with the next chapter outlining a potential practice that flows from this orientation.

What is assessment?

Assessment requires us not just to obtain and combine different types of knowledge and perspectives, but also to use our skills, values, knowledge and theories to analyse and synthesise information. There is a sense in which all of social work is brought together in the practice of assessment. Certainly, assessment is a core part of social work. It is something social workers do almost every day, and some of their assessments can have enormous consequences for people. There are few more far-reaching interventions than, for instance, recommending that a person be given compulsory psychiatric treatment or removing a child. Social workers do not make such immense decisions alone, but their assessments are a key part of the process. Indeed, very often the process does not start if the social worker does not recommend it. Many assessments are less obviously important but can have substantial implications. Whether it be deciding whether a family get financial help, whether adults can become foster carers, or whether a person with a disability should get an enhanced package of care, the assessments and decisions that social workers make are hugely important.

My definition of assessment is that it is the activity we undertake to guide our actions. This simple definition has two benefits. One is that it covers all manner of assessment activities. Sometimes we write about assessments as if they were only in-depth and holistic. This is one important type of assessment, but social workers are also making an assessment when they read a referral and make a decision to do nothing. The second benefit is that it ties assessment organically to action. In fact, as will become apparent over the next few chapters, it is difficult to differentiate assessment and intervention. When we ask questions or contact professionals we are doing things that may impact on the people we are assessing, directly or indirectly. Conversely, when we try to help people, their responses will feed into a deeper understanding of them or their family, and this is an element of our assessment. Assessment and intervention are intertwined and it is something of a fiction to differentiate them. It is, however, perhaps a useful fiction. Considering assessment and helping separately allows us to focus on each before thinking about how they interact, and therefore this chapter and the following one have a focus on assessment and seek to build a rights-focused approach.

This chapter starts by considering some of the biggest challenges that the assessment task poses for social work. Some theories about assessment in social work are then presented and critiqued. This is followed by a critical narrative on the development of policy responses to support and define assessment in child and family social work. It is argued that assessment has some similarities to the research process. In plain language, it is important to be clear about the nature of the knowledge we are gathering and the process of analysis. Assessment is argued to be a form of provisional theory development, synthesising information from multiple sources, and we therefore need to be clear about the theory and practice we use for doing this. This chapter focuses on the theory, while the next moves to consider the practice more.

Challenges for assessment

There are a number of conceptual and practical challenges in carrying out social work assessments. An important one is that most assessments involve gathering multiple perspectives. A social worker may need to capture the views of children, parents and others within the family. Assessments also combine different types of knowledge. A social worker may have directly observed something, for instance a parent appearing to be drunk. They may have been told something, for instance the parent says it was actually medication they were on. They may have information from other sources, for instance a history of police referrals around alcohol-related violence. And it is not uncommon to have to work with evidence that is potentially contradictory, for instance the children insist they have never seen their parents drinking or arguing, despite police reports saying they were present at such incidents. This is complicated, messy stuff. The temptation may be to seek 'the truth', but as we will discuss later in the chapter, the truth is not simply 'out there'. To do assessment well we need to be able to work with multiple truths, recognise that the picture we have is provisional, and yet not let this paralyse us so that we cannot make decisions; ultimately we need to take a position on how we interpret all of this, because without such a position we cannot act – and assessment needs to be a guide to action. This is a key difference between a purely research perspective, which can content itself with solely understanding, and social work assessment. Somehow, from this complexity we need to find sufficient certainty about our conclusions to guide our action.

There are even more challenges with risk assessment. It is difficult enough to assess what has happened or what people currently need: assessing what may happen in the future with complete accuracy is literally impossible. This is an empirical fact. Humans are not terribly good at predicting the future. Work by Wilkins suggests that there is no reason to believe social workers are any different from other humans in this regard, with levels of forecasting in social work cases that were not much better than chance (Wilkins et al, 2020). There is also a conceptual and moral element to the challenge of predicting the future. If we believe in free will and self-determination, then we believe people can change. This creates a moral challenge for risk assessment, because while we may believe that an adult or child is at risk of harm, we also have to be able to offer those we work with opportunities to change. Risk assessment is in important respects a guide to the opportunities we can offer people to change and the protections we need to put in place while this is explored (Forrester and Harwin, 2011). It is one of the places where the rights-focused nature of practice becomes most evident. Sometimes we may look at a case history and feel there is little chance of change. Yet it is vanishingly rare for people not to be given at least some opportunity to change. Providing such opportunities is one of the ethical imperatives for statutory social work, as discussed in Chapter 3. This is not merely technical work, it is also saturated with values about individual freedom, responsibility and harm.

These are big challenges for assessment, and ones that no simplistic approach to assessment in social work is likely to be able to do justice to. So how does the social work literature approach assessment in general, and risk assessment in particular?

Theories of assessment in social work

While assessment is an everyday activity for practitioners it has proved a difficult practice to theorise: 'Although assessment has been recognised as a core skill in social work and should underpin all social work interventions, there is no singular theory or understanding as to what the purpose of assessment is and what the process should entail' (Social Care Institute for Excellence, 2004: 5). This idea is reinforced by a review of textbooks, which identified enormous variety in how assessment was theorised and suggestions for practice (Crisp et al, 2006). It is worth considering some common approaches to assessment. The classic approach to assessment places it within a broader social work process usually defined as consisting of four stages:

1. assessment;
2. planning;
3. implementation; and
4. review.

The stages should not be conceptualised as linear, in fact they form a circle. Reviewing the outcome of implementation feeds into further assessment. So, for instance, your assessment may conclude that children are hungry because the family do not have enough food as their benefits payments did not come through. You plan your intervention, which is to get them a payment now and try to sort out their benefits. Implementation is when you do that. You come back a few days later and find that the children are still hungry. Further assessment follows … maybe the money was not enough? Maybe something else happened? Maybe a parent has a gambling problem and spent the money on that? The outcome will inform your planning and implementation.

Within this process 'assessment' itself has a number of stages. In one of the most widely used models Milner and O'Byrne (2009) suggest five:

1. preparation – think through what data you might collect;
2. data collection;
3. weighing the data (evaluating the elements of the data);
4. analysing the data (bringing together the data); and
5. utilising the data.

This provides a useful way of highlighting the most important thing about assessment, and that is that it involves *thinking*. In three of Milner and O'Bryne's stages thinking is explicit – assessments need to be planned, data has to be weighed and then analysed. Yet there is thinking within the other stages too. Data collection is usually a dynamic and interactive process, particularly when talking with people, and this requires thinking about where to take conversations next and what information to focus on. Similarly, during 'utilisation' the assessment is used to guide action/s, but the actions feed back into assessment.

Milner and O'Byrne are not alone in providing thoughtful accounts of social work assessment. For instance, Coulshed and Orme (2018: 21) give the following definition: 'Assessment is an ongoing process, in which the client participates, the purpose of which is to understand people in relation to their environment; it is a basis for planning what needs to be done to maintain, improve or bring about change in the person, the environment or both.' This is just one example of many definitions that try to capture something of the complexity of the idea and practice of assessment in social work.

A key issue for any approach to assessment is that it needs to have a theory about the nature of the evidence it is gathering and how to make sense of it (Holland, 2010). Whether theorists of assessment or social workers doing assessments are explicit about it or not, this requires developing an approach to what we can know and how we can know it – issues covered in philosophy by concepts such as ontology (theories about what exists) and epistemology (theories about how we can know). Once again, often without knowing it, social workers are acting as practical philosophers.

A problem for social workers is that many of the policy attempts to improve social work assessment have tended to focus on data collection. They have helpfully outlined lots of types of information which social workers should collect. They have then said that analysis is very important, but have had much less to say about what this involves. At its worst, some of these approaches are based on a naïve positivism. Positivism is a philosophical position that believes there is an objectively real world, and that science proceeds by collecting evidence relating to it. It is discussed in more depth in what follows. The problem with this as a basis for social work assessments is that it emphasises collecting data without considering how workers make sense of it. This chapter focuses mainly on the process of analysis, and this and the next chapter argue that if we get analysis right then it can guide what information we seek to gather rather than the other way round. Analysis comes first and last, and is important throughout the process, rather than being something we do at the end once 'evidence' has been 'gathered'.

To place analysis at the heart of assessment it is useful to see it as something akin to research, a comparison that has often been made by social work academics (Shaw and Shaw, 1997; Holland, 2010). The reason we often make this comparison is that researchers have spent long hours debating how to do good research, and how we can rely on the findings of our studies. Not all of this debate is relevant to social work – but some of the key discussions about types of knowledge and how we can think about the process of analysis are of relevance. A helpful place to start is perhaps by understanding and critiquing positivist approaches, because this is a form of misunderstanding about assessment that policy and practice can often slip into.

Research methodology and social work assessment

Positivism was all the rage about a century ago. Science and technology were making huge strides, and it was argued that applying the scientific method to all research would provide similar insights. The problem with positivism was that it had a simplistic and ultimately incorrect vision of what the scientific method was. At its simplest a positivist believes that there are real laws in nature, and that we can discover them by gathering evidence. While both of these propositions are, in my opinion, true, it turns out it is more complicated than that. Two issues are particularly important. The first is that in order to do science or any other type of research you need a theory to get you started, whether you are consciously aware of it or not. The questions you ask, the methods you use to answer them and how you interpret the findings all involve implicit theories. The second is that once you have done the research you will still just have a theory. It may be a better theory, but it will not be 'the truth'. It is worth unpacking these statements, and a useful way to do that is to consider the work of Thomas Kuhn (1969). Kuhn is just one of many critics of naïve approaches to our understanding of science, but his development of the idea of paradigms is a useful way of understanding some bigger issues about how we know things. In the following discussion I talk about research – but the same arguments also apply to social work assessment. The question is: how do we know things?

Kuhn's classic work, *The structure of scientific revolutions*, is a wonderful read. He considers a series of scientific breakthroughs, and develops an argument that science does not proceed through the dispassionate collection of data in the way the positivists suggested. Instead, he suggests that in order to do science you need to have a shared set of ideas. These allow you to understand and communicate with other scientists in your discipline, they frame the sort of questions you ask and the types of answer that qualify as science. This shared way of understanding is supported by the community within the discipline, which, like any community, has hierarchies, ways of defining acceptable and valued behaviour, routes for progression and so on. Taken together these ways of thinking, supported by a community of practice, create a 'paradigm'. Kuhn defines paradigm differently at different points, but in essence it is a shared understanding within a community around a particular topic. Kuhn's argument is that within a paradigm 'normal science' progresses. Normal science involves people elaborating on knowledge within the paradigm. It is what most scientists do most of the time – expanding our understanding within current frameworks. Yet, Kuhn argues, within each discipline there are always fundamental unanswered questions or unquestioned assumptions. As a result, periodically an upheaval occurs. An individual or small group in exploring these issues find their results challenge the paradigm itself, and suggest the need for a profoundly different approach. This happens across every discipline, with steady progress and then dramatic change appearing to be the norm. Perhaps the most famous example came in physics. In 1897 Lord Kelvin stated that 'There is nothing new to be discovered in physics now. All that remains is more and more precise measurement.' (Kuhn, 1969: 12). In 1913 Einstein published his theory of relativity which turned the discipline on its head. This is just the most famous example of paradigm-shifting changes, with similar transformations in ways of thinking found in every discipline.

For our purposes, Kuhn's work has two implications. One is that we cannot approach research without a set of beliefs, a way of understanding both the topic and how to study it. The second is that ultimately what research produces is a theory – it is a way of understanding the world. Of course, these are very powerful ways of understanding the world, and every time we flick a switch for a light to go on or board an aeroplane we show faith in scientific theories. Yet, in practice, these theories are constantly being refined, adapted and improved. What is broadly true for science is even more true for the study of human beings. To date it has proved very difficult to develop strong, replicable theories about human beings and our behaviour, so any theory from the social sciences needs to be treated as provisional.

These insights about research have important implications for social work assessment. As mentioned earlier, we cannot carry out an assessment without a theory about what we are doing. And, in turn, the assessment we produce will be at most a provisional theory about the person and issue we are assessing. Furthermore, theories are not simply generated by individuals – they arise from communities and paradigms that allow us to think about topics. Thus, children's services perhaps offers a paradigm for thinking about and working with problems such as child abuse. It does this through the institutional practices and expectations that surround our work, from how meetings work to what we teach and expect from students, including how work is inspected, managed, rewarded or punished. This creates a language for thinking and talking about the work, a community of people doing the work, and expectations about what we do.

A problem is that many attempts to improve, or at least to standardise, social work assessment have focused on what information to collect. Thus, for instance, the UK government produced the first official guidance on how social workers should do a child protection assessment in 1988 (Department of Health, 1988). Blessed with a bright orange cover it was known as the 'Orange Book'. The Orange Book outlined specific questions workers should ask, and led to quite a prescriptive way of doing assessment. The Assessment Framework superseded it, and is organised around a triangle, with one side focused on the child's needs, the second on parenting capacity and the third on family and environmental factors (Department of Health et al, 2000). Each of these dimensions has several sub-categories. The paperwork and subsequent computer systems sought to reflect this structure with workers completing assessments related to each element. The Assessment Framework provides a useful heuristic for thinking about assessments. For inexperienced workers its structured approach provides a helpful way of ensuring key issues are covered. Yet the problem is that the Assessment Framework, like the Orange Book before it, focuses on gathering evidence and has remarkably little to say about how to analyse it. The Assessment Framework *says* analysis is very important, yet it has relatively little to say about how to actually do it.

There seem likely to be two reasons for this apparent gap. One is that while everyone agrees analysis is important, it is quite difficult to specify what it means. Analysis is a difficult thing to describe in detail, though I make some effort to do so later in this chapter and the one that follows. The second is that the Framework seems to be informed by a naïve positivism. The unexamined assumption seems to be that if a worker gathers all this information they will be able to make the assessment. This is an assumption that has, in my opinion, caused problems in social work with children and families. One problem is that it leads to workers collecting information they do not need to collect, and thus using a lot of worker and family time. A more profound one is that gathering 'holistic' information does not necessarily make for a good assessment. On its own, it just means you have lots of discrete pieces of information. What is needed is a way of interpreting, collating and synthesising the information you need. So, how can we move beyond naïve positivism and what might the implications be for how we do social work assessments, particularly when we strive to be rights focused?

Positivism, social constructionism and realism

Holland suggests that academic approaches to assessment in social work can broadly be understood as positivist or social constructionist (Holland, 2010). Many social work academics have critiqued positivist approaches and instead emphasised the socially constructed nature of our understanding of the world (Parton and O'Byrne, 2000). A social constructionist approach to assessment emphasises understanding the perspectives of those we work with and taking a critical stance towards the way that social 'problems', such as child abuse, are constructed. These are useful contributions, however a problem for a solely constructivist approach is that it is not clear how the various constructions within an assessment can be synthesised. Again, the problem is one of how we do analysis. It is true, for instance, that different people have different perspectives about a particular issue, but there are also facts that are not open to a constructivist interpretation. For example, if a child has bruises and a broken arm these are not merely social constructions – they are also real, physical facts. On their own they do not mean there has been abuse – to have some confidence about that we might need more medical evidence, the accounts of different people, an understanding of the history and more evidence about the child. They also have a constructed element, both at the level of society (for example, whether this is taken as an indicator of abuse) and the level of the individual (for example, how a parent understands the impact of what has happened on their children or the perspective of the child on the injuries). This is the mix of facts, constructions and the social context provided by policies that social workers typically operate in. What is needed is an approach that allows us to combine these different types of knowledge.

In fact, the simplistic antithesis between positivism and constructionism has been largely superseded in contemporary scholarship. Retaining it relies on eliding epistemology and ontology. Specifically, it is based on believing that what *exists* and what we *know about what exists* are the same, and that there is therefore either an objective world we can know objectively, or a socially constructed world that we can only interpret and know subjectively. In fact, it is possible to believe – and I believe – that there is a real world, but that we can never wholly or objectively know it. In this understanding, the real world exists – whether that is a physical injury, a subjective experience of that injury or the accounts different people may give about what caused it. However, we can never fully and objectively understand this real world, in part because our knowledge and our ability to share it with others is socially constructed. This can be thought of as taking an objectivist stance in relation to ontology (the real world exists) and a subjectivist stance towards epistemology (we can never truly know or fully communicate the real world and must do the latter through the social construction of language). There are in fact myriad philosophical positions that combine these beliefs, including pragmatism, neo-positivism and different types of realism (Jackson and Dolan, 2021). While not delving into it in depth, here I take a broadly realist position influenced by thinkers such as Pawson and Tilley (1997), Bhaskar (2013) and by pragmatists such as James (1975) and Rorty (1979).

A realist believes that we cannot fully understand the world, but we can develop increasingly helpful theories about it. These theories can help us understand both the observations we see and deeper factors that may be causing them. That is, while we cannot directly observe causal and structural factors such as class or gender they are nonetheless real (we can observe instances of them but cannot directly see their causal force). So, for instance, a realist can describe the injuries a child has experienced, the accounts and perspectives of different parties and can suggest that underlying factors, such as the acute mental health difficulties of the father who hurt the child, may have contributed to the abuse. Crucially, theories are always provisional, and they can be tested against the real world. We are therefore constantly revising theories, which can never wholly explain the complexity of the world. Our theories allow us to act – which is the purpose of assessment – but they are also tested by action, because what we do feeds back into our developing theory.

Realists see research – and I see social work assessment – as the process of developing theories and testing them empirically. This process combines various types of knowledge, and includes a critical perspective on the definition of the terms being used.

On theories, hypotheses and formulations

So what does developing a theory mean? By theory here I mean a hypothesis or set of related hypotheses that explains a phenomenon. Hypothesis and theory are often used interchangeably, but they differ in two ways. A hypothesis is more provisional than a theory, and it is usually more specific. A theory is often made up of several related hypotheses. When we receive an initial referral we may need to pursue one or two relatively simple hypotheses in guiding our work. Having worked with a family for a while our ultimate theory is likely to be far more complicated, incorporating the views of different people and a variety of other types of evidence. As described in detail in the next chapter, it will take the form of a series of interlinked hypotheses about what happened, why and what might be done about it and it will have a causal element – it presents a plausible explanation for why something happened. It is nonetheless a theory – it is a provisional attempt to synthesise the evidence and be transparent about how you, as the social worker, understand the situation. The name for such a theory is a formulation, and it is the focus of the next chapter.

The development of hypotheses and the combination of them into formulations is the core process required for a good assessment. It is a more coherent and helpful approach to assessment than the naïve positivism that underlies bureaucratic attempts to define assessment. It requires creativity, skill, thoughtfulness and a critical mindset. It also allows us to combine assessment and 'intervention'. It is, in short, the crucible in which we combine all we have learnt as social workers. There are no shortcuts to doing assessments well. Rather, good assessment is a process which requires us to access and use appropriately all our knowledge and experience as a social worker.

For this reason a theory about what assessment is and how to do it is essential for rights-focused practice. The vision of rights-focused practice outlined in this book has emphasised the different perspectives and types of knowledge that social workers need to work with. It has also noted that working with these differences is at the heart of social work. Indeed, the differences are to a large degree why we need social workers. If assessment was merely about gathering information, then like a benefits officer or a housing officer making a decision about eligibility we could follow a comparatively straightforward process. Instead, social workers are faced with the infinitely more complicated, more challenging and more interesting task of thinking about what types of evidence need to be gathered, ensuring the voices of those whose rights are involved are heard, synthesising the different types of evidence and coming to a conclusion about the action that should flow from this process. In doing so social workers are the ultimate realists. The next chapter turns to consider how we might do this in practice, using the development of formulations as a process for developing realist theories.

10

Assessment, formulations and rights

The previous chapter outlined some of the challenges in carrying out a social work assessment. It was argued that an assessment is a theory about what is happening for an individual or a family. The nature of the theory is that it is always provisional, but nonetheless this sort of provisional theory serves to guide our actions and inform our decisions.

Theory development also allows assessment to be transparent. Assessments are made to share. This may be with parents, children or others we work with. It can also be with the organisation – it is common for assessments to be part of making an argument within the local authority for a particular decision to be made or a service provided. Not for nothing, perhaps, do we often refer to the people we work with as 'cases' – working in social work involves constantly 'making a case', in that we are making an argument around needs, risks and services. We also often make a case with other professionals and agencies, for instance explaining our thinking to a court or professionals at a child protection conference.

The shareable nature of assessments also allows for accountability. This is most often conceived of as organisational accountability. An assessment report provides an account of decision-making with an individual or family. It explains why the social worker is doing what they are doing. It is therefore always important, and can be of crucial importance in certain circumstances. If something goes wrong, a well-written assessment is vital. They are also the element of practice that is most thoroughly scrutinised during processes of inspection and management oversight. It is difficult to observe practice directly. In contrast, an assessment is a matter of record. Many people, within and beyond the organisation, read assessments. It is therefore a core element of contemporary social work practice. Yet it is wrong to think of the accountability of a written assessment as being solely for the organisation. We are also accountable to those we work with. A written assessment provides a transparent record of our understanding and how it shaped our decision-making. This can be a fairly immediate occurrence, such as when we share an assessment prior to a key meeting. But assessments stay on case records for a very long time; it may provide an account to a child of decisions we made in relation to them that they read decades later. For all these purposes we need a way of thinking about and doing assessments that allows us to explain our actions and be accountable for them.

This chapter outlines an approach to assessment that is designed to meet these two key functions – assessment as a guide to action and as an accountable record of decision-making that can be shared. The approach taken is one that has become widespread in psychology but is relatively rarely used in social work, and that is the concept of formulation. There are some academic articles on formulation in social work, predominantly from a psychodynamic perspective (for example, Dean and Poorvu, 2008; Lee and Toth, 2016). More recently there has been interest in formulation as a social work practice, with Leeds including formulations in their influential restorative model (Leeds, 2021). I have also worked with colleagues from Kirklees, where they have embedded formulation into their practice (Kirklees, 2021). This chapter benefits from the insights and examples of formulation that they have shared with me. The chapter starts by exploring formulation in psychology. Then it considers formulation as an approach to rights-focused assessment in social work. Finally, it turns to consider a case study example of assessment using formulation.

Origins of formulation

Formulation in psychology developed as an alternative to a narrower medical model that dominated assessment through much of the 20th century and is still extensively used. The medical model has a focus on diagnosis. The psychological issues that people have are generally categorised as mental health or psychological illnesses or problems, such as depression or agoraphobia. Assessment involves gathering information that allows the psychologist to diagnose the issue and then recommend appropriate treatment, in the same way that doctors diagnose illnesses and provide medicines, surgery or other interventions.

Various critiques of this approach contributed to increasing use of formulation in psychology. Diagnosis often has too narrow a focus on identifying a specific pre-defined issue. People's issues often do not fall into neat diagnostic categories. While the diagnostic approach does have some space for the views of those worked with, this was usually fairly marginal; it is fundamentally an expert perspective, in which the psychologist is trained to diagnose the problem for those worked with. Most importantly, a narrow diagnostic focus often does not provide a way of helping people. For instance, concluding that somebody is experiencing agoraphobia has some level of usefulness, in that there are various ways of helping someone experiencing such issues. However, each person and their situation is unique, and a diagnosis on its own does not capture this. A diagnostic approach seeks generalities – essentially fitting people into categories. It struggles with the enormous variability within such categorisations. Formulations strive to understand the unique circumstances of each person, and develop a unique theory about what is happening for this individual, why and what may be helpful. This can include a specific diagnosis, but only as part of a wider understanding of the presenting issue and what might help.

In fact, formulation has roots across different schools within the field of psychology (see Johnstone and Dallos, 2014). Psychodynamic thinking, which proposed explaining symptoms as having both a meaning and a function, provided some of the first attempts to combine subjective experience and observed behaviour. Behavioural and cognitive behavioural therapists started using formulations from as early as the 1950s. This started with behavioural explanations of the environmental factors influencing behaviour, and was then developed to include thoughts and feelings as cognitive behavioural approaches were created. Systemic approaches went even further, focusing on formulations that considered structural factors, and interactions within systems – particularly the family – and the way that these contributed to specific behaviours that might be thought of as problems. A particular contribution was to develop the idea of a working hypothesis as a way of understanding and sharing one's understanding about what might be going on in a family – an idea we return to later. Indeed, formulations can be understood as a group of related hypotheses about an individual or family.

Interestingly, two groups within psychology have been somewhat reluctant to embrace formulation: the humanist and radical traditions (Johnstone and Dallos, 2014). Humanists have been concerned that because formulations involve some element of professional interpretation it is not consistent with a strictly person-centred approach to helping people. Radical psychologists have been concerned that formulations may individualise problems, preferring to emphasise the social and client-centred explanations of the issues they confront. Ironically, of course, these are the two traditions which I have identified as particularly important for rights-focused social work. It is perhaps not a coincidence that these two traditions are so influential in social work and that we rarely use formulation. In this chapter I argue – and then try to demonstrate – that formulation allows the combination of the individual and the social, the client and the professional view, and the objective and subjective perspectives. This is a big promise – so perhaps it is time to explain what formulations actually are.

What are formulations?

At its simplest a formulation 'asks what is wrong, how it got that way, and what can be done about it' (Nurcombe et al, 2002). The Division of Clinical Psychology's *Good practice guidelines on the use of psychological formulations* (DCP, 2011: 2) define formulation as 'both an event and a process [which] summarises and integrates a broad range of biopsychosocial causal factors. It is based on personal meaning and constructed collaboratively with service users and teams'. Johnstone and Dallos (2014) outlined the key features of formulations for psychology. The following list of core features of formulations is slightly adapted, changing references to psychological theory to social work. The core features of a formulation are that it:

1. Summarises the client's core problems.
2. Includes the perspective of the client on the presenting problem.
3. Indicates how difficulties may relate to one another, by drawing on social, social work and psychological theories.
4. Suggests why a problem has developed using these theories, including why at this time and in specific situations.
5. Allows the development of a plan for helping or intervening based on the theories used in developing the formulation.
6. Is always open to revision.

Ultimately formulations will vary depending on the theoretical perspective used to make sense of them. Johnstone and Dallos demonstrate this brilliantly in their edited book on formulation. They use the same two case studies, with different authors writing chapters using formulation from different theoretical perspectives. This produces formulations for the same two situations from the perspective of psychodynamic, cognitive behavioural, systemic, structural and other orientations. The collection as a whole makes for fascinating reading, as it demonstrates formulation as an art rather than a science; the art of applying theory to understand human problems. Each of the formulations provides insights and possible ways of helping, yet each is distinctive. With the kind permission of the authors I am going to use one of the case studies from that book to explore rights-focused formulation and what it might look like in social work. If you are interested in knowing more about formulation and seeing how different theoretical traditions might approach formulation for the same case study then Johnstone and Dallos' book is an excellent read. The case study I have permission to use is in Box 10.1.

How to approach formulation: the four Ps

A common way of approaching formulation in the psychiatric and psychological literature is to start with the 'four Ps'. These are a helpful way to understand presenting issues in relation to four factors. Each of these can be interpreted in various ways. For instance, Cheng (2022) suggests that a biopsychosocial approach can be applied to each factor, giving examples of each. The four are:

1. Predisposing factors
   What background factors make it more likely that this issue might arise? Background factors are present before the development of the problem but they make it more likely. They can operate at any level. For instance, poverty is a background factor that puts families under stress. Biological predisposing factors include genetic and in utero issues, such as foetal alcohol spectrum disorder. Psychological factors might include parents who have been abused finding parenting difficult. Predisposing problems make a problem more likely, but they do not determine that it will happen. Many parents in poverty, or with inherited attention deficit hyperactivity disorder, or who have themselves been abused, do not have problems.
2. Precipitating factors
   These explain why a problem developed. Precipitating factors are primarily concerned with 'why now?' They can take many forms and, as with all the factors, can be present at multiple levels. For instance, a family may have coped until the parents split up, or the mother lost her job and started drinking, or a child became older and started to be more confrontative. Understanding what made a problem appear now and how that interacts with predisposing factors is the beginning of developing a theory about what might be happening.
3. Perpetuating factors
   Usually the problems social workers have to assess and work with are not one-off events. The question is then what keeps a problem going. Again perpetuating factors can operate at multiple levels and often interact with predisposing factors. For instance, the effects of poverty may cause a family to feel ongoing stress that interacts and sustains parental depression. Or a family can get into a cycle of interaction in which parents get angry with a teenager and the more they challenge him the more rebellious he becomes. The question is what factors keep a problem going. Most people, most of the time, sort out the problems they have – why in this instance is that proving difficult?
4. Protective factors
   Even in the presence of all three of the first Ps, many individuals and families overcome difficulties. This is because there are protective factors, which again can manifest at any level. Perhaps there is a supportive relative who provides breaks and wise counsel; maybe a resourceful individual supplements their benefits with money they get from other sources; possibly despite passionate and sometimes violent arguments there is also a lot of love and compassion in a family. Whatever the factors, a formulation tries to identify the positives as well as the negatives, and understand how they interact with other elements to mitigate or prevent difficulties becoming problems.

The four Ps are places to start thinking about formulations. They are higher-level concepts that can be used in any theoretical approach. The theories used will generate different predisposing, precipitating, perpetuating and protective factors. Developing a convincing theory-informed narrative that weaves these together is the art of formulation.

However, there is a danger that on their own the four Ps can become a simplistic checklist. This may be a useful way of starting but a formulation requires two additional elements. The first is a focus on the individual perspectives of those involved. The second is to weave these factors into a narrative. Here a narrative is another word for a tentative theory about what may be happening. In fact, the these two elements are interlinked. As noted in the Division of Clinical Psychology guidance (DCP, 2011: 14), 'personal meaning is the integrating factor in a psychological formulation'. It is ultimately what allows us to build a coherent narrative.

Formulation, rights and social work: three more Ps

Using formulation in a rights-focused way requires some additional thinking around what formulation might look like for this purpose. A useful way to begin to think about this is to add three more Ps:

5. Presenting issue
    It is fairly common in social work literature to question the idea of 'problems' as a starting point (for instance, Turnell and Edwards, 1999). It is argued that this reinforces the problem-saturated nature of the work of statutory services, that it fails to take account of strengths and resilience, and that it can militate against a more holistic assessment that considers people and their situations in the round. There are merits to such arguments, yet for two reasons I think the presenting issue is a good place to start. The first is that this is how individuals and families come to services. There is almost always a specific issue or 'problem' identified by somebody that leads to referral. And in general the people concerned know there is an issue, whether that is a child with a broken arm or a family who have run out of money. Second, and crucially, starting with the presenting issue allows us to start by questioning the nature of the 'problem'.

Most formulations start with a presenting issue. For social work, and particularly social work in any statutory setting, any attempt at formulation needs to start by scrutinising the nature of the presenting issue or 'problem'. What is the 'problem'? Who says this is a problem? For whom is this a problem? What are the potential different perspectives on the problem? For instance, using the social model we should question whether this is a problem for the individual concerned or for others. At every stage of an assessment, questioning the nature of the 'problem' is a core element of social work. This is acutely important in statutory work, where so often people have no choice about involvement. In contrast to, for instance, counselling or most psychology, we need absolute clarity about whether this is a type of problem that justifies our involvement, particularly if some or all of those we work with say they do not want us involved.

6. Personal perspectives
   As already noted, the perspective of those experiencing a problem is an inherent part of psychological formulation. Yet I think they deserve a P of their own for rights-focused social work because we have specific legal duties to understand and represent the views of those we work with. For instance, in protecting a child we have a legal duty to obtain and share their view. Social workers have the power to overrule the views of the child, but to do that they need to find out what those views are. In a rather different way, workers need to understand the perspective of parents. Parents have a right to family life and a right to a high degree of tolerance of different types of parenting. To intervene to limit this we need to understand their perspective. Similar considerations apply in work with adults. If working with someone with dementia or mental illness, there is a legal duty to understand their perspective. In all these situations finding out the perspective of those involved is a fundamental part of what the social worker has to do. It is legally mandated and tied to the reason we are involved.

7. Principles, policies and proportionality
   Rights-focused social work needs to be clear about the mandate for its involvement. Formulation in statutory social work requires a context and analysis which considers the rights of different individuals and the legal and policy basis for the work. This might include relatively simple statements, such as a child protection investigation being required due to concerns about possible significant harm, but it usually requires much more than this. In a statutory assessment the legal basis for work always needs to be clear. It also often needs to justify acting against the views of some or all of those involved, and it needs to ensure that unasked for involvement is proportionate to concerns and their enshrinement in legislation. This is the heart of rights-focused practice. A formulation provides an ideal opportunity to do this work, because it allows us to combine different perspectives, including the view of society as expressed through laws and policy as well as more normative expectations which the social worker can share based on their professional knowledge. This might include, for instance, reference to normal child development or behaviour. A formulation brings this all together, and a rights-focused

formulation is an opportunity to synthesise these different types of knowledge and provide a transparent and justified recommendation for next steps. Consideration of principles and rights should therefore be fundamental to the analysis in rights-focused formulation.

Humanist and social model contributions

To weave the seven Ps together requires a theory or theories to help us make sense of them. As outlined in Part II, the theories I think most useful for rights-focused practice are humanist social work and the social model. There are others that might be useful and fit well. What is needed is the distinctive mix of the individual and the social and, as outlined in Part II, my sense is that humanism and the social model provide that.

Weaving together humanism and the social model is not without its challenges, as considered in Part II. While they are to some degree complementary, arising from a shared Enlightenment tradition that values individual wellbeing and rationality, they remain different and they have the potential to clash, for instance offering different perspectives or allowing different conclusions to be drawn from the same presenting evidence. This illustrates the point made in the previous chapter, namely that assessment is driven by theory and therefore does not consist of simple and objective information gathering. Such clashes require a thoughtful and reflective practitioner to make reasoned choices; the tension between the individual and the social cannot be resolved, indeed it is one of the reasons we need social workers. Yet this is ultimately a creative tension, or at least it can be when worked with in wise and skilled ways. Melding different perspectives allows us to have critical purchase on each and opens up space for new insights and understandings to be developed.

To demonstrate this I now apply a rights-focused social work approach to developing a formulation in relation to the case study of 'Janet' (see Box 10.1). As already noted, this case study is one of two at the heart of an excellent book edited by Johnstone and Dallos. Here, I am illustrating how I might approach developing a formulation for Janet, but I am decidedly *not* saying that this is the 'right' way to do a formulation. Not only are there other theories that might inform very different formulations, but even individuals using the same theoretical lens will generate different formulations. Formulation is an art, perhaps the art of trying to understand people, and therefore the rest of this chapter can only serve to illustrate one approach to rights-focused formulation. I seek to do it through the seven Ps as informed by humanist social work and the social model. I also do not present a finalised formulation, but rather reflections on what might go into the final formulation. However, before doing that it is necessary to consider a key idea in developing a formulation, namely the idea of a hypothesis.

Box 10.1: Janet and her family

Janet, aged nine, was referred by a school nurse to children's social services. Social services had previously been alerted about a number of contacts with the accident and emergency department of the local hospital, although no evidence of abuse had been found. Mary, Janet's mother, had also contacted social services for various reasons including a request for a wheelchair to help with Janet's mobility problems. She was concerned that Janet was not developing properly and wondered if this was linked to Janet's reluctance to travel or use public transport. In addition, Mary and the school nurse had concerns about Janet's low weight. Janet was already being reviewed at yearly intervals by the paediatric consultant because of worries about her development as an infant. On assessment, no physical problems were evident.

Mary, in her late 40s, separated from Janet's father, Colin, when Janet was three. He still lives nearby, and was until recently having overnight contact with Janet at his home. Janet has now said she does not want this to continue, although she still sees her father. Colin is a heavy drinker and was violent towards Mary. Colin and Mary's older child, Andrew, age 12, is doing well at school, both academically and socially. He also lives with Mary and Janet, and hopes to join the police force when he grows up.

Mary says she found it 'hard to bond' with Janet when she was born, and felt sad and depressed for a long time after the birth. At times she wished Janet could be taken away, although she did not feel this way about her other children. This is hard for her to understand, and makes her feel guilty.

Mary has four older children from an earlier relationship, two of whom live in the same street, and Mary is very involved with her infant grandchildren. She is particularly proud of the son who has done well educationally and become a schoolteacher. Mary is also close to her sister, Cindy, who lives locally and has no children of her own but has a special relationship with Janet and takes a close interest in her.

The family have always lived in a very socially deprived location in local authority accommodation, alongside some of the most 'difficult' families in the area. The estate is due for demolition and the family have been waiting to be rehoused for the last two years. They are a Romany family and this is a central part of their identity, one expression of which is a strong interest in spiritualism and clairvoyance. A clairvoyant had told Mary about a white car, which Mary connected with a nightmare Janet had about a white van and her fear of using any form of transport.

At the time of referral, Mary was awaiting a heart operation, having suffered from angina and arrhythmia for a number of years. This means that she easily becomes exhausted.

The referral letter documented Mary's many concerns about Janet, including her weight loss, behaviour at home and refusal to use transport, although she will walk to school, town and therapy sessions. This is paralleled by her mother's limited mobility, which is resulting in them both becoming more withdrawn and isolated, especially from their extended family. Mary describes Janet as being a prisoner in her own home.

Janet was also described as being unable to sleep in her own bed because of night terrors, so that she often ends up sharing Mary's bed; losing her temper (including once setting the dog on her mother); and refusing to eat food prepared for her by Mary, so that she is now seriously underweight. However, she has friends at school, joining in quite enthusiastically, and is achieving adequately for her age.

What are hypotheses and how can we use them in assessment and practice?

Hypotheses are a key step in developing a formulation. A hypothesis may have more complicated definitions, but at heart it is an informed guess about what is going on. Hypotheses are crucially important in helping us think through what may be happening for an individual or a family, and they form the building blocks for developing a formulation – which is ultimately an extended series of hypotheses.

It is preferable to make explicit our hypotheses. An explicit hypothesis allows transparency, accountability and critique. My experience of hypotheses in social work practice has been in doing research and practice related to group systemic supervision. While practice varied, in general this involved a small group discussing a family. Either the presenting worker or the group would then be asked to generate a small number of hypotheses about what might be happening in the family. This process was designed to avoid jumping to conclusions; it deliberately engineered in alternative interpretations. This stood in stark contrast to research David Wilkins, myself and others have done on normal social work supervision (Wilkins et al, 2017). This is characterised by workers giving a long account of what has happened with the family and the manager then providing the solution and telling the worker what to do. Such an approach can work, yet there are multiple reasons for suggesting it is unlikely to be a positive way of making decisions. First, it creates a linear way of thinking. Everything we know about human decision-making suggests that while we love shortcuts, indeed we are hardwired to take shortcuts in decision-making, these often result in poor decisions. This is not just a theoretical issue, problems like this are frequently found in child death inquiries. The abuse of Peter Connelly was partly missed because the mother's cooperation led to workers not seeing the abuse that was happening (Haringey, 2010). They had mentally categorised her as 'cooperative' and therefore did not consider Peter to be at high risk. Victoria Climbié's neglect and abuse was missed in part because workers did not see the severely neglected child in front of them as they thought they were dealing with financial issues (Laming, 2003). In fact, in most child death inquiry reports I have read there have been processes of miscategorisation and over-simplification that are exacerbated by premature conclusions about what is happening for a child. These can be seen as implicit hypotheses that are not questioned.

Second, generating multiple hypotheses provides a guide for action. In research I did with Lisa Bostock and others we found high quality systemic case discussions were strongly correlated with better practice (Bostock et al, 2017). This is, at least in part, likely to be because the hypotheses are tools for practice. Generating different hypotheses guides the next stage of the assessment. If I think a parent may not be answering the door because they have previously had a child removed and are afraid of social workers, then that has implications for how I work with them. If an alternative hypothesis is that they are abusing their child and trying to hide it from us, then working out which is happening is a crucial next step in both assessing and working with the family. Hypotheses are often, perhaps usually, things we share with families. They are therefore about much more than assessment and how to do it. They guide our information gathering and the topics we talk to people about. I will therefore try to generate multiple hypotheses for each of the seven Ps and then incorporate them into a formulation to inform my work with Janet and her family.

Developing a formulation for Janet: the seven Ps

Presenting issue

This is quite a long and rich case study, to encourage the exploration of varied approaches to developing a formulation. In particular, there are many potential causal factors at play and different ways of thinking about what may be going on. Yet the starting point for any social worker is thinking about what the presenting issue/s are for the child and, despite the welter of evidence, there are essentially just two presenting issues. These are:

- Janet seems to have developmental problems. She is of low weight. It is not clear what the other developmental problems are. It is possible that Janet has 'mobility problems', sufficient for the mother to ask for a wheelchair – though she seems able to walk to school, town and to therapy. The concerns are serious enough for a consultant paediatrician to be doing annual reviews. They have not identified any physical problems to be 'evident'.

- Some behaviours of Janet's are reported as problematic, presumably by Mary. These include night terrors, losing her temper and refusing food.

A first place to start with any account of presenting issues in social work is to seek clarification. In particular, more information is needed about the nature and potential causes of the developmental problems that Janet seems to have. We can then turn to think about hypotheses that we might have as a worker.

In child protection, social workers are encouraged and indeed expected to consider the worst case scenario. There are some elements of the case study that generate hypotheses that might suggest serious concerns. For instance, one possibility is that Colin has sexually abused Janet. There is no evidence to prove this, but her concerning pattern of behaviour might be related to sexual abuse and the fact that she does not want to stay overnight with him could also be because of abuse. A social worker would be open to this possibility. On the other hand, we also need to work with other possible hypotheses: perhaps he is just not a good carer. Or perhaps he was abusive in other ways and this contributed to Janet's difficulties.

There are obvious difficulties in the relationship between mother and daughter, by the mother's own account. One hypothesis is that Mary is using and perhaps even developing a narrative of problems around Janet in part so that she can get help. Some of the elements of her behaviour, such as seeking a wheelchair when Janet is reported to be able to walk to town, school and therapy, certainly require further exploration.

The social model is useful for raising questions about the nature of 'problems'. Social model questions for the case study might include:

- How much of what is happening can be explained by multiple individual and social stressors coming together to make it really difficult for Mary to care for Janet? They live in poverty in a poor neighbourhood, Mary has serious health problems and feels socially isolated. Some of the identified problems may be her way of asking for help.
- There is a gendered assumption about care for Janet by Mary, but perhaps her father could or should be caring more for her? We would certainly want to know more about his role, and his potential to make a positive contribution.
- While the Romany identity of the family is considered important, this just seems to be related to clairvoyance. What about attitudes towards family, expectations and supports that might be available? And how might this impact on the perception of social workers? There is strong evidence of high levels of child protection and removal in Romany communities (for example, Allen and Riding, 2018). How might this influence the family engagement with child and family services?

A feature of this case study, which is very common in social work referrals, is that it is not completely clear what the 'problem' is. There is certainly lots to be concerned about, but there are many different shapes that our understanding of what the actual issues are might take – from serious abuse of Janet by her father and mother to an over-anxious mother. Our initial formulation will therefore need to guide us in developing a clearer picture of what the nature of the problem we are dealing with really is.

Before exploring other features of the case study, it is important to explore what is absent. The most glaring gap is that we do not know much about the perspectives of the people involved. This is the focus of the next P – the personal.

Personal perspectives

The most egregious gap is that we do not know what Janet thinks or feels. While she is at the heart of the whole case study, her perspective is largely absent. How is Janet finding life? What is going well and what not so well? What is important to her? What would make her life better? In common with many referrals to children's services this case study does not touch on these crucial questions for the children we work with.

A second gap, and again one we often work with, is that we know little about the father's perspective. Researchers have identified a tendency to see fathers as risks and fail to see them as resources (Maxwell et al, 2012), and this is exemplified in this case study. All we know of Colin is that he is a heavy drinker, that he was violent towards Mary and that Janet does not want to live with him. This begins to paint a picture of him as possibly a serious risk to Janet (and perhaps Mary). It would be easy to imagine marginalising him in our work. On a purely personal level, there would be few workers who would relish the idea of meeting with someone described as a heavy drinking and potentially violent individual. Yet the fact remains that Colin is Janet's father. This gives him rights, and it also makes him an important part of the family situation. He is likely to have parental responsibility under the 1989 Children Act and therefore needs to be consulted on key issues relating to Janet. He is also important from a psychological perspective. Whatever his potential problems, he is Janet's father and he is therefore an important part of Janet's story. That is not to say that involving him should be done in a naïve way. His history of violence towards Mary, and the hypothesis about abuse by him of Janet, mean that his perspective would only be sought after exploring that of Janet and Mary.

In contrast to Janet and Colin, the account is largely about Mary's perspective. Yet it offers an interpretation of this perspective. A humanist approach to social work requires finding out from people directly what is important to them. This account therefore provides a good starting point, but at the heart of the assessment would be finding out in greater depth how Mary sees things.

The humanist tradition is particularly strong for obtaining the accounts of individuals. It provides both the rationale and the skills for doing so. The rationale is that people are the experts on their own lives. To understand and work with them we therefore need to be able to harness this expertise. Furthermore, humanist social workers believe that individuals usually have the potential for change. Tapping into this is central to social work assessment and helping.

The skills involved in this are those touched on in Part I and explored in more depth in the next two chapters. They include, more than anything, an open and curious orientation. This is supplemented by careful listening, open questions, reflections and summaries. Yet these need to be adapted to the social work setting. A humanist counsellor might simply just listen deeply. Even someone using a more directive type of humanist approach, such as Motivational Interviewing, would focus on the individual and their motivations. A humanist social worker also needs to be able to raise difficult or challenging issues. They may need to raise concerns about some elements of Mary's account. For instance, Mary seems to think that Janet's mobility difficulties are physical but if the social worker believes they are not then they need to raise this with her. Chapter 11 considers how to have such difficult conversations from a humanist perspective.

The key point for the development of a formulation is that what is missing is a clear description of the perspective of key actors. Any formulation we develop at this stage would need to capture what we do know about the perspectives of those involved while identifying clearly what further information we need.

Predisposing factors

Using a social model lens there are a multitude of social factors that place the family under stress, and that therefore make caring for children more difficult. The family live in a very socially deprived community, a factor strongly associated with increased risk of coming into care. They are also isolated and the specific neighbourhood they live in is described as having a high number of 'difficult' families. This type of language from a professional might require clarification and some level of challenge – though it is possible that it is a direct quote from Mary and captures her sense that the neighbourhood has high levels of difficulties and problematic social behaviour.

Humanist perspectives allow us to focus on Mary and the multiple difficulties she is trying to cope with. These include serious health problems and associated exhaustion, experiences of domestic abuse and problems with mobility which contribute to her isolation. In addition,

Mary describes finding it hard to bond with Janet and gives an account of what sounds like depression after Janet's birth. This may well be linked to the domestic abuse that Mary described in her relationship with Colin. Mary seems to have ongoing difficulties in her relationship with Janet, which can perhaps be traced back in part to problems in forming a strong relationship at that stage.

Taken together it is easy to imagine these individual and social pressures combining and interacting to make caring for Janet very difficult for Mary. But what has led to the specific referral to social services?

Precipitating factors

Often, a referral has a specific event that precipitates the referral. Yet it is not uncommon for referrals to come due to an accretion of concerns and a sense that other services are not able to help. For this referral the precipitating event seems to be the consultant finding no physical reason for Janet's developmental problems. There does not appear to be a specific event or deterioration of the situation that has led to the current referral. The situation seems to be one of chronic, probably interacting, predisposing factors that have led to Janet and Mary having serious difficulties which may be impacting negatively on Janet and are certainly impacting negatively on Mary.

Perpetuating factors

A key element of any assessment with Janet and her family will be to identify which of the predisposing factors is currently perpetuating the issues. There are myriad potential ones to choose from, ranging from poverty to poor attachment. The key issue in differentiating which ones are most immediately salient is likely to be work directly with Mary and Janet, as well as other members of the family.

Protective factors

As so often happens, having focused solely on problems and what may be causing them by now it might be tempting to feel rather worried about Janet, and perhaps even despairing about her situation, yet there are in fact some very important protective factors. The most important are that in some respects Janet seems to be doing well. At school she has friends, participates 'quite enthusiastically' and is achieving adequately. She also seems to have a fair amount of mobility. She appears able to articulate what she wants, such as saying that she does not want to stay overnight with her father. Crucially, Mary seems able to hear and act upon this.

Janet also has people around her who care deeply for her. Mary is dealing with innumerable problems, but through them she seems to be striving to be a good mother for Janet. Mary's sister, Cindy, has a special and close relationship with Janet. This is potentially an important protective factor. Other members of the family may be protective factors, such as Janet's older brother and four half-siblings who live on the same street. It takes the proverbial village to raise a child, and it looks possible that Janet has some potential support around her.

Principles, policies and proportionality

As already mentioned, a key difference between social work and psychology is that in social work there has to be constant consideration of the legal basis for involvement, and whether involvement – particularly if not wanted – is justified. One element of this is establishing the level of concern for the child or adult that a service is responsible for. Yet decisions about what level of involvement is justified also require us to understand the perspectives of different rights holders, an assessment of the capacity of the child, the likelihood of positive change depending on what choices are made, and knowledge of normative evidence about children and families. The idea of proportionality captures some of this complexity. In the case of unwanted involvement with adults or families we need to be able to justify it both by the level of concern we may reasonably have and by the likely outcome of our different options. This calculus is captured by the idea of proportional involvement.

All this is complicated work that feeds into our formulation. The question is: on what basis are we working with a family? For the case study much will depend on the response of Janet and Mary to our involvement. If they welcome it, then working collaboratively is comparatively straightforward. There are some needs, and some risks, and working together to understand and mitigate these is supported by legislation. The more complicated element of the work is required if Mary, or Janet or Colin, become unhappy about the involvement of children's services. If this happens then the balancing exercise about the level of concern, the rights of individuals, the capacity of the child and the likely outcome of different courses of action needs to be undertaken and made explicit to ensure service involvement is proportionate.

Conclusion

This chapter has built on the argument of the previous chapter that assessment is a type of provisional theory development. Formulation is proposed as a constructive way of approaching such a task because it allows us to blend different perspectives, varied types of evidence and the social work responsibilities to the individual, to society and to our own professional perspective, including ethical and normative elements. Formulation allows us to constructively engage with and ultimately synthesise this complexity. In doing so, it provides an answer to the question at the start of the previous chapter, namely how should we do the analysis that is required in assessment.

While formulation provides a useful way of thinking about and doing assessment, on its own it has little to say about the nature of direct practice. What is needed is a description of practice that allows the worker to work with people and manage the types of conflicts inherent to the social work role. The next two chapters turn to the challenge of how social workers should work with individuals (Chapter 11) and with groups (Chapter 12).

11

Working with individuals and families

This chapter focuses on direct work with individuals and families. It considers two issues that have been central to previous chapters, namely how to work with conflicts and capacity issues. This chapter relies heavily on research I have done over the last 20 years, and it is therefore focused on child and family social work, and particularly on conversations with parents. Throughout I try to identify lessons that are likely to apply more generally, for instance in adult social care.

There is a sense in which the whole book grew from the simple question that this chapter focuses on: how should social workers work with people? Much of my research has focused on this question, and across studies we have recorded more than 800 meetings between social workers and parents and several hundred where a worker talks to an actor playing a parent (called a simulated interview) (Forrester et al, 2008, 2013, 2017, 2019; Bostock et al, 2017). Many of these studies have explored how we might improve social work practice, and a particular interest has been supporting the use of Motivational Interviewing (MI) in child and family social work, with studies of training, whole system change and coaching and feedback (see Forrester et al, 2021).

Like others I identified MI as a helpful approach because I had concerns about the nature of everyday practice. My early studies found that social workers often felt stuck in their work and unsure how to have difficult conversations, and that they received little training or support to do so (Forrester et al, 2008; Forrester and Harwin, 2011). MI seemed to offer a better way to have such conversations. Its respectful values, theoretical focus on understanding and working with 'resistance', and its strong evidence base all suggested it might be useful for child and family social work. Others have undergone similar journeys with other approaches, for instance exploring how solution-focused approaches or systemic practice or restorative justice might be adapted for statutory child and family social work (Turnell and Edwards, 1999; Neff, 2004; Goodman et al, 2011). Yet this adaptation creates substantial challenges, and this book is an attempt to explore and resolve some of these. The first is that when social work practice is observed it seems very unlike counselling. This makes applying MI or other counselling approaches difficult without some preparatory theoretical work. Part I was an attempt to reimagine contemporary social work, explaining why it is so suffused with conflict, what social workers are striving to do and why it is a worthwhile undertaking by focusing on human rights work. Part II introduced humanist perspectives – from which MI emerged – but also emphasised that if used alone any counselling approach risks individualising problems. The importance of the social model is that it provides critical purchase on the nature and goals of practice, ensuring we keep the social in social work. The earlier chapters of Part III have focused on a core element of social work that is absent from MI, namely how workers should do assessments. A practical challenge myself and others have often encountered is that the demands for assessment can be at odds with the principles of MI if we do not think about how they can be combined. In many ways these earlier chapters have provided the theoretical context for the focus of this chapter on how social workers should work with people. More specifically, how might workers do rights-focused work in ways that are consistent with the lessons of previous chapters – for instance, informed by a love ethic, respectfully and purposefully working with tension, and combining social and individual perspectives.

Much of my personal journey has involved thinking about how MI might be useful for social workers. The more I have looked at this, the more I have begun to think that the key is that therapeutic skills can be used to facilitate purposeful dialogue. Purposeful dialogue is a way of respectfully working with differences of opinion or perspective. This concept was introduced in a previous book and is elaborated upon in this chapter (Forrester et al, 2021).

The next section starts by summarising some of our findings from varied studies about how social workers talk to parents. The chapter then focuses on how to manage difficult conversations where there may be clashes of rights, before concluding with some thoughts on working with capacity issues. Taken together it is hoped that it provides an introduction to how social workers can ethically and helpfully manage the challenges these difficult conversations can often involve.

How do social workers talk to people?

Social work in any setting is a difficult job. In the context of child protection it is hard to imagine a more difficult situation for working with an individual. Similar challenges exist in other safeguarding situations. There is evidence that social workers do not receive the training or supervision they need to do this difficult work (Wilkins et al, 2017). Furthermore, there are strong institutional imperatives to operate in a confrontational and perhaps authoritarian manner (Sheehan, 2022). In general, my experience is that most social workers are striving hard to do their job well – but that a lack of guidance and support, combined with these pressures to work in ways that are confrontational, produce a form of practice that is unlikely to be particularly good at protecting children or helping families. The practice we identified in studies of direct practice, which indicated rather unempathetic and often confrontative practice, would readily be identified by most people as not what we should strive for in social work (see Forrester et al, 2018). This finding is consistent with qualitative accounts of parents of their experiences of children's services (for example, Dale, 2004; Davies, 2011). The final chapter considers some of the reasons why this may be the case and what we can do about it. In this chapter, I want to consider two particularly common problems we found in practice and think about how we might improve practice, using a rights-focused approach undergirded by the insights from previous chapters. These two problems are a lack of purpose and a tendency to what Featherstone et al (2014a) have called 'muscular authoritarianism'.

The examples are all taken from simulated interviews, where a real social worker demonstrates their practice with an actor playing a parent. I am using simulated interviews for three reasons. First, it is not necessary to explain the context for each example, because they all have the same background, as outlined in Box 11.1. Second, they are all high challenge. We have many recordings of relatively mundane and everyday practice, but this chapter focuses more on difficult conversations – such as that in this simulated interview. Finally, all workers had the same scenario (with some variation in level of concern), which means differences between workers can be more easily identified.

Purposeless practice

A surprisingly common feature of practice was that it was often very difficult to work out what the purpose of the meeting was. This was more common in real practice. Whittaker reanalysed 138 recordings of practice from a study we did and found in about a third that she could not work out what the point of the meeting was. In another third the focus seemed to be collecting information for an assessment. Only about a third had a focus on actually helping parents or children (Whittaker, forthcoming). This sense of a lack of clarity about why a worker is involved was not just experienced by researchers, it was probably the most common point made by parents we talked to. They often did not understand why they had a social worker in general, nor what the point of a specific meeting had been.

This lack of clarity about what social workers are doing is not a new finding. Indeed, similar results were found in key studies of social work going back to the 1960s. Reid and Shyne (1969) identified a lack of clarity in the work in recordings of practice, which contributed to the development of task-centred practice. Mayer and Timm (1970) found clients did not know why they had a social worker. Goldberg and Warburton (1974: 12) sought to work out what social workers thought they were doing but were confounded by the 'vastness and the vagueness of the social work task'.

Box 11.1: Simulated interview scenario

Jeanette is the mother of Charlie, aged five. They live alone together and Charlie's father is not around. Charlie was made subject to a child protection plan one month ago. There have been concerns around Jeanette's care for Charlie, and in particular her drinking, for some time. Fourteen months ago the first police notification of Jeanette being drunk in charge of Charlie while shopping was received. Charlie was placed with a supportive neighbour. Over the next year there were a total of seven further notifications from police, neighbours and the school of concerns about Jeanette's drinking and her ability to care for Charlie when under the influence.

Two months ago the police were once again involved when a neighbour called stating Charlie was home alone. Jeanette was home but appeared unconscious due to alcohol consumption. Charlie was placed with a neighbour and a social worker was allocated.

The worker identified a number of concerns. The school stated that while Charlie was very able, his attendance was very poor, including unexplained absences and lateness. They also had concerns about his presentation as he often appeared unkempt with dirty clothes. An anonymous call from a 'concerned friend' said that Jeanette was drinking very heavily, that she was regularly seen staggering around the estate, that Charlie would go to a neighbour asking for dinner and that the neighbour thought Jeanette was drinking to unconsciousness regularly – perhaps every day. They also said she smoked 'puff'. At the subsequent case conference the chair and social worker both stated that they were very concerned about the situation and that if there was not an improvement care proceedings would be considered.

There are then two scenarios. In scenario A there had been substantial improvement, with Charlie attending school regularly and Jeanette broadly cooperating. In scenario B there had been little change, with concerns continuing and care proceedings being likely if there is not immediate change.

In simulated interviews the purpose is usually much clearer, as there is a specific scenario and pressing issues. Yet even here workers often did not agree an agenda with parents, and often the focus of the interview was dictated by the worker and not negotiated with the parents. For instance, here is a fairly typical start:

Worker: OK. From my point of view I would just like to see how things are going from your point of view and your understanding of the child protection plan at the last case

	conference, just so I'm clear that you understand things from our point of view as well.
Jeanette:	So you want me to tell you now?
Worker:	Yeah, just sort of how things are sort of going from your point of view.
Jeanette:	Well things are going fine. Just same as ever really, you know, everything is OK.
Worker:	Everything is OK?
Jeanette:	Everything's alright, I think.
Worker:	Right, OK. I mean, you are aware, I mean, at the last case conference, which you attended, a plan was drawn up in which the department asked you to do certain things. Could you just give us some indication that you have an understanding of what we have been asking for you to do?

On the face of it the social worker says they want to obtain the parent's perspective – but do they? The parent says things are going fine, which is not explored by the worker and quickly leads to a fairly confrontational interaction. This is, of course, because the context for this conversation is serious concerns about Charlie. The social worker therefore has to raise difficult issues, and that is a challenge in conversations. In this instance – and many we saw in other interviews – asking for the parent's perspective is simply a way of opening a conversational opportunity for the worker to raise concerns and begin to talk about consequences. It is the beginning of the 'muscular authoritarianism' described in the next section. Before considering that, it would perhaps be helpful to reflect on what purposeful practice might look like.

Purposeful practice

The most important pre-condition for purposeful practice is for the worker to be clear what the purpose of their work generally and this specific meeting is. Indeed, without such clarity it is not possible to do good social work, and in many respects this book has been an attempt to provide some of the intellectual resources workers might find helpful in being clear about what they are trying to do. The next step is to be able to share this purpose and then negotiate a joint understanding of the meeting with the person worked with. Interviews should be dialogues, and therefore their purpose should be negotiated. Purposeful practice requires an ability to negotiate this. This is something that should happen at the start of almost every encounter, but that can take place throughout.

The level of negotiation that is possible depends in part on how serious the issues are. Where they are very serious, then the worker may need to be very directive and authoritative. For instance, a different way of starting the previous interview might have been:

> 'Thank you for coming in to see me Jeanette. What I would like to do is have a talk about how you and Charlie are doing. I'd like to start by sharing some of the things I have heard from the school and the alcohol service – and then you can tell me how you think things are going, and what you think about what they have to say. Is that OK?' (Worker)

Here I am intending to start by raising concerns, but doing so in a way that makes clear that I want to hear what Jeanette has to say about them. It is not perfect – communication is never perfect – but on balance I think this brief agenda-setting statement provides a relatively clear sense of how I would like the interview to go. It also leads with me as the worker raising concerns, which the parent can respond to, rather than asking for their view just so that I can then raise concerns. Where concerns are less serious it might be better to have a genuinely open question, asking for instance what Jeanette would like to talk about. All communication, including social work interviews, requires a fit between context and communication.

Purposefulness is not just agreed at the start of the meeting. It is negotiated throughout. Micro-skills – like a decision about whether to ask an open or closed question, or what to ask questions about – shape the purpose of a meeting in real time. At a slightly more meta-level the purpose can be renegotiated at any time. For instance, here 'Jeanette' asked if she had to go to the alcohol service but the worker does not wish to address that issue at this point: "OK, well let's go through the rest of the plan and then we might come back to that because I am going to let you know, obviously I have done my report and what my concerns continue to be and then we can address that then."

Another time when it is usually best if purpose is explicitly negotiated is at the end of the interview. The ideal might be some sort of agreement about what happens next, perhaps followed by some lighter chat. In fact, ending any conversation is a remarkably difficult activity, with conversation analysts finding in everyday interactions that, without realising it, we work quite hard to negotiate endings that ensure nobody loses face by the encounter being ended (Hall et al, 2006). Similar issues can be found in social work interviews, though they are exacerbated by the power differences involved – making ending particularly difficult. In broad terms we tended to find two types of ending predominated. In real practice, a slightly vague ending is most common – without clarity about what the plan or expectations are, except perhaps the time of the next meeting. This is of a piece with the general sense that it is often difficult to be sure of the purpose of interviews from listening to them.

Where the purpose of interviews is obvious there was a strong tendency for the concerns to be more serious. In these interviews the next steps were generally largely imposed by the worker, with little indication of negotiation. For instance:

Worker: I need to think about, just wrap it up a little bit, I know for the, the review conference I need to have a think about what, what sort of recommendations we have … normally at a review conference you do a little bit like what we've done today and just review how things have been, it's been really helpful actually talking to you today because it gives me more insight into how it is for you and what it is that you need. I think, you know, from, err, the point of view of, of a review conference is going to be looking at, well what were the original concerns and how, what happened with the, care plan and what, what should need to happen now really. And it's only been a couple of months since the case conference and generally we need to, with something, with so … with something like, you know, children and worrying about children we need to probably give it a bit of time, so you say what, what you were saying earlier about well maybe you might think about trying [alcohol service], just trying a different way of, of coping with things well then maybe we should give a bit of time for that to happen.

Jeanette: Yeah. Sort them out. Joking. That's fine, no I'll wait, I will try you know.
[Social worker starts coughing leading to digression.]

Worker: Erm, where was I? Oh yeah sorry, give it a bit of time, will that be all right, just to see how erm, how you get on and erm see what else you might think might find supportive. And we'll see how Charlie's continuing at school, I know he's done really well, and I know that you know, a lot of, of changes have happened in the last couple of months so I think at this stage we would be just sustaining that change, how to, to keep things going in a way that you're happy and that er Charlie's happy? Erm, so that, that would mean if, if er, in order to do that if, if Charlie's name stays on, on the child protection plan for another few months and we'll have another review, erm, just while these other things are happening and the other agencies are, you have the chance to sort of really feel for yourself and decide for yourself if they're helpful or not.

Jeanette:	OK.
Worker:	Does that sound OK?
Jeanette:	Yeah it sounds good.
Worker:	Do you have any questions?
Jeanette:	No.

This was a clearly caring social worker and there did seem to be the beginnings of a good relationship between worker and (simulated) parent. Yet, nonetheless, the 'plan' comes from the worker and by extension the agency. It is not clear in this interview as a whole, as in many others, whether the parent is actually in agreement – the worker tended to talk a lot and the parent would monosyllabically agree, as in this interchange. Of course, there are serious concerns in this scenario and it is appropriate for the worker to be clear about them and to be directive. However, if that results in a form of practice that does not engage parents in a dialogue it is less likely to create change, and it is also not adequately respecting the rights of the parent. Which leads on to the second issue, the tendency for practice to display a 'muscular authoritarianism' and what might be done about it.

Muscular authoritarianism or good authority?

'Muscular authoritarianism' was typical in our simulated interviews and in real interviews where there was something serious to discuss. Social workers do not appear afraid to raise concerns nor to be confrontative. The drivers for this have been touched on in previous chapters but are worth recounting. The main one is a series of child death inquiries which have repeatedly identified workers as being unable or unwilling to challenge parents. These have been reinforced through inspection regimes, bureaucratic processes and organisational cultures that have emphasised the importance of being able and willing to challenge parents. Sometimes this is described as being 'child focused', sometimes as 'authoritative child protection practice' (Haringey, 2010), but it always requires social workers to be able to have difficult conversations, raise concerns and be clear about consequences (Laming, 2003).

There have been powerful critiques of this type of practice. It is argued to be symptomatic of a system, and indeed perhaps a profession, that has lost its way (Featherstone et al, 2014a). The argument of this book is that in liberal democracies we need a profession and processes like those undertaken by social work in working with children and adults at risk of harm. Yet the practice described here, and found in so many observational studies of social work that it must surely be accepted as normal practice by now, is not that which we would aspire to. While a focus on rights suggests that such difficult conversations are necessary as part of a liberal society, it is possible to suggest we could combine authority with empathy, care and love to move away from 'muscular authoritarianism' to something more like the 'good authority' discussed in Chapter 3. Yet what is relatively lacking is a detailed account of what this might involve.

Good authority requires social workers to be able to *combine* an ability to focus on the child and possible risks to them with a focus on the parent who they are working with, and a recognition that they are worthy of respect and care in our work with them; that our work should be infused with an ethic of love for both child and parent or others involved. A specific concept I want to outline here is the idea of 'purposeful dialogue'; I want to suggest that social work conversations about risk are very different from counselling or other helping conversations. For all the reasons discussed here, workers need to raise and discuss difficult issues, but they should do so in ways that are respectful and encourage dialogue. This involves four key elements:

1. Raising difficult issues (such as concerns, but also consequences).
2. Exploring the parent's perspective – including showing the parent that you understand their point of view.
3. Bringing the two into a *dialogue* – a conversation in which each hears and reacts to the other.
4. Seeking some type of resolution – this is the ultimate *purpose* of the conversation.

The 'dialogue' element is to capture the fact that this should be a genuinely two-way conversation. Of course, all professional conversations involve two people, however in conversations where either one person is doing all the listening or they are telling the other person what to do the conversation does not involve a two-way interaction in the sense meant here. A useful concept here is Rollnick and colleagues' idea of a spectrum of directiveness (2005). At one end is simply listening to the other person. Sometimes counselling can feel like this. At the other end is telling the person what to do. Rollnick et al make the point that there is no right way to interact with people – sometimes we need to listen and sometimes we need to tell. They suggest that for helping people the key is an ability to move between positions. They are particularly interested in interactions that are neither following nor telling but that occupy a middle area. They call these 'guiding' interactions – where the helper seeks to guide the person they are helping to consider issues that may be useful for them. In a similar way, rights-focused social work involves a lot of guiding. It uses the skills of counselling, but to achieve a dialogue about difficult issues rather than to provide psychological help. While sometimes we will listen, and on other occasions we may need to raise difficult issues, what we should strive to do is bring this back to a genuine interaction. This involves skilled guiding, something the rest of this chapter focuses on.

The 'purposeful' element of the interaction is to understand, and try to create a shared understanding, of what we are trying to do. In a conversation around child protection issues the ultimate purpose is to ensure the child is safer than they were. This involves trying to build a shared understanding of the nature of the concerns and, where possible, jointly build a plan to do something about it. A plan may be a complicated thing involving lots of people – but it may be focused on a specific issue in a particular conversation. The point is that the purpose of the dialogue is to help ensure children are safer than without the conversation. To achieve this requires advanced level communication skills. I have found those outlined in MI particularly useful and they inform the following discussion. In Forrester et al (2021) we discuss their use in child protection in greater depth.

Good authority and purposeful dialogue in practice

What might this look like in practice? Here, we consider a fairly typical interaction in a simulated interview – in fact a continuation of the introduction covered earlier. I then – with the advantage of time to pause and reflect and consider in detail how we might respond – offer some alternative responses that might have been used in the interview which are designed to combine authority and a love ethic to build a purposeful dialogue. They are not some magical trick that ensures that the process or outcomes of the interview would necessarily go differently. Rather they are an attempt to make explicit the values and theories discussed in previous chapters. They try to unpack the nature of 'purposeful dialogue'. It may be that however we do it, telling somebody we are thinking about removing their child will result in them becoming angry towards us. The question is nonetheless how do we as professionals – and how do we as a society – think such conversations should happen?

So, we left the interview when the social worker said "Could you just give us some indication that you have an understanding of what we have been asking for you to do?" Here is how the interview proceeded:

Worker:	Right, OK. I mean, you are aware, I mean, at the last case conference, which you attended, a plan was drawn up in which the department asked you to do certain things. Could you just give us some indication that you have an understanding of what we have been asking for you to do?
Jeanette:	Basically to stop drinking alcohol, to go to some classes or some sessions or whatever, basically that's it. Make sure Charlie is alright.
Worker:	OK. Can I ask you have you been doing any of those things?

Jeanette: Yeah, well I haven't been drinking really. Charlie is fine, you know, he has been going to school when he hasn't been ill and stuff and yeah, everything's OK.

There is a disjuncture here between what the worker has heard from other agencies and what the parent is saying. So the worker moves to focus on the alcohol service – perhaps because there is concrete information about the parent not attending:

Worker: Because I understand that you haven't been to the alcohol advisory service or to ATA, which is an agency that works with people who have an alcohol problem, there is all kinds of group work, one-to-one work and some counselling. Is there a reason that you haven't gone to that?

Jeanette: Yeah because I'm actually not an alcoholic, um, you know I have a drink but I am not an alcoholic. I don't really think that that is for me at the moment, you know, so I don't want to waste anyone's time.

Worker: OK. So, um, in terms of the concerns that were raised at the conference in terms of, there were referrals saying that you had been using alcohol and that you had been presenting to the school under the influence of alcohol, um, that you were found at home unconscious under the influence of alcohol. I mean how could you explain that to me in terms of, this is how it presents to us that you have got a problem and you are sort of saying that you haven't.

This is a fairly strong and direct challenge. The worker is making clear that there are concerns around drinking and asking the parent to give their account. This leads to a fairly rapid escalation in the emotional temperature of the conversation:

Jeanette: So how do you find out this information? Only because people tell you that, isn't it?

Worker: So you are saying, one of the referrals from a neighbour, are you saying there is an issue with you and the neighbour?

Jeanette: Yes and I'm saying there is an issue, everyone seems to have an issue with me, don't ask me why. Well, I think I know why but I'm not going to go into that anyway. They are all in on it, the school, even the bloody newsagent, they all just don't like me. You know, their silly little games are not going to get to me.

Worker:	OK. The school are very clear that you have been presenting under the influence of alcohol and that you smell of alcohol and they are very clear about that.
Jeanette:	Well, maybe if I do smell of alcohol maybe I have had a glass of wine at lunchtime or whatever.
Worker:	So what are you saying, that your drinking is more social …
Jeanette:	Yeah that is exactly it.
Worker:	… than a problem. OK, well obviously the department are taking a different view to that. We are of the opinion that there is cause for concern. So from our point of view we have asked you to go along to the support agencies, ATA and the alcohol advisory service, to have an assessment so at least if you met a worker and sort of discussed things from your point of view we could then have some idea and get a clear indication of how much alcohol you are using. Would you be prepared to go if I said that I would go along with you?

The social worker is working hard to get the mother to go to the alcohol service, but the mother pushes back:

Jeanette:	But I am not going to tell them anything different to what I've been telling everybody all along, you know what I mean? You know, obviously if you are saying that this is the last thing, you know, I have to do this or they are going to take Charlie obviously I'll do it.
Worker:	Right but we are saying … what we are saying, and it was said at the last case conference, that we have an expectation that you would carry out certain things and those were going to the alcohol advisory service and to remain alcohol-free and to make sure that Charlie got to school. So yes I am asking you to go along to that because given the fact that you have not carried out any of the things that we have asked with regards to the last child protection plan we would say to you that the recommendation would be that the children do remain on the plan and that, yes, we are actually saying to you that you do need to go along to the services as we will be looking at a legal meeting.
Jeanette:	So basically if I don't go he is gone? That's it?
Worker:	It's not as clear-cut as that. I mean what I am saying to you is that you need to take into account that we do have serious concerns.

From Jeanette's perspective this is probably quite frustrating. She does not want to go to the alcohol service, but will go if she would otherwise lose Charlie. Yet it is rare for a social worker to be able to give a completely straight answer to questions like this. Their decisions are surrounded by checks and balances: whatever the worker feels, they will need to get agreement from their manager, perhaps more senior managers, the local authority solicitor and then the court. And attending the alcohol service is just one consideration – what would the worker do if Jeanette does everything else asked of her but refuses the alcohol service? Often parents talk about social workers being unclear about their expectations – yet it can be difficult for workers to provide such clarity.

What might a different approach be like?

I have already noted a different way of starting the interview, starting with me explaining my concerns and then offering Jeanette an opportunity to respond.

Assuming that Jeanette allows me to continue, the next job from a rights-focused perspective is to share the concerns so that Jeanette can provide her account of what is happening. To do this I might try to frame it in an explicitly rights-focused way – with one of the principles of rights-focused practice being transparency. So I might say something like:

> 'One of the things I will always try to do is to be honest with you. I'll always tell you if anyone tells me anything worrying about Charlie. And I will always try to find out what you think about things. So, I'm afraid I have to start with some things that I am worried about. The biggest one is that Charlie has not been going into school very much at all since we had the case conference. What's being going on?' (Worker)

Assuming that Jeanette gives her account I would focus on listening carefully, using communication skills like non-verbal attentiveness, open questions and reflective statements. Yet this is not a counselling session, and at some point I need to draw the listening to an end, and move it on to consider how we might move forward together. A particularly useful skill in this respect is a summary statement. It is surprising that we rarely hear social workers use summary statements, because they serve multiple functions. They demonstrate that we have been listening and have hopefully understood what the person we are talking with has said. Also, if they are broadly accepted, they help to end one portion of a conversation and allow us to move onto another in a respectful manner. In the next imagined response I am going to use a summary statement to perform these two functions. I also use it to set up one of the most difficult things any social worker has to do, namely explore the possibility that somebody is lying:

> 'So let me see whether I have got this. You feel that Charlie *has* been going to school, and the times he has not gone he has had a bad cold and you say you phoned the school and told them this. You also feel that the school are always picking on you, that they think you do not fit in with the other 'posh' mums, so they report any little thing you do, and that it was the things the school said at the case conference that led to Charlie going on a child protection plan. In fact, you are really angry with them and thinking of taking Charlie out of school. Have I understood everything?' (Worker)

Now, at this point it would be easy to escalate the level of challenge. For instance, the worker could point out that it is not just the school but also the police and others who had concerns. Or they could suggest that it is unlikely the school would make things up. These types of responses are fairly common in simulated and in real interviews with high levels of concerns; they have the advantage of being clear about concerns and avoiding any sense of collusion with 'Jeanette', but they also tend to lead to resistance – and it is questionable whether they further the ultimate purpose of the meeting, namely to better protect Charlie.

To avoid this, one option might be to move on to another topic. For instance, it might be appropriate to ask about Jeanette's drinking. In fact, I think that is probably what I would do. However, it would be potentially dangerous practice to *finish* the interview without offering some level of challenge. The issue, for me, is that often social workers think they need to offer that challenge immediately. I think in this interview I might be inclined to log the issue about the school in my head, and ensure I came back to it before the end. This requires workers to be able to have skills to respond appropriately in the moment while simultaneously being able to strategically manage the interview. This combination is something we explore in our book on MI (Forrester et al, 2021). As an aside it is worth noting how extraordinarily complicated these conversations are. It would be possible to write many thousands of words about a five-minute child protection conversation. In the real world, workers have to make these choices in real time, surrounded by the feelings, sounds and smells of the family home and often with a pounding heart and awareness of risks to self and child.

To allow us to explore challenge within purposeful dialogue I am going to choose to raise some level of challenge around the schooling issue here – but seek to do so in ways that might encourage further conversation. Here are some ways I might do this. I do not know which is best: what do you think?

1. Worker: So, I guess that leaves us with a bit of a problem. On the one hand I've got you being really unhappy with the school. On the other hand, it is really important that Charlie gets into school every day. What do you think we should do about it?

2. Worker: What do you think we can do to improve your relationship with the school? Because making sure Charlie is going to school every day is really important.

Or we could decide to be more probing: "I guess the problem is that it looks quite bad if there is a plan to protect Charlie that says he is to go to school every day and it is not happening. What do you think we could do about it?"

Or, if we are very concerned (and we are), this might be the point where we are clear about our concerns, and the consequences of not sorting this out:

> 'I have to be honest with you Jeanette, I am really worried about Charlie – and him not going to school is a big part of that. You need to know what will happen if he does not start going regularly. I would be so concerned that I would recommend that we need to start care proceedings. That is the last thing I want to do, but if he is not going in every day then that is what I feel I have to do. Do you understand why I think that, or would you like me to explain more?'

This is a confronting intervention. It goes beyond raising concerns to explaining consequences, and in this instance raises very serious consequences – perhaps the most difficult thing that a worker has to do. In this imagined excerpt I did this by emphasising what I would do. In practice, social workers rarely do this. When difficult things need to be said they tend to talk about 'we', saying things like 'we would need to consider care proceedings'. On the one hand this reflects the truth that this decision is not made solely by the social worker. On the other hand, I think it can be difficult for parents to know who 'we' are, and it can make understanding the role of the social worker more difficult. During the interview as a whole it will be important to explain processes – they are a key element of rights-focused practice. Now might be the time to do that, but the priority seemed to be to create a dialogue about the concerns. So the statement of consequences seeks to understand 'Jeanette's' point of view.

We do not know how Jeanette will respond – that is the nature of all human interaction. However, my priority would be to try to understand and show to her that I understand her response whatever it is. To do this I would suggest using skills that are central to MI, such as reflective and summary statements. For instance, even if Jeanette is very angry at me for raising the possibility of care proceedings this might be appropriate:

Jeanette: You have got to be fucking kidding me! I do everything for that boy. And I tell you the school are out to get me and all you can say is "We're going to take him away". You must be fucking joking. Over my dead body will you take him. That ain't never going to happen.

Worker: You're really pissed off with me for even saying he might come into care. And you think I haven't listened to the troubles you have had with the school.

Jeanette: You're just like all the other social workers, and the teachers and everyone. You just judge me, and now you're threatening to take Charlie off me. You're the worst of the lot. I want a new social worker. I want to speak to your manager!

There are a lot of responses that may be tempting at this point. Maybe you feel like leaving the room to get your manager might be a good idea, and would allow Jeanette some time to cool down. It might be tempting to argue back, saying something like: "The thing is Jeanette, at the child protection conference everyone spoke about how worried they were for Charlie and since then things seem to have just got worse." I think a confident professional response needs to acknowledge Jeanette's comments and offer her further opportunities to enter into a dialogue about what is going on. For instance:

> 'You're pissed off with me. You love Charlie, so me talking about him even *maybe* coming into care makes you angry. I can arrange for you to speak to my manager, but she's not around right now. I can explain a bit more about what might happen, but before we do that I'd really like to hear more what you think should happen. At the conference there were lots of worries about Charlie and we put together a plan to keep him safe. Him going to school every day was the most important part of that, which is why I am worried. What do you think should happen now to make me and the other professionals less worried?'

This may not be the best response – maybe you can think of a better one? What this response tries to do is be clear about power and authority, while acknowledging the feelings of 'Jeanette' and seeking to engage her in a purposeful dialogue about Charlie and what might happen next for him. Who knows how Jeanette might respond, and whether this might be the best way of talking to her? Much would depend on the context for the dialogue that we cannot read here – such as Jeanette's body language and the setting. And we can never know what the right thing to say was, we can merely do our best.

So far, the picking apart of the dialogue has explored the first three elements of developing a purposeful dialogue. These are being clear about our professional perspective, seeking the view of those we are working with and where possible bringing these two into dialogue. This involves the types of skills and approaches discussed. The final part of purposeful dialogue is crucial, and that is creating a resolution from the dialogue about what should happen next.

Purposeful practice requires the application of complex skills across the whole of an interview. Yet the bedrock for it is, as already noted, that each interview should usually start and end by clarifying its purpose. We covered this for the start of the interviews earlier. Equally, the end of interviews should involve some element of summarising key things from the interview and what will happen next. Yet this is also comparatively rare. Often this is because workers know they have to be quite directive about serious concerns. How should we proceed if we, as workers for a statutory agency, need to be more directive about the plan?

In practice, what tends to happen is that social workers often tell people what to do. For instance, the following is the end of a meeting in the scenario with the more serious concerns about Charlie, and the worker had already skilfully raised the possibility of care proceedings. In bringing the meeting to the end she was purposeful and did create a plan, but she also almost entirely dictated it:

Worker:	I mean with things like Charlie getting to school and that being much much closer to 100 per cent, I'd say 100 per cent or 99 per cent, it needs to be very high. Making the appointments and meeting with the social worker, those are very practical things that you can show yes I've done this, all right? With regards to alcohol service I think you would need to show an ability to change within those meetings as well. I mean we're looking for slightly more than attending and sitting down crossed arms not saying a word and leaving at the end of the day, you know?
Jeanette:	Yeah.
Worker:	Those are fairly simple, practical things to do. OK?
Jeanette:	Yeah.
Worker:	And if we saw that those were changing and there was sustained change, because I don't think we're out of the woods. Even if this was all 100 per cent in the next two weeks we're not out of the woods for a while are we?
Jeanette:	No.
Worker:	So that would be my suggestion.
Jeanette:	OK.

Worker: So if we arrange to meet next week, 5 o'clock on Thursday and we'll do that as a weekly thing, what I'll do is just write down the points that we've had in this conversation for us both to sign so that we're in agreement. So you're saying yeah, actually I agree with these points and I'm going to try and do that.

In practice, in this (simulated) interview my sense was that the worker had done enough to engage the parent and take her with her. Many workers seem good at an approach which could be characterised as 'firm persuasion'. They are clear about problems and then tell the parent what they have to do, and they do so in an obviously warm and compassionate way. This seems to me a much better type of practice than interviews which failed to raise difficult issues, or those characterised by vagueness and uncertainty. In the context of very serious concerns – and this scenario is close to care proceedings – then it is dishonest to pretend that the plan is genuinely collaborative. It is more honest to be transparent about power and consequences, as discussed at length in Chapter 3.

Nonetheless, despite the positives about this practice, from a rights-focused perspective it does not do enough to engage the parent in dialogue. To make the excerpt more purposeful and rights-focused I would suggest fairly minor but important changes. Where the worker said "So that would be my suggestion", I might change it to: "That would be my suggestion. What do you think about the actions I have suggested?" and then have a dialogue in response to that. I would then ask "Is there anything you feel needs to be part of the plan to make sure Charlie is OK?" And, if time allowed, I would also want to ask "Is there anything you need from me as Charlie's social worker that would be helpful?" These are relatively minor changes, but they are important. They move towards a more collaborative and dialogical process in which plans can be more truly shared and agreed.

This provides a sense of what might be involved in a rights-informed purposeful dialogue, particularly in difficult conversations where there may be conflict or tension. It is not possible in the space we have to cover every issue that even this single case study raises, but the intention is to give a flavour of purposeful dialogue as a rights-focused practice. The next section turns to consider another key element of rights-focused practice, namely working with people where their capacity may (or may not) be an issue.

Working with capacity issues

This book has repeatedly made the point that one of the fundamental reasons why social workers are needed in statutory work is because we often work with people where there may be capacity issues. Most people are able to make decisions about their lives without the involvement of professionals, however in some groups there can be issues about the capacity of individuals to make reasonable decisions. These groups include children and young people, those with mental illness, learning difficulties, dementia or other conditions that might affect the ability of individuals to make reasoned decisions. It is not a coincidence that social workers are often the lead professional to work with such groups. Capacity issues immediately raise challenges around rights and how to make decisions with or for people. Social work, as a rights-focused profession, is well placed to carry out such work. In this section, some of the issues in working with capacity issues are considered.

The first and most obvious point to make is that while in the groups identified there may be individuals where there are capacity issues, there may be many where this is less of an issue or not an issue at all. Most people with mental illness, learning difficulties or dementia, for instance, are still able to make decisions about their lives. Many young people are also able to make key decisions. Indeed, a good starting point for working with capacity issues is an assumption that individuals have capacity. The Mental Capacity Act (2005) includes the principle that we should assume capacity to make decisions unless there is evidence that this is not the case. It also emphasises that unwise decisions do not mean a lack of capacity. Both of these principles can be applied to working with children and young people

There are some fairly important issues to consider when working with capacity issues. Our first job is to try to discover the individual's views and feelings about key issues affecting them. This is not primarily a technical issue, in which the right style of questioning may unlock people's wishes and feelings. It is, instead, about building a relationship. To understand what people want, at least about important decisions in their lives, we need to know them, and ideally know them well. For them to share with us we need to build their trust in us – and the key to do that is by demonstrating that we are trustworthy.

Building relationships is easiest when we have time. When we get to know a child or adult over months or years, spending times together that are not always focused on a specific task but are just for fun, we are best placed to be a good advocate for what they need and to understand why sometimes they may not be able to make reasonable decisions. For me, my best work as a social worker was often done when I was simply having fun with children – or adults. I remember taking children to football matches or out for something to eat, and when I worked to help people with mental health challenges I remember trying (rather badly) to help in buying carpet for a flat and us singing loudly along to the radio as we inexpertly laid it. Time spent together just having fun is time well spent, because it allows us to develop a deeper and more rounded understanding of the people we are working with and for.

It is not always possible to build such a relationship. Sometimes social work happens in times of crisis, for instance because there has been a serious injury to a child or the behaviour of an adult is causing grave concern. The investigation may be the first time a social worker meets the person whose interests they represent. In such circumstances, an ability to build trust quickly is one of the most important skills a social worker can have. I do not think there is any template for building trust, nor set of skills that shows we are trustworthy, but I think there are some principles worth noting.

The first is that if we want people to trust us the most important thing we can do is to be trustworthy. Genuinely wanting the best for the person we are working with is the most important thing we can do to build trust. This is the heart of the ethic of love discussed at length in Chapter 6. Often, though of course not always, people can detect whether you genuinely want the best for them. However, genuinely wanting the best for them is the essence of our job. It is not therefore a means to an end; it is more true to say that when we are doing our job well people are more likely to trust us.

The second is to strive to understand their perspective. How do they see things? What do they want and why? For some groups it may be relatively straightforward to explore such questions. They may be articulate and able to express themselves clearly. For others we may need to be more creative. Children and, indeed, many adults may prefer to express themselves artistically or through play. Social workers for children should have available play materials to allow such non-verbal communication constantly, and similar approaches can sometimes be helpful with other individuals, such as some people with learning difficulties. A genuine curiosity about the person we are working with is another key social work attribute. What is important to the person I am working with and for, and why?

A third key feature of working with people to understand what is important to them is to share our understanding of what they are saying. This can be done in conversation using communication methods such as reflective and summary statements. These methods allow us to offer back to the individual our understanding of what they are telling us. Similar feeding back of our understanding can be done whatever methods we are using to discover what people really want.

For some people we work with even creative methods may not be a feasible option. For instance, a baby of a few weeks old or some individuals with very severe learning disabilities may not be able to engage in meaningful work around what they want. In such circumstances building up a picture of what seems important to them by observing and interacting with them and talking with those who spend the most time with them is crucial. While the needs of babies are fairly generic, and meeting these needs is likely to form the foundation of our assessment, nonetheless each child and adult is unique and understanding this should inform our work if we are to champion their rights.

A final point about working around capacity is that sometimes we need to tell people we do not agree. Understanding what a person wants or thinks they need does not mean we will necessarily agree that they should have it. We are appointed to represent their interests, and we therefore must understand what they want and why they want it. Yet sometimes we may decide this is not in their interests. For instance, most children will want to keep living with even an abusive parent and we may need to decide that in their interests that is not possible, at least for a period of time. Being honest and sharing that this is the situation in framing our work with people is therefore important.

Finally, if we want to build trust it is important to do what we say we will do. As a foster carer, almost every social worker our children have had has been kind, caring and interested in children. But some do what they say they will, and some do not. However lovely a worker, if they do not follow through then it is difficult to build a trusting relationship. And if that is true for us as foster carers, how much more likely is it to be true for people with less power and control, such as the children we look after whose interests the social workers are employed to represent? Apparently trivial things, such as being on time, following up on issues discussed and letting people know if you have to change arrangements are of foundational importance in building a relationship.

Conclusion

This chapter has tried to outline a form of practice that allows workers to engage with conflicting rights in a purposeful and respectful way. As emphasised at the beginning, the skills of direct practice need to be the servant of higher-level values and theories. The idea of purposeful dialogue is an attempt to make a reality of a rights-focused practice, undergirded by a love ethic and informed by humanist and social model traditions.

This chapter has focused on working with individuals or families. This is a legitimate element of rights-focused practice, yet applying a social and critical lens to rights entails us thinking about the social in our work, and considering ways of working that avoid a focus on the individual. This is explored in the next chapter which considers rights-focused practice beyond the family, looking at Family Group Conferences, Contextual Safeguarding and challenging accepted wisdom or existing policies as part of rights-focused practice.

12

Rights beyond the individual and the family

As noted in the previous chapter social work practices have tended to focus on the individual and the family, despite the values, beliefs and even the name of the profession emphasising the social. The social model helps to counteract this tendency. As discussed in Chapter 9, the social model emphasises a critical view of the nature of the 'problems' we work with, focuses on the social causes and emphasises moving away from individualised responses. This chapter considers approaches to social work that emphasise a rights orientation and a move away from individualised practice. This includes Family Group Conferences (FGCs), Contextual Safeguarding, policy-aware practice and political or policy change. The chapter concludes with a more general discussion of lessons for how to develop new ways of understanding rights-focused social work.

Family Group Conferences

FGCs seek to involve the wider network of family and others in decision-making and helping children where there may be issues or problems. This is done through a meeting – a FGC - that includes everyone with an interest in a child. The FGC is independently facilitated and the process involves professionals sharing concerns and then withdrawing to allow the family network to have private time to form a plan to address issues (Brown, 2003).

FGCs were developed in New Zealand, where Maori communities and professionals felt that the intrusive and individualised practice of child protection services did not reflect the importance of wider family and community. Community meetings that are a feature of Maori culture inspired the creation of the FGC approach (Fulcher, 1999). A number of other types of meetings with similarities to FGCs have also been developed (Stabler et al, 2019). They share the aspiration to involve the wider family (and relevant others) in decision-making and the support and protection of children, though they differ in important elements, such as whether the facilitator is independent and whether private family time is provided.

The values and practices of FGCs are consistent with those of a rights-focused perspective, or indeed those we associate with social work more generally. They emphasise the rights of the wider family to be involved in decision-making, conceptualise the child not as just an individual but as part of a community, and the ethos is collaborative and participatory. Like any rights-focused service, there are ethical conundrums in the delivery of FGCs, such as how to work with domestic abuse and what the limits are on family-led decisions (Parkinson and Rogers, 2018; Stabler et al, 2019).

The qualitative evidence about FGCs is consistently positive. Professionals tend to strongly value the approach, and family members speak positively about the experience and the sense of being involved. Perhaps for these reasons there has been increasing interest in applying FGCs into other social care and social work settings, such as work with older people or those experiencing mental distress (Metze et al, 2015). FGCs are now very extensively used across England and Wales and many other countries. This spread has happened despite some questions about the evidence base in relation to outcomes for children and parents. Reviews of the evidence found little support for the idea that FGCs are more likely to keep children at home than normal service, and the few that have examined whether parents feel more involved where there is an FGC have not found it makes much difference (Dijkstra et al, 2016). More recently a large randomised controlled trial in England found a significant reduction in children being in care (Taylor et al, 2023). These findings have contributed to a debate about the place of evidence in relation to rights. These issues are returned to in the final chapter. For now FGCs provide an excellent example of a rights-based approach to practice that moves beyond working with the individual or the isolated 'nuclear' family.

Another area where new ways of working are being developed and evaluated is in relation to the exploitation of children outside the home. The next section considers Contextual Safeguarding in particular.

Child sexual and criminal exploitation and Contextual Safeguarding

The exploitation of children sexually and in other ways outside the family has highlighted problems in the way we conceptualise and respond to abuse. The development of new practices in this area also demonstrates the profound ways in which the conceptualisation of a 'problem' and our professional response to it are interlinked. Sexual abuse has been identified as unacceptable and more common than previously accepted, and over time we have developed stronger and, in general, better responses to abuse both in the home and outside it. Yet much of this response is predicated on ideas of childhood innocence and the abuse of that innocence, and with a focus on the family (Melrose, 2002, 2010). Professional and public responses have been more confused when there appears to be some element of agency in the activities of children and young people. This is particularly true when the abuse takes place outside the home. For instance, until comparatively recently official guidance talked about children involved in sex work as child prostitutes, and they were criminalised (Melrose, 2010). In a similar way, children involved in gang activity were seen as criminals rather than as themselves victims (Children's Commissioner, 2019; Maxwell et al, 2019). Indeed, this can still be the case, not least because such young people are in complicated and potentially ambivalent positions, sometimes for instance being at the same time victims and perpetrators of crime or intimidation. Responses also tend to be individualised, focusing on specific children rather than groups of young people (Firmin, 2018).

The campaigning of researchers and activists has led to a transformation in the conceptualisation of such activity. First, concepts such as child sexual exploitation and more recently criminal exploitation have emphasised that children are children and as such the victims of exploitation – and therefore have rights to protection and help (Children's Commissioner, 2019). Second, they have considered the knotty issue of children's agency and the ways in which exploitation works to involve them in abusive situations. A practice and policy challenge is that often these young people do not feel, at least initially, that they are being abused. They may feel that the person who is considered their abuser is their boyfriend, or they may feel that being involved with gang activity gives them respect from others. Initially, the idea of grooming helped in understanding some of these issues (see Maxwell et al, 2019). More recently the idea of exchange has been argued to be helpful, with some young people making choices to engage in behaviours that are abusive because they obtain things they value, which may be money or affection or prestige, in exchange (Hallett, 2017). Given the power relations involved this is still abusive, but for those involved exchange can represent a clearer description of their lived experience.

The third 'problem' for the system has been that this abuse takes place outside the home. An implicit assumption in much of this book and in the development of society's responses to abuse and neglect is that abuse takes place in the family (Firmin, 2018). This is the place where, typically, rights are seen to be in conflict and careful professional practice is needed to help individuals and families. The system therefore struggled with abuse that was outside the home, for instance often not identifying abuse because it was categorised as a criminal matter rather than an issue of child protection.

There have been various responses to these challenges in recent years, including complex safeguarding (Maxwell, 2023), transitional safeguarding (Holmes, 2022) and Contextual Safeguarding (Firmin and Lloyd, 2023). Here I focus on Contextual Safeguarding because it is probably the best known and because it is an excellent example of thinking beyond the family. Contextual Safeguarding was created by Professor Carlene Firmin, who identified that social services were often failing to help children experiencing abuse (Firmin, 2018). Her work identified that too often these responses focused on family, for instance investigating whether parents were adequately protecting children. They did not recognise the ways in which factors such as specific places or groups might create risks of abuse or exploitation. The child protection system was designed to respond to harm within the family and struggled to respond to harm in other places or from other people. This applied to children who were sexually or criminally exploited, but also included challenges in responding to other abuse outside the home, such as in romantic or sexual relationships or violence in the community (Gorin and Jobe, 2013; Firmin, 2018; Firmin and Knowles, 2022).

Contextual Safeguarding seeks to protect children and young people from harm outside the family home. It does so by focusing on children in their ecological context and seeks to bring together the multiple agencies with an interest in carrying out such work. Crucially, the focus is often on changing the context in which exploitation or abuse may take place, for instance if a dark stairway is a nexus for gang activity then lighting and regular police visits might be part of a solution. However, usually responses need to take place at multiple levels, including working directly with children and their families in a supportive and relationship-based way (see Firmin and Lloyd, 2023).

Contextual Safeguarding has five core values at its heart (Firmin and Lloyd, 2023). The first four are that it is:

- collaborative (seeking to work with people not doing to them);
- ecological (seeing problems in their structural and social context);
- strengths-based (at the level of the individual and the community it seeks to identify and build on positives); and
- rooted in the young person's understanding of their lived experience.

Of particular interest for this book is the fifth core value: an emphasis on rights. Firmin and Lloyd characterised this in this way:

> [Contextual Safeguarding] engages with the full range of young people's rights when developing responses to extra familial harm. This would not only include rights to protection, but a right to have their views heard and considered, a right to privacy, and a right to spend time with others and so on. Directly engaging with, rather than ignoring, any tensions that might emerge when trying to protect all those rights in safeguarding processes is critical. (Firmin and Lloyd, 2023)

One might add that it also engages with other rights, such as those of families and others to proportionate intervention, and a right to family life.

Contextual Safeguarding is in its infancy. A range of interesting research and evaluation is being carried out around Contextual Safeguarding and other approaches to protecting children outside the home. It is too early to say whether it 'works' – and indeed, it is unlikely that such a simplistic question is even appropriate. What is becoming clearer over time is the difference it can make for some children, what is needed to deliver it well, the obstacles to such delivery and how they can be overcome. Contextual Safeguarding has made an impressive start to addressing these issues.

The focus on Contextual Safeguarding here is to illustrate that a focus on rights has implications beyond working with individuals. Applying a social model and critical perspective about rights helps us move away from individualised practice towards thinking about family and community. It also sometimes requires us to carry out social work at the macro level – the level of politics and policy. This is the focus of the next section.

Social work at the macro level and the 'smacking ban' in Wales

The social in rights-focused social work means that we sometimes need to strive for change at the macro level of politics and policy. This is certainly true if we have a focus on human rights. As argued in previous chapters, social workers need to operate in the often uncomfortable space between the views of those we work with, the views of society as expressed in law, policy and resource provision, and the professional knowledge and values we have. In working with individuals this often creates tensions and conflicts, and good practice strives to work constructively with such differences. A more difficult situation arises when we believe that one of these perspectives is unacceptable. This may happen when we work with individuals, for instance because we believe that what they have said or what they believe is not acceptable. Much of this book, and particularly Chapters 3 and 11, has considered the challenge that this creates. Yet social workers are not mere agents of the state, mindlessly carrying out the diktats of a higher power – or at least we should not be. Our professional identity provides us with a more independent position, and one which can be critical about either the state's provisions or our own professional evidence base. This can and should lead social workers to question and perhaps even work to change elements of our professional knowledge or state provision.

In recent years there are many examples of academics seeking to change the 'general knowledge' which guides social work practice. For instance, Bywaters and colleagues have carried out a programme of work that seeks to establish the central place of deprivation in understanding why children come into care, and challenge the individualised narrative that focuses on parental risk factors such as substance use, mental illness or domestic abuse (Bywaters et al, 2016, 2017). Colleagues including Morris, Bilson and Krumer-Nevo have developed practical suggestions for how to work with people experiencing poverty (Krumer-Nevo, 2020; BASW, 2021b). Featherstone, Devaney and others have been active in seeking better ways of understanding and working with domestic abuse in the context of child protection (Featherstone and Peckover, 2007; Maxwell et al, 2012; Devaney, 2015; Skafida et al, 2022). Broadhurst and colleagues have highlighted the repeat removal of children from mothers (Broadhurst and Mason, 2017). Louise Roberts has worked with care-experienced mothers to highlight the extraordinarily high rate of child removal for such mothers, and to develop a charter to influence good practice (Roberts, 2021). Bernard has explored the lived experience of Black children who have been abused (for example, Bernard and Harris, 2019). The list could go on. These academics and many others are striving to introduce new ways of thinking about and responding to issues and problems in social work.

At a micro level, the collective strivings of academic social workers and others rarely produce a set of knowledge and ideas that workers can simply apply. Rather, they provide insights and evidence for practice and policy. Such knowledge is a core element of assessment and practice, yet it is far from a monolithic or objective body of evidence. It is more akin to a set of ways of understanding and interpreting the issues that we encounter in practice. Social workers therefore need to be equipped with critical, thoughtful and reflective abilities to allow them to use the knowledge appropriately.

There are similarities in the way in which social workers need to engage with the social mandate, as set out in laws, policies and resource provision. This provides the context for the work we do, at least in all statutory work, yet it is not a context we need to accept unquestioningly. Indeed, the price and the privilege of our professionalism is that we are expected to question this social mandate. There are many non-professional bureaucrats within the welfare state whose primary job is to follow predetermined procedures to establish eligibility criteria. The status of the social worker as a professional both enhances and restricts our capacity to critique the social mandate for our work. It enhances it because professionalism requires and enables some element of independent critique. This is more true for social workers than for most professionals, because our work typically takes place at the intersection of the individual and the social; because we work with human rights, and these require us to strive for those we represent to have the rights they deserve. We cannot therefore simply treat the social mandate 'as if' it were objective (Sheppard, 1995).

Yet our role also restricts the extent to which we can critique the mandate. Being employed to deliver a service requires some willingness to deliver the service. For those practising or leading services a moderate critical engagement with rights is expected and appropriate. This critical engagement takes place at two levels. The first is the level of individual practice. Social workers need to act as advocates for those they work with at the micro level. For instance, in Chapter 4 when I talked about arguing for money for a family, or in Chapter 2 with the case study of a social worker lobbying for children to be moved to a new school, social work is often about fighting for the rights of our clients within and across systems. Every day social workers are appealing housing decisions, supporting benefits claims, arguing with managers about resources and in general making a nuisance of ourselves in the interests of those we work with.

At a higher level, sometimes social workers may feel law or policy is not adequate. They may then believe they need to be involved in changing it. This is usually the job of those who have more senior roles, but it can be something any social worker has to do. Social workers often have key roles in shaping policy and law. A recent example is in making physical chastisement of children illegal. This first happened in Sweden in 1979 and has been illegal in Scotland since 2020. Working in Wales I saw the way that a campaign largely led and supported by social workers, and backed by the Children's Commissioner (also a social worker – Sally Holland) was eventually successful in passing a law making smacking and other physical chastisement illegal. It was passed into law in 2022 by First Minister Mark Drakeford – another social worker who decided he could make a bigger contribution to society by changing policy than in practice or the academy.

Conclusion

A focus on rights in social work requires us to have a critical view of the way we work with people and the policies and resources provided for our work. It means we need to move beyond the individual in our focus. Sometimes that means we need to lobby, advocate and challenge within our organisation, sometimes it means we should strive to improve the rights and resources provided for the people we work with. As in every chapter throughout this book, there are no simple answers about when we work with individuals, when we strive to change social contexts or policies, or when we do both. In fact, it is *because* there are no simple answers that we need professional social workers who can wrestle with these complicated and important political and practical conundrums and make wise judgements about the best course of action.

13

Social work, rights and society

In this concluding chapter I want to explore the wider implications of a focus on rights for social work. These include some consideration of what the arguments mean for social work as a profession, including the nature of social work as political struggle. The extent and potential limits of a focus on rights within social work are reviewed. The way we think about policy and research in social work are also changed if we take a rights-focused perspective. Finally, I consider the role of social work in society and argue that social work is an essential profession for any enlightened society and one that we should be proud to be part of.

Rights-focused practice and social work

One of the initial motivations for writing the book was as an apologia for social work in general and child and family work in particular. There have been increasingly vociferous critiques of the profession from within and close to the profession, including calls for the profession to be abandoned published in the academic journal of the British Association of Social Work – the professional association that is meant to champion the profession (Maylea, 2021). Others have been more temperate in their conclusions, but no less scathing in their critique of current practice (Featherstone et al, 2014a). I have also been concerned about the practice I have observed in my own research and have read about in the research of others. Child and family social work seems to have lost its way, with much practice that seems authoritarian and also often a lack of clarity about the purpose of the practice. Any apologia therefore has to be married to a critique, and this in turn requires an account of what social work should be. This book seeks to provide the beginnings of such an account, at least from my perspective.

When confronted with the shortcomings of contemporary social work practice it is tempting to call for services and the profession to do something completely different. Thus, for instance, there have been calls for more community work, or a social model, or more help and less intervention. These all seem eminently sensible suggestions, which I would wholeheartedly support. The danger is if they are used to avoid addressing the challenge of how to do the work we currently call 'child protection'. I have been in debates with eminent academics who have argued that if we moved to genuine community-based work we would not need to do 'child protection'.

This seems to me to be untrue. It is a form of naive wishful thinking. Three things would massively reduce the need for child protection work: a more equal society, excellent universal services and more effective help for families that are struggling. Yet even in combination it seems to me ludicrous to suggest there would be no need for something like 'child protection' – and by child protection I mean the difficult balancing of rights involved when parents are unable or unwilling to care for their children well enough that is the focus of this book. One does not have to have read many child death inquiries, nor worked with many children who have been sexually abused, to realise that not all parents want the best for their children. And once we as a society recognise this difficult fact, then there is a need for a rights-focused profession such as social work to deal with the challenges that it creates.

Considered another way, this is a classic liberal position. While utopians of the left and right have often argued that individuals or society can be perfected, the outcomes of such beliefs have too often been the brutality of the re-education or concentration camp, mass killings and the suppression of dissent. In contrast, the liberal perspective is that neither individuals nor society can ever be perfect. Humans and the organisations we create are capable of extraordinary achievements and kindness; but we are also capable of cruelty, selfishness and abuse. We therefore need to create societies that protect individuals from our worst tendencies. Social work has a central role to play in this enterprise.

The specific contribution of this book is to consider how this difficult work can perhaps be done. The temptation is to suggest that if we provided enough help there would be no need for protection. Instead, the argument here is that we will always need protection and, given that is the case, what should it look like?

The extent and limits of a rights focus for social work

A focus on rights helps us understand much of the work of children's services; it is a good description of what workers seem to be trying to do. It fits better than, for instance, 'helping' or 'promoting social justice'. This is perhaps unsurprising, as the ideas for this book were developed through a process of reflecting on my practice and research in this area. It is more open to question how useful a focus on rights is as a framework for thinking about social work more generally. This applies in two ways. First, does it work as a way of thinking about social work with other client groups? Second, does it work as a way of thinking about other types of practice?

This book has been largely focused on child and family work, but it is obvious that many of the same considerations apply to other areas in which social workers often work. Social workers are involved with capacity issues and as a consequence work around rights for some people with mental illness, learning difficulty, dementia and other issues where capacity may (or may not) need to be considered. My hypothesis is that many of the arguments of this book apply to these other areas, though those with more expertise would be able to explore this far better than I can. Certainly when workers are safeguarding and protecting then the work appears to have many similarities. Yet I think a rights-focused approach probably applies more broadly.

This touches on the second question. One way of framing this is to ask whether social work is rights focused when workers are providing services to meet needs? For instance, is a worker putting together a care package for an older person coming out of hospital after a knee replacement working in a rights-focused way? For child and family social work I have argued that this is rights-focused work. More specifically, in Chapter 4 I argued that the nature of the needs which social workers assess means that there are likely to be tensions between what people may want and what they receive. Ultimately, these tensions are about rights and social need, and I think a rights-focused approach is therefore helpful for understanding this type of work. I have also alluded to the importance of workers struggling for the rights of people, including examples of workers who have left the profession to become politicians.

Rights are an ideal framework for thinking about social work because they are the site where the individual and the social intersect. Rights are provided by society for individuals. That is one of the reasons social workers are so often involved at this intersection. Our involvement is particularly likely when there may be tensions or conflict about rights. This tension becomes a core element of social work; it reverberates out to create other tensions, such as that between the client's perspective, that of society and the expert knowledge of the worker; between the care and control elements of the work; between objective and subjective evidence. These uncomfortable tensions are the very stuff of social work, and to a large degree this book has been an attempt to map out how social workers might constructively work with such potentially conflicting imperatives.

I am not sure whether all of social work can be understood through a rights-focused lens. I tend to think that where there are not tensions related to a focus on rights then what we are talking about is not really social work. For instance, a qualified social worker working as a counsellor is probably not doing social work; nor is one who has become a politician. These are both vital occupations, but neither has the tension around individual rights that I consider characteristic of social work. In contrast, a community worker striving for the rights of girls to an education is probably doing social work as I understand it. Nonetheless, while I think a rights focus probably does define social work I am not completely convinced that this is the case yet.

It is worth mentioning the choice of the phrase 'rights focused' rather than 'rights based'. I decided to use the phrase focused to indicate that there is no conflict between relationship based, or indeed evidence based or any other 'base' for social work, and a focus on rights. More than this, rights are the focus of the work rather than the basis upon which we do it. So rights focused seems a better term.

The critique of current practice

The purpose of this book, at least for me, was to try to articulate a vision of social work – at least statutory social work with children and families – that described the actual challenges of the work while still recognising it as worthwhile. Such a vision serves a second function: it allows us to critically engage with current practice. This involves being able to recognise that often the service received is not good enough, that too often the rights of children or parents are inadequately supported, while not abandoning the enterprise altogether.

Instead, my hope is that a focus on rights allows us to point towards forms of practice that may be better than some of the things we currently do. This book has been an attempt to outline some of the approaches I think may be most useful. A recurring theme has been working with conflicts and tensions, and seeking to outline ways in which workers might constructively be able to do so. I hope that this focus is broadly complementary to key critiques of 'child protection' from recent years (e.g. Featherstone et al, 2014a), while providing more focus on the intricacies of direct practice. A second contribution is to suggest some of these issues apply beyond child and family work, to social work more generally.

What I strongly believe is that it is not appropriate to talk about social work or train workers as if what we do is akin to helping people. Most social workers move into child and family work, and encounter the tensions associated with this. We therefore need to develop a social work theory and practice that takes seriously the difficult nature of this work.

Rights, policies and research

Moving the focus of social work from helping to rights has implications beyond practice. In recent years I have been involved directly and indirectly in several major policy initiatives, as well as extensive programmes of research. It has become apparent to me that often these initiatives are undergirded by an often unexamined utilitarianism. By this I mean the assumption that social work services for children are there to improve outcomes. In other words, they are primarily there to help children and their families. There are several problems with this position.

The first problems are empirical. There is not much evidence that child and family social work does improve outcomes. Certainly, for the massive outlay of time and cost involved the evidence we have of positive differences is paltry. Furthermore, when people look at what social workers do when they meet people in research, it is not really helping people – at least in any straightforward sense that we might understand. This is not to say that social workers or children's services do *not* help people. It is just that any approach predicated on the idea that they improve outcomes does not seem a good fit. Workers are doing all sorts of things, trying to build relationships, raising concerns, monitoring and checking up, and other things but fairly rarely are they actively working to create change and improve outcomes.

The next problems are more conceptual. The first is that not all services should be measured by the outcomes they produce. Imagine that for some reason your family is subject to a child protection investigation. Assuming there was no real reason for the intervention, for instance because it was a malicious referral, how might we evaluate it? It would be inappropriate to consider outcomes; the investigation could not be expected to change outcomes, not least because they are not necessarily of concern. Rather, it is exploring whether or not an intervention is necessary. We might evaluate this by whether the involvement was proportionate, and whether the process was clear, respectful and professional. In other words, like the workings of the court or the police or other rights-based processes, the appropriate standard for evaluation is not about outcomes but about whether processes are fair and just. This thinking influenced the development of the outcomes framework for the What Works for Children Centre, which prioritised rights, before considering outcomes (What Works for Children, 2021).

A second issue is to unpack the fact that so many of the families worked with do not want a social worker. This is not a trivial issue. On the contrary, it is fundamentally important. As noted in the introduction, child and family services are akin to Nanny McPhee's statement that 'When you need me, but do not want me, then I must stay. When you want me, but no longer need me, then I have to go.' Why is this the case for so much of statutory social work? The answer is because we deal with conflicts and tensions. Where a parent wants help in looking after their child, they can usually be provided with a support service. Such services are there to help people, they are often staffed by social workers and measuring them in relation to the outcomes they produce is wholly appropriate. Crucially, however, there is not a conflict about rights here. We can work with the broad assumption in our society that the rights of most children and parents are broadly in accord, because in general parents want the best for their children. Most support services are provided on this basis.

Yet if a parent does not want 'help', maybe because they do not think they can change, or they do not see a problem with what they do, or because they are covering up abuse or they are concerned about their child being removed, then what are we to do? This is when child protective services will typically become involved. There is an immediate difference between the situation of someone wanting help and being helped and that of working with a family where the adults feel they do not want help, or maybe are actively hostile to it. How should we think about or evaluate a service where this is the case?

At the least it would be unrealistic to expect the service to be as successful in helping people as one that worked with people who are seeking help. Put another way, if one still believes that the purpose of social services is primarily to help people it might be possible to measure the effectiveness of such help against some outcomes that seem relevant. Yet, the impact of even evidence-based interventions for people who want help is not enormous. Indeed, it is perhaps surprisingly modest. What might we realistically expect the impact of a service working with people who do not want help to be? I think the answer would have to suggest a very modest impact, because it is very hard to create change when people do not want change (though of course, as discussed in Chapter 3, motivation is a complicated idea).

Moving away from the assumption that services are there to help people and improve outcomes has some important implications for both research and policy. For both it places greater emphasis on the process. Rights-focused processes have intrinsic worth, and can reasonably be measured against these intrinsic measures. So, for instance, I would suggest child protection investigations should be clear about their rationale, proportionate and timely, and the workers should be respectful, authoritative and kind. Others might use other words, but the key point here is that we need to be able to articulate a rights-focused process not merely justify services by the outcomes they allegedly produce. This is a challenge for research, and comparatively rarely is the process itself evaluated in its own right (rather than as a means to producing outcomes). I will just leave a related thought here: perhaps one of the reasons we have had so much trouble proving anything works in social work is that we have been looking at the wrong things, focusing on outcomes rather than rights supporting processes?

Of course, for evaluative research the key is to have a good fit between the aims of the service and the outcomes one is measuring. It would be a brave, and perhaps foolhardy, person who tried to measure outcomes for the National Health Service as a whole. Instead, we need to be clear what each element is striving to achieve and measure it against that. In a similar way, if an assessment service is seeking to be proportionate and timely in its assessments then perhaps that can be captured. A separate service for families where there is domestic abuse does perhaps seek to improve specific outcomes, though even here it is more likely and probably more appropriate to measure it against a direct aim of the service, such as reducing incidents of domestic abuse, than against a more distal aim, such as improving the mental health of the children. There are many factors that may influence children's mental health, and for this reason we might need a very large number to be confident in identifying the difference a service makes. Instead, strong evidence of a reduction in domestic abuse combined with what we know about the impact domestic abuse can have on children may be all we need.

Similar considerations apply to national and local leadership of children's services, and I am sure to adult and other services. A key issue for leaders is clarity about what the aims of the service are, both as a whole and in relation to specific elements of the service. When I work with leaders at national and local level I am often struck by the difficulty we have articulating what the purpose of our service is. Participants can provide definitions of teaching, medicine and policing that are broadly consistent with those of professional associations. Yet for their own service there is far move variation between individuals, and there is far more likely to be disagreement with the public definitions such as the International Federation of Social Workers' definition of social work. This reflects the sense of a gap that prompted me to start writing this book, but it has important implications for leadership and management of services. If we cannot define and describe what we are doing – what we are trying to achieve and how we seek to do so – then we are unlikely to be able to lead the system effectively. In outlining a rights-focused vision for children's services and social work more generally I am seeking to make a positive contribution to clarifying what the purpose of child and family social work is – and by doing so to hopefully shed some light on other types of social work.

On rights and love

A key element of the book that was not planned at the outset was the discovery of bell hooks' love ethic, and the exploration of its application to social work practice. I have spoken before about love and social work, though I have been reluctant to write about it for fear of a lack of academic rigour. For instance, my inaugural lecture as a professor was titled 'Faith, hope and love: reflections on evidence based social work'.

My interest in love comes in part from my Christian background, and in part from a sense that I felt a kind of loving when I was doing social work well – yet there seem to be few ways of speaking about this. It was certainly not something I talked about in the office or supervision, and as outlined in Chapter 6 social work spends a great deal of effort to avoid talking about the powerful emotions which it evokes. hooks' work provides a way of recognising love not as a noun but as a verb, and therefore not as something that happens to us but something we choose to do. It therefore can become a guide to all our actions and relationships, not just those we 'feel' love about. From this perspective a love ethic became a natural fit with the complex challenges of working in a rights-focused way. It provides principles, values and an ethical framework that can guide us in this complicated and often fraught work. The question we need to constantly come back to is how to work in a loving way.

There is a sense in which a love ethic seems a poor fit for rights-focused work. The former seems emotional and not concerned with the rational. The latter is more clearly associated with Enlightenment ideals, and in particular with rational decision-making. Yet this is a misunderstanding of both the love ethic and rights. A love ethic is not primarily about emotions, and can encompass rationality. It is about relating to people in ways that genuinely value them and wanting the best for them. And decision-making about rights, at least in the context of social work, are rarely solely about rational decision-making. Rather they encompass the whole of each person we work with, including their emotional and embodied reality. Rights-focused practice is what we seek to do, while a love ethic is how we should do it.

The need for much of contemporary social work is created by the sort of rights-focused conundrums this book has focused on. We need social workers because individual rights can and do come into conflict, certainly around capacity issues and probably far beyond these. The question we fundamentally need to ask is how do we, as a society, wish for these conflicts to be handled? The answer to this question is in some senses very complicated – this book may just be the start of an answer. Yet in another sense it is very simple, instead of asking the abstract question about society we can consider how we would like such conflicts to be handled if it was us or our family that was involved in them; if it was we who had a social worker involved with us. The answer to this question is, I believe, best understood as 'with love'.

In seeking to provide the practice for others that we would hope to receive I am drawn to a love ethic. It is what I would hope for from social workers, and what I have seen from many. Yet it is more than simply about individual practice, because how we handle conflicts about rights also shapes the society we are creating. Thus, in practising in a loving manner we contribute to creating a loving society. We literally become the change we want to see. That is why a love ethic is essential for rights-focused practice.

Social work and the Enlightenment

How does all of this relate to the Enlightenment and its ideals? Here I want to argue that the Enlightenment has been a tremendous success, and that its ideals are fundamental to the tangible progress human beings have made in recent history. I then want to conclude that social work is made necessary by the ideals of the Enlightenment and is therefore an essential part of building a humane and liberal society.

As mentioned in Chapter 2, progress was part of the rationale for and the justification of the Enlightenment. If Enlightenment ideals have not contributed to improved human wellbeing over the last 300 years then perhaps it is time we looked for new ideals? In fact, there are strong grounds for optimism about both the idea of human progress and the specific contribution that social work makes to this.

There is such widespread scepticism about human progress that when I suggest to students or social workers that we are making progress it is often greeted with disbelief. We are constantly bombarded with depressing and distressing stories and pictures, tales of poverty and hunger, war and environmental degradation, of extreme weather and more recently the COVID-19 pandemic and the Russian invasion of Ukraine. Amidst all this gloom the suggestion that things are actually getting better seems improbable to many people. Yet there are grounds for suggesting that we are not just making progress, but that our progress is extraordinary. It is something we should be celebrating. And it is, to at least some degree, based on Enlightenment ideals, with social work a core part of a progress in human welfare.

The Enlightenment has been having something of an intellectual renaissance in recent years. After the rather unproductive focus on postmodernism in the late 20th century, key thinkers have been returning to the Enlightenment to provide the foundations for a progressive politics (see Bronner, 2004; Todorov, 2010). A contributor to this process has been Stephen Pinker, whose work empirically exploring the idea of progress has been particularly important. In two key books – *The better angels of our nature* and *Enlightenment now* – he amasses a compelling case for human progress (Pinker, 2011, 2018). *Better angels* argues that we are hurting and killing each other at a lower rate than at any point in human history. Amassing a wealth of empirical data, Pinker argues that far fewer people are being killed by other people now than at any time in human history. This is not just about wars. The levels of murders and assaults are reducing long term. The level of domestic abuse has reduced substantially. What seems certain is that now is the time in all history when we are least likely to be killed by another human being.

In *Enlightenment now*, Pinker widens his analysis and broadens his argument. He seeks to support Enlightenment ideals and ideas by arguing that we are seeing human progress, measured in a variety of ways. On the most basic level, life expectancy has shot up. In 1800 no country had a life expectancy above 40 and now every country has a life expectancy higher than that. Since 1900 life expectancy has doubled. This increase is not evenly spread between countries, but recent decades have seen extraordinary increases among many of the poorest countries. Pinker quotes Norberg as noting that in the ten years following 2003 life expectancy in Kenya increased by ten years. This is just one example of huge recent increases in life expectancy across much of Africa. This is partly about reductions in infant mortality, but it is also about successes that impact health across the life course and social changes, including reduced conflict and more democratic countries.

Pinker's analysis extends beyond life expectancy. He argues that people have more access to basics, such as food, and that far fewer are in absolute poverty, that social spending to support welfare has increased massively as a percentage of gross domestic product, that not only has war reduced but so has terrorism, that there has been a huge and continuing spread of democracy. He also argues that there has been an increase in rights within countries, as demonstrated by recognition of rights for women, racial minorities, gay, lesbian and bisexual people, substantial reductions in executions and a variety of other measures. He shows that people are more educated and that education is more likely to be provided for all, including excluded groups, such as poorer people and girls. People in developed countries are working fewer hours, spend more time on leisure and have a higher proportion of their income to spend on non-essentials. These factual changes would suggest people are better off – they have more freedom, health, education, resources and so on. He also argues there is some tentative evidence that people are happier – and highlights some unexpected findings, such as that US teenagers are less lonely than they used to be.

One does not have to accept all of Pinker's descriptions of the evidence – I have major reservations about elements relating to inequality and the environment– yet the overall depiction of a world in which there is substantial and accelerating progress as measured in relation to overall human wellbeing is hard to deny. An important question then is why do we tend to feel the opposite? The news, amplified by online 'doom-scrolling', leads us to focus on the negative. There is an old journalistic adage that 'if it bleeds, it leads', which captures the fact that bad news gets people's attention. This is even more true online where, in the battle for our attention, tragedies and disaster grab people's focus. Good news is barely news at all. During the COVID-19 pandemic how many people noticed that we developed life-saving medicines for cystic fibrosis and made enormous strides in preventing malaria? The focus on the negative leads to a real and important perceptual bias: we tend to think things are worse than they are and we have a strong tendency to think things are getting worse. And this tendency becomes more pronounced the older we are (Pinker, 2018).

The flip side of this tendency to focus on the negative is perhaps that the price we pay for progress is a restless discontent with the current situation. The reason things are getting better is not because it is preordained: it is precisely because we tend to focus on bad things that need to change. So, for instance, it seems certain that there have been massive reductions in male domestic violence towards women over the last 100 years. It was so widespread in the past that it was barely worthy of a mention, wives were legally a possession of men and men were entitled in law and in custom and practice to use violence. If we focus solely on the fact that there is now less violence then there used to be that might undermine positive change, suggesting complacency about the current situation. Instead, organisations and individuals continue to highlight the – still shocking, still completely unacceptable, still requiring urgent action – number of women killed by men each year in the United Kingdom, and campaign to improve society's responses. We focus not on what has been achieved but on what we still need to do in overcoming problems. A similar pattern can be seen in many other areas, for instance racism, homophobia or the abuse of children – where we focus on the problem. This drives the restless struggle for us to do better that fuels progress, but perhaps leads us not to appreciate how far we have come.

Pinker's argument is not just empirical – that as a matter of fact things are getting better – but it has policy and theory implications. He believes Enlightenment ideas – the rational pursuit of human welfare, rights and democracy – have been fundamental to the gains we have enjoyed. Pinker thinks it important to articulate this success story in response to a loss of faith in Enlightenment ideals. He is particularly concerned with the lack of regard for truth and democracy associated with 'populist' and nationalist politicians such as Trump in the United States, Orbán in Hungary and Putin in Russia, and also the fundamentalism linked to groups such as the Taliban and Islamic State. As I write, Putin has launched an invasion of Ukraine which typifies this type of anti-Enlightenment thinking, where his nationalist vision of Russia entitles him to use force to oppress the Ukrainian people and deprive them of democracy and individual freedoms. Pinker's argument is that we need to rearticulate and champion the importance of rational debate, individual rights and freedoms and the progress that ensues when we dedicate society to such principles.

This book shares Pinker's positive view about the ideas of the Enlightenment and the contribution that they have made to human progress. It is possible to have other ideals, such as a religious fundamentalism or a belief in a specific leader or the idea of a nation state. For me, Enlightenment ideals and ideas, and specifically belief in a society based on the equal worth of each of its members, their freedom to pursue the life they want to live, and rationality and debate as the best way of ensuring progress, are inherently better ideals; but they are also ideals that deliver – they contribute to the improvements in human flourishing that we have seen in recent centuries. There are many legitimate concerns and caveats about such arguments, but a full discussion of them is beyond the remit of this book. Certainly, we need to apply such thinking to key current challenges such as global warming, the loss of nature on a massive scale and the continuing scourge of poverty and inequality. Nonetheless, the central point remains true: the Enlightenment ideas and ideals have enabled human progress, and that progress is a real and positive thing. I want to argue that by promoting human rights in difficult situations social work can justifiably claim to be making an important contribution to the progress we are making as the human species. This is because the Enlightenment does not just explain why we need social work, it also helps us understand the essential contribution that social work makes to a just, humane and caring society.

Social work and progress

Social work can lay claim to contributing to the progress that Pinker outlines so persuasively in his books. Of course, improvements in medicine and political changes are primary drivers for many of the improvements Pinker identifies. Yet in many areas social workers can take some credit. Pinker argues that we may think that abuse in the family or of children is going up, when in fact it is almost certainly falling while our awareness of it is increasing. In this, social workers have played a key part. In carrying out the essential balancing of rights required by our role, social workers have been a key group who have identified and sought to publicise and address key causes of harm – usually by listening to those experiencing it. We have been at the forefront of identifying sexual abuse and physical abuse, neglect and emotional abuse (Parton, 1985). More recently, we have been central to identifying the harm that domestic abuse can inflict on children and in developing better professional responses and in recognising and working to mitigate and prevent child sexual and criminal exploitation (e.g. Mullender et al, 2003; Stanley, 1997; Devaney, 2015). Social workers have also had key roles in changing and expanding the rights of children and women, by for instance expanding the rights of children to be heard or campaigning against the right of parents to hit their children (Holland, 2022). Social workers were a central part of arguments to close psychiatric and other hospitals and help those with learning difficulties, physical disabilities and mental health problems live in the community. They continue on a daily basis to work to support such people and maximise individuals' ability to live a free life in the place of their choice.

There is a danger here of appearing to slip into a rather Panglossian view of the world. Professor Pangloss was a satirical character created by Voltaire. Pangloss argued that 'all is for the best in this best of all possible worlds'. As already argued, the picture is more complicated than such a simplistic assertion: progress is not constant, and it is achieved through struggle against forces dedicated to protecting the interests of those with power. It is also important to recognise and reflect on the fact that social workers have colluded with abuses of rights and as a profession we are implicated in shameful practices such as the forced adoptions of indigenous people in Australia and Canada (Sinclair, 2004; Fronek and Cuthbert, 2013). Yet that is not the whole picture, social work has often also helped challenge such abuses and has contributed to many of the positive changes we have seen in society in recent decades, as outlined earlier.

This book is unashamedly optimistic. It believes we – as human beings and in our society – have made progress through a dedication to Enlightenment principles; that social work wrestles with some of the complexities of a commitment to individual liberty, the equal worth of people and building solidarity that come with such a dedication; and that as such we, as social workers, have made and continue to make a central contribution to a humane, liberal and caring society. Rights-focused social work is crucial because it is an essential element of an Enlightened society.

References

Allen, D. and Riding, S. (2018). *The fragility of professional competence: A preliminary account of child protection practice with Romani and Traveller children.* https://e-space.mmu.ac.uk/623526/1/the-fragility-of-professional-competence-january-2018.pdf

Androff, D. (2015). *Practicing rights: Human rights-based approaches to social work practice.* Routledge.

Baginsky, M. (2023). Parents' views on improving relationships with their social workers. *Journal of Social Work*, 23(1), 3–18.

Bailey, R.V. and Brake, M. (eds) (1975). *Radical social work.* Pantheon.

Barber, J.G. (1991). *Beyond casework.* Bloomsbury.

Barney, D.D. and Dalton, L.E. (2006). Social work under Nazism: An analysis of the 'profession-in-the-environment'. *Journal of Progessive Human Services*, 17(2), 43–62.

BASW (British Association of Social Workers) (2021a). *Code of ethics for social work.* https://www.basw.co.uk/about-basw/code-ethics#:~:text=Principles%20of%20social%20justice%2C%20human,life%20challenges%20and%20enhance%20wellbeing

BASW (British Association of Social Workers) (2021b). *Anti-poverty guide.* https://www.basw.co.uk/system/files/resources/Anti%20Poverty%20Guide%20A42.pdf

Bennett, B., Zubrzycki, J. and Bacon, V. (2011). What do we know? The experiences of social workers working alongside Aboriginal people. *Australian Social Work*, 64(1), 20–37.

Beresford, P. (2012). What service users want from social workers. *Community Care*, 27 April. https://www.communitycare.co.uk/2012/04/27/what-service-users-want-from-social-workers/

Beresford, P., Perring, R., Nettle, M. and Wallcraft, J. (2016). *From mental illness to a social model of madness and distress.* Shaping Our Lives.

Berlin, I. (2017 [1967]). Two concepts of liberty. In *The liberty reader* (pp 33–57). Routledge.

Bernard, C. and Harris, P. (2019). Serious case reviews: The lived experience of Black children. *Child & Family Social Work*, 24(2), 256–263.

Berrick, J.D. (2018). *The impossible imperative: Navigating the competing principles of child protection.* Oxford University Press.

Bhaskar, R. (2013). *A realist theory of science.* Routledge.

Bhui, K. (2001). Over-representation of Black people in secure psychiatric facilities. *The British Journal of Psychiatry*, 178(6), 575.

Bilson, A. (2007). Promoting compassionate concern in social work: Reflections on ethics, biology and love. *British Journal of Social Work*, 37(8), 1371–1386.

References

Bilson, A. and Martin, K.E. (2017). Referrals and child protection in England: One in five children referred to children's services and one in nineteen investigated before the age of five. *British Journal of Social Work*, 47(3), 793–811.

Binion, G. (1995). Human rights: A feminist perspective. *Human Rights Quarterly*, 17(3), 509–526.

Boserup, E. (1970). *Woman's role in economic development*. Allen & Unwin.

Bostock, L., Forrester, D., Patrizo, L., Godfrey, T., Zounouzi, M., Antonopoulou, V., et al (2017). *Scaling and deepening the reclaiming social work model*. Department for Education.

Bradshaw, J. (1972). Taxonomy of social need. In G. McLachlan (ed) *Problems and progress in medical care: Essays on current research*, 7th series (pp 71–82). Oxford University Press.

Brendtro, L.K. (2006). The vision of Urie Bronfenbrenner: Adults who are crazy about kids. *Reclaiming Children and Youth*, 15(3), 162–166.

Brent (1987). *A child in trust: Report into death of Jasmine Beckford*, chaired by Louis Blom-Cooper. Brent Council.

Broadhurst, K. and Mason, C. (2017). Birth parents and the collateral consequences of court-ordered child removal: Towards a comprehensive framework. *International Journal of Law, Policy and the Family*, 31(1), 41–59.

Bronner, S.E. (2004). *Reclaiming the enlightenment: Toward a politics of radical engagement*. Columbia University Press.

Brown, L. (2003). Mainstream or margin? The current use of family group conferences in child welfare practice in the UK. *Child & Family Social Work*, 8(4), 331–340.

Burford, G. (2017). *Family group conferencing: New directions in community-centered child and family practice*. Routledge.

Bywaters, P., Brady, G., Sparks, T. and Bos, E. (2016). Child welfare inequalities: New evidence, further questions. *Child & Family Social Work*, 21(3), 369–380.

Bywaters, P., Kwhali, J., Brady, G., Sparks, T. and Bos, E. (2017). Out of sight, out of mind: Ethnic inequalities in child protection and out-of-home care intervention rates. *British Journal of Social Work*, 47(7), 1884–1902.

Carey, K.B., Scott-Sheldon, L.A., Garey, L., Elliott, J.C. and Carey, M.P. (2016). Alcohol interventions for mandated college students: A meta-analytic review. *Journal of Consulting and Clinical Psychology*, 84(7), 619–624

Carmalt, J.C. (2007). Rights and place: Using geography in human rights work. *Human Rights Quarterly*, 29(1), 68–85.

Children's Commissioner (2019). *Keeping kids safe: Improving safeguarding responses to gang violence and criminal exploitation*, February. https://www.childrenscommissioner.gov.uk/resource/keeping-kids-safe/

Christensen, D.N., Todahl, J. and Barrett, W.C. (2020). *Solution-based casework: An introduction to clinical and case management skills in casework practice*. Routledge.

Christie, G. (2003). Law, theory and aboriginal peoples. *Indigenous Law Journal*, 2, 67–73.

Coady, N. and Lehmann, P. (eds) (2016). *Theoretical perspectives for direct social work practice: A generalist-eclectic approach*. Springer.

Coulshed, V. and Orme, J. (2018). *Social work practice*. Bloomsbury Publishing.

Crisp, B.R., Anderson, M.R., Orme, J. and Lister, P.G. (2006). What can we learn about social work assessment from the textbooks? *Journal of Social Work*, 6(3), 337–359.

Croft, S. and Beresford, P. (1992). The politics of participation. *Critical Social Policy*, 12(35), 20–44.

Croft, S. and Beresford, P. (2002). A participatory approach to social work. In C. Hanvey and T. Philpot (eds) *Practising social work* (pp 49–66). Routledge.

Crummell, A. (1891). *Africa and America: Addresses and discourses*. Willey & Company.

Dale, P. (2004). 'Like a fish in a bowl': Parents' perceptions of child protection services. *Child Abuse Review: Journal of the British Association for the Study and Prevention of Child Abuse and Neglect*, 13(2), 137–157.

Davies, M. (2007). *The essential social worker: An introduction to professional practice in the 1990s*. Ashgate.

Davies, P. (2011). The impact of a child protection investigation: A personal reflective account. *Child & Family Social Work*, 16(2), 201–209.

Dean, R.G. and Poorvu, N.L. (2008). Assessment and formulation: A contemporary social work perspective. *Families in Society*, 89(4), 596–604.

Declaration of the Rights of Man (1789). https://avalon.law.yale.edu/18th_century/rightsof.asp

Department of Health (1988). *Protecting children: A guide for social workers undertaking a comprehensive assessment*. HMSO.

Department of Health, Department for Education and Employment and the Home Office (2000). *Framework for the assessment of children in need and their families*. The Stationery Office.

Devaney, J. (2015). Research review: The impact of domestic violence on children. *Irish Probation Journal*, 12–18.

Dijkstra, S., Creemers, H.E., Asscher, J.J., Deković, M. and Stams, G.J.J. (2016). The effectiveness of family group conferencing in youth care: A meta-analysis. *Child Abuse & Neglect*, 62, 100–110.

Dingwall, R., Eekelaar, J. and Murray, T. (2014). *The protection of children: State intervention and family life* (Vol 16). Quid Pro Books.

Dinham, A. (2006). A review of practice of teaching and learning of communication skills in social work education in England. *Social Work Education*, 25(8), 838–850.

DCP (Division of Clinical Psychology) (2011) Good practice guidance on the use of psychological formulation. British Psychology Society. https://explore.bps.org.uk/content/report-guideline/bpsrep.2011.rep100

Dominelli, L. (2002). *Feminist social work theory and practice*. Macmillan International Higher Education.

Dominelli, L. (2017). *Anti-racist social work*. Macmillan International Higher Education.

Doyal, L. and Gough, I. (1984). A theory of human needs. Critical Social Policy, 4(10), 6–38.

Doyal, L. and Gough, I. (1991). *A theory of human need*. Springer.

Du Bois, W.E.B. (2015). *The souls of black folk*. Yale University Press.

Dubois, L. (2006). An enslaved Enlightenment: Rethinking the intellectual history of the French Atlantic. *Social History*, 31(1), 1–14.

Duchet, M. (1971). *Anthropology and history in the century of the enlightenment.*, Hachette

Edwards, H.P., Boulet, D.B., Mahrer, A.R., Chagnon, G.J. and Mook, B. (1982). Carl Rogers during initial interviews: A moderate and consistent therapist. *Journal of Counseling Psychology*, 29(1), 14–22.

Eysenck, H.J. (1994). The outcome problem in psychotherapy: What have we learned? *Behaviour Research and Therapy*, 32(5), 477–495.

Featherstone, B. (2023). Can we go on? Child protection in a broken place. *Families, Relationships and Societies*, 12(1), 1–11.

Featherstone, B. and Peckover, S. (2007). Letting them get away with it: Fathers, domestic violence and child welfare. *Critical Social Policy*, 27(2), 181–202.

Featherstone, B., Fraser, C., Ashley, C. and Ledward, P. (2011). Advocacy for parents and carers involved with children's services: Making a difference to working in partnership? *Child & Family Social Work*, 16(3), 266–275.

Featherstone, B., Morris, K. and White, S. (2014a). A marriage made in hell: Early intervention meets child protection. *British Journal of Social Work*, 44(7), 1735–1749.

Featherstone, B., Morris, K. and White, S. (2014b). *Re-imagining child protection: Towards humane social work with families*. Policy Press.

Featherstone, B., Gupta, A., Morris, K. and White, S. (2018). *Protecting children: A social model*. Policy Press.

Ferguson, H. (2011). *Child protection practice*. Bloomsbury.

Ferguson, H. (2016). What social workers do in performing child protection work: Evidence from research into face-to-face practice. *Child & Family Social Work*, 21(3), 283–294.

Ferguson, H. (2017). How children become invisible in child protection work: Findings from research into day-to-day social work practice. *The British Journal of Social Work*, 47(4), 1007–1023.

Ferguson, H., Warwick, L., Cooner, T.S., Leigh, J., Beddoe, L., Disney, T. and Plumridge, G. (2020). The nature and culture of social work with children and families in long-term casework: Findings from a qualitative longitudinal study. *Child & Family Social Work*, 25(3), 694–703.

Ferguson, I. and Woodward, R. (2009). *Radical social work in practice: Making a difference*. Policy Press.

Ferrone, V. (2015). *The enlightenment*. Princeton University Press.

Fine, M. and Glendinning, C. (2005). Dependence, independence or interdependence? Revisiting the concepts of 'care' and 'dependency'. *Ageing & Society*, 25(4), 601–621.

Firmin, C. (2018). Contextual risk, individualised responses: An assessment of safeguarding responses to nine cases of peer-on-peer abuse. *Child Abuse Review*, 27(1), 42–57.

Firmin, C. and Knowles, R. (2022). Has the purpose outgrown the design? *Safeguarding Young People: Risk, Rights, Resilience and Relationships*, 129.

Firmin, C. and Lloyd, J. (2023). *Contextual safeguarding: The next chapter*. Policy Press.

Firmin, C., Horan, J., Holmes, D. and Hopper, G. (2016). *Safeguarding during adolescence: The relationship between contextual safeguarding, complex safeguarding and transitional safeguarding*. Contextual Safeguarding Network. https://uobrep.openrepository.com/bitstream/handle/10547/625045/Safeguarding-during-adolescence-Briefing_Jan19_v1.pdf?sequence=2

Foren, R. and Bailey, R. (2014). *Authority in social casework*. Elsevier

Forrester, D. and Harwin, J. (2011). *Parents who misuse drugs and alcohol: Effective interventions in social work and child protection*. John Wiley & Sons.

Forrester, D., McCambridge, J., Waissbein, C. and Rollnick, S. (2008). How do child and family social workers talk to parents about child welfare concerns? *Child Abuse Review: Journal of the British Association for the Study and Prevention of Child Abuse and Neglect*, 17(1), 23–35.

Forrester, D., Westlake, D. and Glynn, G. (2012). Parental resistance and social worker skills: Towards a theory of motivational social work. *Child & Family Social Work*, 17(2), 118–129.

Forrester, D., Westlake, D., McCann, M., Thurnham, A., Shefer, G., Glynn, G. and Killian, M. (2013). *Reclaiming social work? An evaluation of systemic units as an approach to delivering children's services*. University of Bedfordshire.

Forrester, D., Lynch, A., Bostock, L., Newlands, F., Preston, B. and Cary, A. (2017). *Family safeguarding Hertfordshire: Evaluation report*. https://orca.cardiff.ac.uk/id/eprint/121973/1/Family_Safeguarding_Hertfordshire.pdf

Forrester, D., Westlake, D., Killian, M., Antonopoulou, V., McCann, M., Thurnham, A. et al (2018). A randomized controlled trial of training in Motivational Interviewing for child protection. *Children and Youth Services Review*, 88, 180–190.

Forrester, D., Westlake, D., Killian, M., Antonopoulou, V., McCann, M., Thurnham, A. et al (2019). What is the relationship between worker skills and outcomes for families in child and family social work? *The British Journal of Social Work*, 49(8), 2148–2167.

Forrester, D., Killian, M., Westlake, D. and Sheehan, L. (2020). Patterns of practice: An exploratory factor analysis of child and family social worker skills. *Child & Family Social Work*, 25(1), 108–117.

Forrester, D., Wilkins, D. and Whittaker, C. (2021). *Motivational interviewing for working with children and families: A practical guide for early intervention and child protection*. Jessica Kingsley Publishers.

Forslund, T., Granqvist, P., van IJzendoorn, M.H., Sagi-Schwartz, A., Glaser, D., Steele, M. et al (2022). Attachment goes to court: Child protection and custody issues. *Attachment & Human Development*, 24(1), 1–52.

Fox-Harding, L.F. (2015). *Perspectives in child care policy*. Routledge.

Foxcroft, D.R., Coombes, L., Wood, S., Allen, D., Santimano, N.M.A. and Moreira, M.T. (2016). Motivational interviewing for the prevention of alcohol misuse in young adults. *Cochrane Database of Systematic Reviews*, 7.

Fronek, P. and Cuthbert, D. (2013). Apologies for forced adoption practices: Implications for contemporary intercountry adoption. *Australian Social Work*, 66(3), 402–414.

Fulcher, L.C. (1999). Cultural origins of the contemporary family group conference. *Child Care in Practice*, 5(4), 328–339.

Garcia, H. (2012). Islam and the English Enlightenment, 1670–1840. Johns Hopkins University Press.

Gibson, M. (2015). Shame and guilt in child protection social work: New interpretations and opportunities for practice. *Child & Family Social Work*, 20(3), 333–343.

Gibson, M. (2016). Constructing pride, shame, and humiliation as a mechanism of control: A case study of an English local authority child protection service. *Children and Youth Services Review*, 70, 120–128.

Gibson, M. (2020). The shame and shaming of parents in the child protection process: findings from a case study of an English child protection service. *Families, Relationships and Societies*, 9(2), 217–233.

Gilbert, P. (2009). Introducing compassion-focused therapy. *Advances in Psychiatric Treatment*, 15(3), 199–208.

Godden, N.J. (2017). The love ethic: A radical theory for social work practice. *Australian Social Work*, 70(4), 405–416.

Goldberg, E.M. and Warburton, R.W. (1974). *Ends and means in social work: The development and outcome of a case review system for social workers*. Routledge.

Goodley, D. (2001) 'Learning difficulties', the social model of disability and impairment: Challenging epistemologies. *Disability & Society*, 16(2), 207–231.

Goodman, S., Trowler, I. and Munro, E. (2011). *Social work reclaimed: Innovative frameworks for child and family social work practice*. Jessica Kingsley Publishers.

Gough, I. (1979). *The political economy of the welfare state*. Palgrave Macmillan.

Greenwich (1987). *A child in mind: Protection of children in a responsible society*. Report of inquiry into death of Kimberly Carlile, December.

Greer, G. (1971). *The Female Eunuch*. Paladin.

Hachtel, H., Vogel, T. and Huber, C.G. (2019). Mandated treatment and its impact on therapeutic process and outcome factors. *Frontiers in Psychiatry*, 10, 219–231.

Hall, C., Slembrouck, S. and Sarangi, S. (2006). *Language practices in social work: Categorisation and accountability in child welfare*. Psychology Press.

Hallett, S. (2017). *Making sense of child sexual exploitation: Exchange, abuse and young people*. Policy Press.

Harding, L.F. (2014). *Perspectives in child care policy*. Routledge.

Haringey (2010). *Serious care review child A, Haringey*. https://assets.publishing.service.gov.uk/government/uploads/system/uploads/attachment_data/file/595135/second_serious_case_overview_report_relating_to_peter_connelly_dated_march_2009.pdf

Hart, R. (1980). *Slaves who abolished slavery: Blacks in rebellion* (Vol 2). University of West Indies Press.

Hayek, F.C.J. (1945). *The road to serfdom*. Routledge.

Herman, A. and Bishop, J. (2002). *The Scottish enlightenment: The Scots' invention of the modern world*. Fourth Estate.

Hester, M. (2011). The three planet model: Towards an understanding of contradictions in approaches to women and children's safety in contexts of domestic violence. *British Journal of Social Work*, 41(5), 837–853.

Hoffman, L. (1985). Beyond power and control: Toward a 'second order' family systems therapy. *Family Systems Medicine*, 3(4), 381.

Holland, S. (2010). *Child and family assessment in social work practice*. Routledge.

Holland, S. (2022). Commissioner: 'Let's provide children with the same protection in the law as adults'. https://www.childcomwales.org.uk/2018/01/commissioner-lets-provide-children-protection-law-adults/

Holmes, D. (2022). Transitional safeguarding: The case for change. *Practice*, 34(1), 7–23.

Honneth, A. (1987). Enlightenment and rationality. *The Journal of Philosophy*, 84(11), 692–699.

hooks, b. (2000). *All about love: New visions*. Perennial

hooks, b. (2001). *Salvation: Black people and love*. Perennial.

hooks, b. (2002). *Communion, the female search for love*. Perennial.Hopkins, B. (2015). *Restorative theory in practice: Insights into what works and why*. Jessica Kingsley Publishers.

Hothersall, D. and Lovett, B.J. (2022). *History of psychology*. Cambridge University Press.

Howe, D. (1998). Relationship-based thinking and practice in social work. *Journal of Social Work Practice*, 12(1), 45–56.

Howe, D. (2014). *The compleat social worker*. Palgrave Macmillan.

References

Howe, D., Kohli, R., Smith, M., Parkinson, C., McMahon, L., Solomon, R. et al (2018). *Relationship-based social work: Getting to the heart of practice*. Jessica Kingsley Publishers.

Hunt, L.A. (2008). *Inventing human rights: A history*. W.W. Norton.

Ife, J. (2018). *Human rights and social work* (second edition). Cambridge University Press.

Ife, J., Soldatić, K. and Briskman, L. (2022). *Human rights and social work* (third edition). Cambridge University Press.

IFSW (International Federation of Social Workers) (2001). Global standards. https://www.ifsw.org/global-standards/

IFSW (International Federation of Social Workers) (2014). Global definition of social work. https://www.ifsw.org/what-is-social-work/global-definition-of-social-work/

Ignatieff, M. (1984). *The needs of strangers*. Palgrave.

Ihara, C.K. (2004). Are individual rights necessary? A Confucian perspective. In *Confucian ethics: A comparative study of self, autonomy, and community* (pp 11–30).

Independent Review of Children's Social Care (2022). Josh McAlister, Department for Education – unavailable online at time of writing

Ingram, R. (2015). Exploring emotions within formal and informal forums: Messages from social work practitioners. *The British Journal of Social Work*, 45(3), 896–913.

Jackson, P.T. and Dolan, L. (2021). Positivism, post-positivism, and social science. In *Research methods in the social sciences: An A–Z of key concepts* (p 214).

James, C.L.R. (1989). *The black Jacobins: Toussaint L'ouverture and the San Domingo revolution*. Vintage.

James, W. (1975). *Pragmatism* (Vol 1). Harvard University Press.

Jobe, A. and Gorin, S. (2013). 'If kids don't feel safe they don't do anything': Young people's views on seeking and receiving help from Children's Social Care Services in England. *Child & Family Social Work*, 18(4), 429–438.

Johnstone L. and Dallos R. (eds) (2014). *Formulation in psychology and psychotherapy: Making sense of people's problems* (second edition). Routledge.

Kirklees (2021). *Kirklees pre-birth model*. https://westyorkscb.proceduresonline.com/files/kirklees_pre_birth_model.pdf

Kirschenbaum, H. (2003). *The history of the person-centered approach*. https://adpca.org/the-history-of-the-pca/

Knight, C. (2013). Humanistic–existential and solution-focused approaches to psychotherapy. In K. Wheeler (ed) *Psychotherapy for the advanced practice psychiatric nurse: A how-to guide for evidence-based practice* (pp 289–328). Springer.

Krumer-Nevo, M. (2020). *Radical hope: Poverty-aware practice for social work.* Policy Press.

Kuhn, T.S. (1969). *The structure of scientific revolutions.* University of Chicago Press.

Laming, H. (2003). *The Victoria Climbie inquiry.* HMSO.

Lee, E. and Toth, H. (2016). An integrated case formulation in social work: Toward developing a theory of a client. *Smith College Studies in Social Work,* 86(3), 184–203.

Lee, S. (2015). Lord Denning, Magna Carta and magnanimity. *The Denning Law Journal,* 27, 106.

Leeds (2021). *Rethink formulation guide.* https://www.leeds.gov.uk/docs/One%20minute%20guides/Rethink%20Formulation.pdf

Lewis, C.S. (1960). *The four loves.* Houghton Mifflin Harcourt.

Lewis, J. (1997). Gender and welfare regimes: Further thoughts. *Social Politics: International Studies in Gender, State & Society,* 4(2), 160–177.

Lloyd, G. (2017). Rationality. In A. Garry, S.J. Khader and A. Stone (eds) *The Rougledge companion to feminist philosophy* (pp 163–172). Routledge.

Lundahl, B., Moleni, T., Burke, B.L., Butters, R., Tollefson, D., Butler, C. and Rollnick, S. (2013). Motivational interviewing in medical care settings: A systematic review and meta-analysis of randomized controlled trials. *Patient Education and Counseling,* 93(2), 157–168.

Lundy, C. (2011). *Social work, social justice & human rights: A structural approach to practice.* University of Toronto Press.

Marland, H. (2013). *Women and madness.* https://warwick.ac.uk/fac/arts/history/chm/outreach/trade_in_lunacy/research/womenandmadness/

Marmot, M. (2020). Health equity in England: The Marmot review 10 years on. *BMJ,* 368.

Maroto, M. and Pettinicchio, D. (2014). Disability, structural inequality, and work: The influence of occupational segregation on earnings for people with different disabilities. *Research in Social Stratification and Mobility,* 38, 76–92.

Maslow, A.H. (1943). A theory of human motivation. *Psychological Review,* 50, 370–396.

Maslow, A.H. (1968). *Toward a psychology of being* (second edition). D. Van Nostrand.

Maxwell, N. (2023). Complex Safeguarding Wales. https://complexsafeguardingwales.org

Maxwell, N., Scourfield, J., Featherstone, B., Holland, S. and Tolman, R. (2012). Engaging fathers in child welfare services: A narrative review of recent research evidence. *Child & Family Social Work,* 17(2), 160–169.

Maxwell, N., Wallace, C., Cummings, A., Bayfield, H. and Morgan, H. (2019). *A systematic map and synthesis review of child criminal exploitation.* https://orca.cardiff.ac.uk/id/eprint/131950/1/Child%20Criminal%20Exploitation%20Report%20Final.pdf

Mayer, J.E. and Timms, N. (1970). *The client speaks: Working class impressions of casework*. Routledge.

Maylea, C. (2021). The end of social work. *The British Journal of Social Work*, 51(2), 772–789.

McLeod, A. (2010). 'A friend and an equal': Do young people in care seek the impossible from their social workers? *British Journal of Social Work*, 40(3), 772–788.

McLeod, S. (2003). Humanistic approach in psychology (humanism): Definition & examples. *Simply Psychology*. https://www.simplypsychology.org/humanistic.html#:~:text=Humanistic%20psychology%20is%20a%20perspective,their%20potential%20and%20self%2Dactualize

McMurran, M. (2009). Motivational interviewing with offenders: A systematic review. *Legal and Criminological Psychology*, 14(1), 83–100.

Melrose, M. (2002). Labour pains: Some considerations on the difficulties of researching juvenile prostitution. *International Journal of Social Research Methodology*, 5(4), 333–351.

Melrose, M. (2010). What's love got to do with it: Theorising young people's involvement in prostitution. *Youth and Policy*, 104, 12–31.

Mende, J. (2021). Are human rights western—And why does it matter? A perspective from international political theory. *Journal of International Political Theory*, 17(1), 38–57.

Mental Capacity Act (2005). https://www.legislation.gov.uk/ukpga/2005/9/contents

Metze, R.N., Kwekkeboom, R.H. and Abma, T.A. (2015). 'You don't show everyone your weakness': Older adults' views on using Family Group Conferencing to regain control and autonomy. *Journal of Aging Studies*, 34, 57–67.

Mill, J.S. (1989 [1859]). *'On liberty' and other writings*. Cambridge University Press.

Millar, A., Devaney, J. and Butler, M. (2019). Emotional intelligence: Challenging the perceptions and efficacy of 'soft skills' in policing incidents of domestic abuse involving children. *Journal of Family Violence*, 34, 577–588.

Miller, N.S. and Flaherty, J.A. (2000). Effectiveness of coerced addiction treatment (alternative consequences): A review of the clinical research. *Journal of Substance Abuse Treatment*, 18(1), 9–16.

Miller, W.R. (1983). Motivational interviewing with problem drinkers. *Behavioural and Cognitive Psychotherapy*, 11(2), 147–172.

Miller, W.R. and Rollnick, S. (2012). *Motivational interviewing: Helping people change*. Guilford Press.

Milner, J. and O'Byrne, P. (2009) *Assessment in social work* (third edition). Palgrave Macmillan.

Morley, L. and Ife, J. (2002). Social work and a love of humanity. *Australian Social Work*, 55(1), 69–77.

Mullender, A., Hague, G., Imam, U.F., Kelly, L., Malos, E. and Regan, L. (2002). *Children's perspectives on domestic violence*. Sage.
Mulvany, J. (2000). Disability, impairment or illness? The relevance of the social model of disability to the study of mental disorder. *Sociology of Health & Illness*, 22(5), 582–601.
Murphy, D., Duggan, M. and Joseph, S. (2013). Relationship-based social work and its compatibility with the person-centred approach: Principled versus instrumental perspectives. *The British Journal of Social Work*, 43(4), 703–719.
Neff, R. (2004). Achieving justice in child protection. *The Journal of Sociology & Social Welfare*, 31(1), 137.
Normand, R. and Zaidi, S. (2008). *Human rights at the UN: The political history of universal justice*. Indiana University Press.
Nozick, R. (1974). *Anarchy, state, and utopia* (Vol 5038). Basic Books.
Nurcombe, B., Drell, M., Leonard, H. and McDermott, J.F. (2002). Clinical problem solving: The case of Matthew, part 1. *Journal of the American Academy of Child & Adolescent Psychiatry*, 41(1), 92–97.
Nussbaum, M. (2007). Human rights and human capabilities. *Harvard Human Rights Journal*, 20, 21.
O'Brien, K. and O'Brien, K.E. (2009). *Women and enlightenment in eighteenth-century Britain*. Cambridge University Press.
Oates, R.K. (1996). It's time to have another look at the medical model. *Child Abuse & Neglect*, 20(1), 3–5.
Oliver, M. (1984). The politics of disability. *Critical Social Policy*, 4(11), 21–32.
Oliver, M. (2017). Defining impairment and disability: Issues at stake. In E.F. Emens and M.A. Stein (eds) *Disability and equality law* (pp 3–18). Routledge.
Oliver, M. and Barnes, C. (2012). *The new politics of disablement*. Bloomsbury.
Owens, J. (2015). Exploring the critiques of the social model of disability: The transformative possibility of Arendt's notion of power. *Sociology of Health & Illness*, 37(3), 385–403.
Parkinson, K. and Rogers, M. (2018). Addressing domestic abuse through FGCs. In D. Edwards and K. Parkinson (eds) *Family group conferences in social work* (pp 123–140). Policy Press.
Parton, N. (1985). *The politics of child abuse*. Macmillan.
Parton, N. (2014). *The politics of child protection: Contemporary developments and future directions*. Bloomsbury.
Parton, N. (2017). The politics of child protection in contemporary England: Towards the 'authoritarian neoliberal state'. In *Transdisciplinary perspectives on childhood in contemporary Britain* (pp 191–209). Routledge.
Parton, N. and O'Byrne, P. (2000). *Constructive social work: Towards a new practice*. Palgrave.
Pascall, G. (1997). *Social policy: A new feminist analysis*. Psychology Press.
Pawson, R. and Tilley, N. (1997). *Realistic evaluation*. SAGE.

Payne, M. (2010). *Humanistic social work: Core principles in practice*. Lyceum Books.

Pinker, S. (2011). *The better angels of our nature: The decline of violence in history and its causes*. Penguin.

Pinker, S. (2018). *Enlightenment now: The case for reason, science, humanism, and progress*. Penguin.

Plant, R. (1998). Citizenship, rights. In J. Franklin (ed) *Social policy and social justice: The IPPR reader* (p 57). Polity Press.

Plant, R. (2009). *Social and moral theory in casework*. Routledge.

Plant, R. (2019). Needs, agency, and welfare rights. In J.D. Moon (ed) *Responsibility, rights, and welfare* (pp 55–74). Routledge.

Porter, R. (2000). *The creation of the modern world: The untold story of the British Enlightenment*. WW Norton & Company.

Potter-Efron, P.S. and Potter-Efron, R.T. (1986). Promoting second order change in alcoholic systems. *Journal of Strategic and Systemic Therapies*, 5(3), 20–29.

Pritchard-Jones, L.G. (2018). Revisiting the feminist critique of rights: Lessons for a new older persons' convention? In L. Pritchard-Jones (ed) *Ageing, gender and family law* (pp 109–124). Routledge.

The Promise (2021). *Independent review of children's social care in Scotland*. https://www.carereview.scot/wp-content/uploads/2020/02/The-Promise.pdf

Reid, W.J. and Shyne, A.W. (1969). *Brief and extended casework*. Columbia University Press.

Reith-Hall, E. and Montgomery, P. (2022). The teaching and learning of communication skills in social work education. *Research on Social Work Practice*, 32(7), 793–813.

Roberts, D.R. (2022). Abolish child protection. https://www.motherjones.com/crime-justice/2022/04/abolish-child-protective-services-torn-apart-dorothy-roberts-book-excerpt/

Roberts, L. (2021). *The children of looked after children: Outcomes, experiences and ensuring meaningful support to young parents in and leaving care*. Policy Press.

Rogers, C.R. (1942). *Counseling and psychotherapy: Newer concepts in practice*. Houghton Mifflin Company.

Rogers, C.R. (1946). Significant aspects of client-centered therapy. *American Psychologist*, 1, 415–422.

Rogers, C.R. (1951). *Client-centered therapy: Its current practice, implications, and theory*. Houghton Mifflin.

Rogers, C.R. (1959). A theory of therapy, personality and interpersonal relationships as developed in the client-centered framework. In S. Koch (ed) *Psychology: A study of a science. Vol. 3: Formulations of the person and the social context*. McGraw Hill.

Rogowski, S. (2015). From child welfare to child protection/safeguarding: A critical practitioner's view of changing conceptions, policies and practice. *Practice*, 27(2), 97–112.

Rollnick, S., Butler, C.C., McCambridge, J., Kinnersley, P., Elwyn, G. and Resnicow, K. (2005). Consultations about changing behaviour. *BMJ*, 331(7522), 961–963.

Rorty, R. (1979). *Philosophy and the mirror of nature*. Princeton University Press.

Rose, H. and Rose, S. (2010). *Alas poor Darwin: Arguments against evolutionary psychology*. Random House.

Rose, S., Lewontin, R.C. and Kamin, L. (1984). Not in our genes: Biology, ideology and human nature. *The Wilson Quarterly*, 152.

Roth, A. and Fonagy, P. (2006). *What works for whom? A critical review of psychotherapy research*. Guilford Press

Rubak, S., Sandbæk, A., Lauritzen, T. and Christensen, B. (2005). Motivational interviewing: A systematic review and meta-analysis. *British Journal of General Practice*, 55(513), 305–312.

Ruch, G. (2005). Relationship-based practice and reflective practice: Holistic approaches to contemporary child care social work. *Child & Family Social Work*, 10(2), 111–123.

Ruch, G., Winter, K., Morrison, F., Hadfield, M., Hallett, S. and Cree, V. (2020). From communication to co-operation: Reconceptualizing social workers' engagement with children. *Child & Family Social Work*, 25(2), 430–438.

Sen, A. (1985). *Commodities and capabilities*. Elsevier Science.

Sen, A. (1999). *Development as freedom*. Anchor Books.

Shaw, I. and Shaw, A. (1997). Keeping social work honest: Evaluating as profession and practice. *The British Journal of Social Work*, 27(6), 847–869.

Sheehan, L. (2022). Fixing change: An ethnographic study of child protection practice. Doctoral dissertation, Cardiff University.

Sheppard, M.C. (1995). *Care management and the new social work: A critical analysis*. Whiting & Birch.

Sinclair, R. (2004). Aboriginal social work education in Canada: Decolonizing pedagogy for the seventh generation. *First Peoples Child & Family Review: A Journal on Innovation and Best Practices in Aboriginal Child Welfare Administration, Research, Policy & Practice*, 1(1), 49–61.

Skafida, V., Morrison, F. and Devaney, J. (2022). Prevalence and social inequality in experiences of domestic abuse among mothers of young children: A study using national survey data from Scotland. *Journal of Interpersonal Violence*, 37(11–12), NP9811–NP9838.

Skegg, A.M. (2005). Brief note: Human rights and social work: A Western imposition or empowerment to the people? *International Social Work*, 48(5), 667–672.

Social Care Institute for Excellence (2004). Communication skills in social work education. SCIE.

Stabler, L., O'Donnell, C., Forrester, D., Diaz, C., Willis, S. and Brand, S. (2019). *Shared decision-making: What is good practice in delivering meetings? Involving families meaningfully in decision-making to keep children safely at home: A rapid realist review*. https://www.researchgate.net/profile/Ulugbek-Nurmatov/publication/333080348_Reducing_the_number_of_children_in_statutory_care_a_systematic_scoping_review/links/5cda8f77a6fdccc9ddaac8b5/Reducing-the-number-of-children-in-statutory-care-a-systematic-scoping-review.pdf

Stanley, N. (1997). Domestic violence and child abuse: Developing social work practice. *Child & Family Social Work*, 2(3), 135–145.

Stevens, A., Berto, D., Frick, U., Hunt, N., Kerschl, V., McSweeney, T. et al (2006). The relationship between legal status, perceived pressure and motivation in treatment for drug dependence: Results from a European study of quasi-compulsory treatment. *European Addiction Research*, 12(4), 197–209.

Susser, M. (1990). Disease, illness, sickness; impairment, disability and handicap. *Psychological Medicine*, 20(3), 471–473.

Sutton, T.E. (2019). Review of attachment theory: Familial predictors, continuity and change, and intrapersonal and relational outcomes. *Marriage & Family Review*, 55(1), 1–22.

Tanner, D. (2020). 'The love that dare not speak its name': The role of compassion in social work practice. *The British Journal of Social Work*, 50(6), 1688–1705.

Taylor, S., Blackshaw, E., Lawrence, H., Stern, D., Gilbert, L. and Raghoo, N. (2023). *Randomised controlled trial of family group conferencing at pre-proceedings stage*. https://foundations.org.uk/wp-content/uploads/2023/06/Randomised-controlled-trial-family-group-conferencing.pdf

Todorov, T. (2010). *In defence of the enlightenment*. Atlantic Books.

Tomaselli, S. (2017). The enlightenment debate on women. In J. Moore (ed) *Mary Wollstonecraft* (pp 111–134). Routledge.

Treby, L. (2022). What is the relationship between supervision and practice in child and family social work? An analysis of 12 case studies. Doctoral dissertation, Cardiff University.

Trotter, C. (2015). *Working with involuntary clients: A guide to practice*. Routledge.

Turnell, A. and Edwards, S. (1999). *Signs of safety: A solution and safety oriented approach to child protection casework*. Norton.

Twelvetrees, A. (2008). *Community work*. Macmillan International Higher Education.

United Kingdon Supreme Court (2016). Case 51, The Christian Institute and others versus the Lord Advocate. https://www.supremecourt.uk/cases/docs/uksc-2015-0216-judgment.pdf

Werb, D., Kamarulzaman, A., Meacham, M.C., Rafful, C., Fischer, B., Strathdee, S.A. and Wood, E. (2016). The effectiveness of compulsory drug treatment: A systematic review. *International Journal of Drug Policy*, 28, 1–9.

Weston, T. (2011). *The clinical effectiveness of the person centred therapies: The impact of the therapeutic relationship.* https://ueaeprints.uea.ac.uk/id/eprint/33506/1/Tony_Weston's_PhD_thesis.pdf

What Works for Children (2021). *Outcomes framework.* https://whatworks-csc.org.uk/research/outcomes-framework-for-research/#:~:text=Why%20we%20created%20a%20framework,first%2C%20high%2Dlevel%20overview

White, S., Gibson, M. and Wastell, D. (2019). Child protection and disorganized attachment: A critical commentary. *Children and Youth Services Review*, 105, 104415.

Whittaker, C. (forthcoming). The relationship between social worker skills and parental talk. PhD, Cardiff University.

Wilkins, D. (2020). Disorganized attachment does not indicate child maltreatment. *Journal of Social Work Practice*, 35(2), 219–220.

Wilkins, D., Forrester, D. and Grant, L. (2017). What happens in child and family social work supervision? *Child & Family Social Work*, 22(2), 942–951.

Wilkins, D., Foster, C., Sanders, M. and Reid, L. (2020). Good judgement and social work decision-making: A randomised controlled trial of brief interventions to improve forecasting. What Works for Children's Social Care, January.

Wilkins, D., Pitt, C. and Addis, S. (2022). What do child protection social workers talk about when they talk about helping children and families? An observational study of supervision. *Practice*, 1–19.

Williams, A., Reed, H., Segrott, J., Rees, A. and Kitchiner, N. (2022). How does a restorative approach work? Supporting military veteran families affected by Post Traumatic Stress Disorder (PTSD). *The Internet Journal of Restorative Justice*.

Wilson, K., Petrie, S. and Sinclair, I. (2003). A kind of loving: A model of effective foster care. *British Journal of Social Work*, 33(8), 991–1003.

Wolff, L. and Cipolloni, M. (eds) (2007). *The anthropology of the enlightenment.* Stanford University Press.

Wollstonecraft, M. (2008 [1792]). *A vindication of the rights of women & a vindication of the rights of men.* Cosimo.

Wood, E.M. (2012). *Liberty and property: A social history of western political thought from the renaissance to enlightenment.* Verso Books.

Yao, L. and Kabir, R. (2023). Person-centered therapy (Rogerian therapy). StatPearls.

Index

References to endnote or footnotes show both the page number and the note number.

A

abuse 25, 35, 37, 47, 154–155, 170–171
  see also child abuse; domestic abuse; sexual abuse
accessibility 91
accountability 114–115, 123
actions 104, 151, 165
  unloveable 73–74
activists (activism) 25, 90–91, 93, 98–99, 154
Addams, Jane 24
adjustments, reasonable 91
Adler, Alfred 82
adoption, forced 40, 170
affection 68, 70
agape 67
agency 56, 79, 80, 153–154
alcohol addiction (problems) 45, 53–54, 62, 86–87, 89, 93
analysis, data 107, 110
Anti-racist social work 97
apartheid (anti-apartheid) 19, 92
assessment formulations and rights 114
  conclusion 129–130
  definition 116–121, 123–124
  developing a formulation for Janet 124–129
  origins 115–116
Assessment Framework 109–110
assessment theory development 103
  challenges 104–105
  definition 103–104
  positivism, social constructionism and realism 110–112
  and research 108–110
  theories 106–108
  theories, hypotheses and formulations 112–113
assessments 61, 65, 132
attachment 65–66, 66n1
authoritarianism, muscular 133
  see also muscular authoritarianism
authorities, local 8, 28–30, 97–98, 114
authority 14–15, 44, 146
authority, good 138–140
  purposeful dialogue 140–143
autonomy 23, 57, 59

B

behaviourism 79, 81, 83, 84
behaviours 50, 86, 87, 116
  parental 51

beliefs 56, 109
beliefs, humanist 84
belonging, sense of 81
benefits 60–61
Bernard, C. 157
Berrick, J.D. 36
better angels of our nature, The 167
Bhaskar, R. 111
bias 168
Bilson, A. 70, 93, 156
Black people 17, 92
body language 85, 146
Bostock, Lisa 124
boundaries, professional 72
Bradshaw, J. 59
British Association of Social Work (BASW) 31, 159
British Journal of Social Work 1
Broadhurst, K. 157
Bronfenbrenner, Urie 68
Bywaters, P. 93, 156

C

campaigners 90–92, 97
campaigns 18–19, 91, 93, 154
capacity limitations (issues)
  direct practice 148–151
  Enlightenment 21–22, 26
  freedom and protection 35–37, 52
  positive freedom 55, 60
  rights and social work 32–33
  social work, rights and society 160–161, 166
capitalism 17
care 9, 44–46, 139, 160–161
  assessment 104, 125, 129
  human connection 68, 70–71
  rights and social work 28, 33
  see also in care; social care
Case Con Manifesto 97
case studies
  children in need 53–54
  Janet 121–123
  Mancini family 38–42
  Ted and Cara 27–31
change 86, 164, 171
  assessment 105, 109
  freedom and protection 40–41, 44, 50–51
  parental 42–43
chastisement, physical 158

child abuse 94, 109–110
child-centred, concept of 41
child protection 87, 109, 125
  freedom and protection 40–41, 46, 48–49, 51
  social work, rights and society 159–160, 162
  traditions 91, 93–94
  see also protection
children 24, 29, 61, 68, 92
  freedom and protection 36, 39, 51
  social work, rights and society 164, 170
Children Act (1989) 53, 126
children's services 48, 49
choice 51
church (faith) 14–15
citizenship 28
clarity 44, 51, 133
clients 5, 61–62, 69, 133, 158, 161
  traditions 84, 86
Climbié, Victoria 124
coercion 11, 24, 51, 92
cognitive behavioural therapy (CBT) 84, 85, 87
collaboration 44, 84, 148
  assessment 117, 129
  beyond individuals and families 153, 155
colonialism (anti-colonialism) 17–18
commitment 12, 13–14, 26, 100, 171
  human connection 68, 70, 73
  rights and social work 32, 34
common good 56
communication 30, 50
  direct practice 136, 140, 143, 150
  humanism 82, 87
communities 24–26, 61, 94, 109, 127, 170
  Maori 152–153
  Romany 125
  see also human connection
compassion 70, 71, 74, 84, 87, 118
concerns 6–7, 68–69, 95
  freedom and protection 37, 39–40, 44–46, 49–52
  social work, rights and society 163, 169
  see also families, working with; Janet; Williams family
conflicts 4–10, 71, 100, 166
  direct practice 131, 148
  freedom and protection 29–30, 32–34
  positive freedom and need 60, 62
confrontation 46, 48, 86, 132, 135
connections 25, 34, 74
Connelly, Peter 49, 123–124
consensus 58, 95
consequences 51, 145, 148
consequences, ladder of 35, 39–40, 41, 42–43
  working with 44–47

consistency 43, 66, 88, 100, 116, 165
  direct practice 132–133
constructionism 110–112
contact, parental 27, 29, 33, 36, 68, 73
  see also Janet; Mancini family
contexts 23, 56, 111, 120, 157
  direct practice 136, 146
Contextual Safeguarding 12, 152–156
control 25, 93, 151, 161
  freedom and protection 41, 44, 46
  humanism 80, 82, 85
  see also coercion
conversations 131, 138, 139
  see also talking (conversations), social workers
conversations, difficult 8–9, 127
  direct practice 131–133, 138, 148
  freedom and protection 41, 48
Coulshed, V. 107
counselling (counsellors) 69, 100
  direct practice 131–132, 139
  freedom and protection 37, 41, 44, 50
  humanist social work 79, 82–83, 86–87
counter-transference 69
creativity 80, 112
crime 73, 87, 96, 154
critiques 15, 23, 94–95, 157, 159, 162
  assessment 115, 123, 138
Crummell, A. 17
cultures 25
  Maori 152
  organisational 138
current practice, social work 162

D

Dallos, R. 117, 121
data 106
deaths, child 40, 49, 124, 138, 160
debates 15–16, 58, 100, 169
decision-making 114–115, 123, 152, 166
decisions 15, 90, 149, 153
  assessment 123, 129
  Family Group Conferences 24
  freedom and protection 35–36, 39
  positive freedom 55, 58
  rights and social work 29, 32
decisions, organisational 30
decisions, social worker 103–105, 114
declarations 31–32
definitions, international 32
dementia 5, 9, 21, 120, 149, 161
democracy 10, 12, 33, 58, 96
  Enlightenment 13, 15–16, 19–21
  freedom and protection 35–36
  social work, rights and society 168–169
deprivation 156
Devaney, J. 156–157
dialogue, purposeful 11, 60, 151
  see also families, working with; individuals, working with

dignity 31
dilemmas, unsolvable 99
disability (disablism) 32–33, 104, 170
  Enlightenment 18, 19
  positive freedom 57, 62
  traditions 89–93, 95
discrimination 18, 19, 91, 99
discussions, case 124
diversity 57
Division of Clinical Psychology 116, 119
domestic abuse 60, 65, 167, 170
  assessment, formulations and rights 127–128
  beyond individuals and families 156–157
  rights and social work 33, 37
  social model 93–94
Dominelli, Lena 97
Doyal, L. 57, 59
Drakeford, Mark 158
drug addiction (issues) 6, 86
  human connection 64, 71, 73
  traditions 89–90, 93
  see also Mancini family
Du Bois, W.E.B. 17

E

Einstein, Albert 109
eligibility 10, 60, 113, 157
emotions 11–12, 23, 83, 165–166
  freedom and protection 38, 50
  human connection 69, 70, 72, 74
empathy 44–46, 139
employers 91
Enlightenment 13–14, 121, 166–170
  criticisms 16–20
  definition 14–16
  rights 20–26
Enlightenment now 167
environments 25, 90, 107, 168
equality 18, 19, 22–23, 34, 55, 92
  see also inequality
equity 26, 92
  see also inequity
Erickson, Eric 82
European Convention on Human Rights 31–32
evidence 83–85, 103, 153, 157, 162
  assessment 105, 107–108, 110, 113
expectations 62, 143
  assessment 109, 120, 125
  freedom and protection 49, 51
experts (expertise) 59, 66, 83, 91, 127, 161
  see also social workers
exploitation 17, 153–156, 170
  see also abuse
exploration 69, 85, 124, 165

F

factors (four Ps) 117–119
facts 111
families 61, 68, 87, 129
  assessment 104, 116
  Enlightenment 24–25
  freedom and protection 35–38, 44
  traditions 91, 93–94
  see also Family Group Conferences
families, working with 131–132
  capacity issues 148–151
  different approach 143–148
  good authority and purposeful dialogue in practice 140–143
  how social workers talk to people 132–135
  muscular authoritarianism or good authority 138–140
  purposeful practice 135–138
Family Group Conferences 24, 94, 152–153
Family Rights Group 94
Family Safeguarding Model 6, 87
fathers 126
Featherstone, B. 93, 94, 133, 156
feedback loops 85
feelings 51, 69
feminism 17, 23, 24, 57, 59
Firmin, Carlene 154–155
formulations 112–113
  definition 116–121, 123–124
  origins 115–116
  four Ps 117–119
frameworks 4, 6, 87, 108, 165
  freedom and protection 41, 48, 50
free will 79, 81, 82, 105
freedom
  limitations 36
  negative 21–22
  positive 22–23
French Revolution 21, 63
fun 149
fundamentalism 169
futures, prediction 105

G

gangs 154, 155
Gbowee, Leymah 24
gender 19, 93, 94, 111
global warming 169
Godden, N.J. 70
Goldberg, E.M. 133
good practice 48, 51, 71, 156
Good practice guidelines on the use of psychological formulations 116
Gough, I. 57, 59
governments 49, 60, 97–99
grooming 154

guidance 28, 154
  assessment 109
  direct practice 132
  freedom and protection 41
  human connection 65
  traditions 95

H

handicaps 90, 91
harm principle 21, 35, 36, 57
helping 37–42, 163–164
hierarchy of needs 81
Holland, S. 110
homophobia 18, 169
honesty 71–72, 74, 148, 151
hooks, bell 63, 67, 70, 71, 83, 165
hospitals 56, 62, 161, 170
human connection 25–26, 63
  complications in applying love ethic to rights-focused practice 72–74
  implications of an ethic of love 74–75
  a kind of loving 70–72
  social work and loving relationships 68
  social workers and love 69–70
  what's love got to do with it? 65–68
  Williams family 63–65
human welfare 12, 14–16, 167, 169
humanism 13, 15, 121
  helping 83–85
  history 79–83
  later developments 86–87
  and social work 87–88
Hume, David 24
hypotheses 112–113, 116, 121, 123–124

I

identity 24, 156
  Romany 122, 125
Ife. J. 23, 70
Ignatieff, M. 55–56, 58
immigration 29–30, 33
impairment 89–90
implementation 106
in care 65, 127, 148, 153, 156
  rights and social work 27–29, 33
  traditions 93–94
  see also Ted and Cara
inclusion 18, 73, 75, 87
indigenous communities (people) 17, 170
individuals, working with 131–132
  capacity issues 148–151
  different approach 143–148
  good authority and purposeful dialogue in practice 140–143
  how social workers talk to people 132–135
  muscular authoritarianism or good authority 138–140
  purposeful practice 135–138

industrial actions 19
inequality 93, 168–169
  see also equality
inequity 91
  see also equity
information 103, 109, 110, 113, 124
inquiries, empirical 15, 100
insights 5, 12, 55, 79, 92–93, 157
  assessment 108, 121
inspections 114, 138
institutions 23, 25, 39
interactions, guiding 139
interdependency 23
International Federation of Social Work (IFSW) 31
interventions 6, 39, 61, 65, 87, 164
  assessment 103–104, 106, 112, 115
interviews 136, 138, 143, 147–148
interviews, simulated 134
investigations 164

J

James, W. 111
Janet 121, 122–123, 124–129
Jenny 53–56, 59, 61–62, 63–65, 70, 72–73
Johnstone, L. 117, 121

K

Kant, Immanuel 24, 51
Kelvin, Lord (William Thomson) 109
kindness 26, 71, 74, 160
knowledge 103–104, 107–108, 111–112, 120–121, 161
  professional 156–157
Krumer-Nevo. M. 156
Kuhn, Thomas 108

L

ladder of consequences 35, 39–40, 41, 42–43
language 56
  assessment 104, 109, 111, 127
  body 85, 146
  human connection 66, 69
laws 14, 120, 157–158
  positive freedom 58, 60, 62
  rights and social work 32–33, 35
leaders (leadership) 15, 19, 165
leads, negative 168
learning difficulties 89, 93, 149, 150, 161, 170
legislation 26, 32, 55, 65, 98
  assessment 120, 129
Lewis, C.S. 67, 68
liberty 21–22, 34, 75
  change in protection 44
  conclusion 52
  how should social workers talk with people 50–51

ladder of consequences 44–47
ladder of consequences and parental change 42–43
rights and capacity issues 35–37
rights and helping 37–42
social workers talking to people 48–49
life expectancy 167–168
listening 85, 127, 139, 143
Lloyd, G. 155
Locke, John 24
L'Ouverture, Touissant 18, 19
love 65–68, 70–72, 150, 165–166
implications for social work 74–75
and professional boundaries 72
social workers 69–70
unloveable people and actions 73–74
lying 144

M

Mancini family 38–42, 52
manipulation 51
Maori people 24, 152
Marx, Karl 56
Maslow, Abraham 66, 79, 80–82
Mayer, J.E. 133
Maylea, C. 97
medical model 89–90
men, White, Western 16–18, 23–24, 80
Mental Capacity Act (2005) 149
mental distress 153
mental health 115, 160, 164, 170
traditions 89, 91, 93
mental illness 14, 32, 120, 149, 156, 160
freedom and protection 35, 37
theories 66, 93
Mill, J.S. 21
Miller, William R. 84, 86
Milner, J. 106
models 106
medical 89–90
Morley, L. 70
mothers 47, 49, 93, 157
Motivational Interviewing (MI) 79, 82, 85–87, 131, 144–145
motivations 42–43, 50, 51, 79, 127
movements, social 17, 19, 57, 91, 93
muscular authoritarianism 133, 135, 138–140

N

nature, loss of 169
needs 22–23
negative freedom 21–22
negative leads 168
negotiation 135, 136, 137
networks 152
news, online 168
non-directive listening 85

non-judgemental 73–74, 84
nurture 68

O

Oates, R.K. 89
objective need 56–59
obligations 23
O'Bryne, P. 106
offenders 87
Oliver, Michael 91
opinions 27, 99, 132
oppression 23, 35, 95
Enlightenment 17–20
Orange Book 109
Orme, J. 107
outcomes 30, 34, 162–163, 164
Owens, J. 95

P

paradigms 108–109
parents 138
beyond individuals and families 153, 155–156
freedom and protection 35–37, 39, 42–43, 49
rights 29–30
Pawson, R. 111
peers 94
permanence 66
perpetuating factors 118, 128
person-centred counselling (PCC) 82, 83, 85, 86
perspectives 100, 121, 132, 156
assessment 103–104, 110
direct practice 147, 150
personal 120, 126–127
philosophers (philosophy) 33, 67
assessment 107, 111
positive freedom 54, 56, 58, 62
Pinker, Stephen 167–168, 170
places, physical 20, 23–25, 66, 154, 170
planning 106–107
Plant, R. 57
play 150
policies 14, 32–33, 156–158, 169
assessment 107, 111, 120–121, 129
freedom and protection 35, 49
national 28
positive freedom 58, 60, 62
rights and society 162–165
politics 13, 31, 58, 88, 156
traditions 90, 96–99
politics of disability, The 91
positive freedom 22–23, 53
case study 53–54
equality, positive rights and social need 55
individual and social need 55–60
social need 54–55

social needs and rights 60–61
uncomfortable nature of social work 61–62
positive rights 22, 24, 55, 95
positivism 107, 108, 110–112
poverty 92, 93, 168, 169
power 20, 25, 48, 136, 148, 154
practice, purposeful 135–138, 147
practice, rights-focused 159–160
  critique 162
  extents and limits 160–162
practices, humanist 85
precipitating factors 118, 128
predisposing factors 118, 127–128
presenting issue 119–120, 124–126
Prince, Mary 18
principles 120–121, 129, 165
privilege 23, 24
problems 90, 91, 92, 119–120, 125–126
procedures 32, 103, 157
processes 163
  bureaucratic 138
professionalism 157
professionals 47, 99, 153
progress 15, 167, 168, 169, 170
progress and social work 170–171
proportionality 120–121, 129
protection 29, 35, 36, 39, 44
  see also liberty
protective factors 118, 128–129
provision, controlled 59
Ps, four 117–119
psychoanalysis 79–80, 81
psychology 79, 115–116
purposeful dialogue 140–143

Q

questions 149
questions, open 83, 85, 125, 127, 136, 143

R

race 93
racism (anti-racism) 17–18
rationality 13–15, 23, 100, 121, 166
rationing 60
realism 110–112
reason 14
reflections (reflective statements) 83, 85, 127, 143, 145, 150
Reformation 14
Reid, W.J. 133
relationships 82, 94, 128, 155, 165
  direct practice 138, 149–150
  freedom and protection 41, 44
  human connection 66, 68
  rights and social work 23, 25–26, 29–30, 34
  see also love

religion 57, 68, 84, 169
research 107, 108, 109, 112, 162–165
  rights and society 162–165
researchers 107, 126, 133, 154
resistance 144
  Enlightenment 17–20
resources 33, 157
  Enlightenment 22, 24
  positive freedom 55, 57–58, 60–61
respect 70, 100, 139
  mutual 23
responses 144
responsibilities 25, 70
reviews 40–41, 65, 87, 106, 124, 153
rights 13, 16, 70, 71, 162–165, 168
  case study 27–31
  criticisms and third generation 23–26
  first generation 21–22
  and love 165–166
  second generation 22–23
  social work and human 31–34
  third generation 74
  see also liberty; practice, rights-focused
rights and society
  current practice 162
  Enlightenment 166–170
  extent and limits 160–162
  love 165–166
  policies and research 162–165
  rights-focused practice and social work 159–160
  social work and progress 170–171
risk assessments 105
Roberts, Louise 157
Rogers, Carl 79, 82–83, 84, 86
Rollnick, Stephen 86, 87, 139
Roosevelt, Eleanor 24
Rorty, R. 111
Rosa 30, 33–34

S

safe spaces 69
safeguarding 10, 51, 132, 151, 161
  contextual 12, 152–156
  see also Family Safeguarding Model
sanctions 39
schools (schooling) 28–30, 34, 53, 144–145, 158
  assessment 116
  humanism 84, 87
  traditions 96
  see also Janet; Williams family
Scientific Revolution 14, 17
Second World War 22, 79
self-actualisation 81
self-care 72
self-determination 58, 88, 105
self-esteem 81

Sen, A. 25, 57
sexism 18
sexual abuse 73, 125, 153, 170
shame 48
Sheppard, M.C. 58, 59, 61, 99
Shyne, A.W. 133
Signs of Safety 87
skills 11, 30, 60
  assessment 103, 127, 132, 136
  caring 44
  communication 50, 140, 143
  counselling 139
  direct practice 144–145, 147, 150–151
  freedom and protection 37, 41
  human connection 62, 71
  humanism 82–83, 86–87
  see also communication; counselling (counsellors)
slavery 17, 18
smacking bans 156–158
social care 36, 38, 131, 153
  see also Mancini family
social control 41
social justice 31, 55, 73
social model
  development of 90–94
  limitations of 94–95
  medical model 89–90
  rights and humanist approaches 100
  rights and social work 95–100
social needs see positive freedom
social work
  critique 162
  and the Enlightenment 166–170
  extents and limits 160–162
  practice, rights 31–34
  and progress 170–171
  rights-focused practice 159–160
  see also positive freedom
social workers 33, 45, 99
  assessment 103, 110, 120
  beyond individuals and families 156, 158
  how they talk to people 132–135
  human connection 69–70, 74–75
  see also positive freedom
societies 58, 103, 160–161, 170
  Enlightenment 15, 22, 25
  traditions 90, 92
Society for the Prevention of Cruelty to Children 82
solidarity 25–26, 34, 63, 95
Somerset, James 18
spaces, safe 69
spectrum of directiveness 139
stability 66, 68
state provision 156
statements 143, 146, 150
stigma 48

structure of scientific revolutions, The 108
struggle 19–20
subjective needs 59, 103
  see also perspectives
summary statements (summaries) 127, 143, 146, 147, 150
supervision 48, 49
support, lack of 48
surveillance 39, 49

T

Taft, Jessie 82
talking (conversations), social workers 45–46, 48–51
Tanner, D. 70
Ted and Cara 33
tensions 13, 61–62, 99–100, 148, 161
  rights and social work 29–30, 32, 34
  see also conflicts
theories 109, 112–113, 169
thinking 109, 157
Thomson, William (Lord Kelvin) 109
thriving, human 23
Tilley, N. 111
Timm, N. 133
tool 100
traditions 100, 116
  Maori 24
transference 69
transparency 44, 71, 114, 121, 123, 148
Treby, L. 49
trust 41, 70, 84, 149, 150, 151
truths 105, 108, 169

U

uncertainty 148
unconditional positive regard 82, 84
United Nations Universal Declaration of Human Rights (1948) 22, 31
unloveable people and actions 73–74

V

vagueness 133, 148
values 103
  ecological 155, 165
  humanist 84
  professional 32
vigilantes 73
violence, domestic 168
  see also domestic abuse
Voltaire 170

W

Wales, smacking bans 156–158
Warburton, R.W 133
welfare 29, 61, 168
  see also human welfare
welfare states 19, 22, 53, 95, 98, 157

wellbeing 6, 12, 100, 121, 167–168
 Enlightenment 15, 20
 positive freedom 56, 61
What Works for Children
 Centre 163
Whittaker, C. 46, 133

Wilkin, David 48, 105, 123
Williams family 63–65
Wollstonecraft, Mary 16
women 17, 18, 24–25, 170
work progress 34
writers 24–25

www.ingramcontent.com/pod-product-compliance
Lightning Source LLC
Chambersburg PA
CBHW051546020426
42333CB00016B/2118